Breaking the Learning Barrier for Underachieving Students

For Leslie
And in grateful appreciation of all the wonderful teachers
who sacrificed much to share with me their love of life and learning.

Breaking the Learning Barrier for Underachieving Students: Practical Teaching Strategies for Dramatic Results

George D. Nelson

Corwin Press
A Sage Publications Company
Thousand Oaks, California

For information:

Corwin Press
A Sage Publications Company
2455 Teller Road
Thousand Oaks, California 91320
www.corwinpress.com

Sage Publications Ltd.
1 Oliver's Yard
55 City Road
London EC1Y 1SP
United Kingdom

Sage Publications India Pvt. Ltd.
B-42, Panchsheel Enclave
Post Box 4109
New Delhi 110 017 India

Printed in the United States of America

Library of Congress Cataloging-in-Publication Data

Nelson, George D.
Breaking the learning barrier for underachieving students: Practical teaching strategies for dramatic results/George D. Nelson.
p. cm.
Includes bibliographical references and index.
ISBN 1-4129-1484-1 (cloth)—ISBN 1-4129-1485-X (pbk.)
1. Learning disabled children—Education—United States. 2. Learning strategies—United States. 3. Students with social disabilities—Education—United States. I. Title.

LC4691.N45 2006
371.826'94—dc22 2005014946

This book is printed on acid-free paper.

05 06 07 08 09 10 9 8 7 6 5 4 3 2 1

Acquisitions Editor: Kylee Liegl
Production Editor: Beth A. Bernstein
Copy Editor: Freelance Editorial Services
Typesetter: C&M Digitals (P) Ltd.
Proofreader: Scott Oney
Indexer: Rick Hurd
Cover Designer: Michael Dubowe
Graphic Designer: Scott Van Atta

Contents

Preface

Never before had she been this excited about anything associated with school.

Now, for the first time in her life, learning was rewarding and satisfying. Even the thought of missing school, for any reason, was simply out of the question. How could this be the same young woman who used to find every possible excuse to stay home?

Now she worked hours on her own, without compulsion, to prepare for class. She felt that she had discovered a vast secret, and she longed to share it with everyone she met. Every search seemed to lead to new answers. New answers led to new questions. In her mind, she was beginning to picture her educational journey like the ever-splitting branches of an enormous tree. What an adventure! What a thrill! The world looked like a completely different place. Something new and different was happening, and she liked the change. Even the thought of missing school, for any reason, was simply out of the question. How could learning and study be fun? Was it even possible? How many times in the last little while had she blessed the name of the teacher who helped her to see what she had never imagined?

Is this not the dream of every educator: to be the person responsible for changing the life of a student? There is no amount of money that can replace the thrill and joy of seeing a young mind come alive with wonder. In truth, most teachers endure all the associated headaches of academia for these moments. Lured by this dream and not by money, fame, or status, teachers everywhere have been willing to pay a high personal price to have this effect in the life of a student.

If this dream is what has drawn people to the teaching profession, then by now the practice of teaching should be an exact and perfected science. By the sheer weight of these aspirations, pedagogical formulas, theories, and practices should have been carved in stone years ago. The improvements in knowledge, theory, and practice in other fields of endeavor that are only a few decades old cast shame on those of us who have chosen to make teaching our profession. What has happened? Why are we still caught in quagmires of revolving thought and reworked ideas when our motives are so right? Why, in all these years of experience, have we come so few steps forward?

As a teacher of teachers, I am deeply troubled by the universal confusion that surrounds teaching and the preparation of teachers. I ponder this dilemma every day with questions like these: "Why don't we get it?" "What's so mysterious about learning?" "Is there something more I can do to ensure that my teaching efforts will help my students learn better and become better teachers?"

My search for these answers has led me down many divergent paths. I've observed the practice and researched the ideas of many different educators; some have provided exciting insights and hope, but just as many have deepened my confusion and doubt. How could this task be so difficult? Why, in this time of ultimate access to information and knowledge, are we seeing more and more students turn their backs on learning? I recently addressed a group of twenty-five hundred teachers in Alaska as they prepared to return for a new school year. I voiced this frustration to them in this fashion: "Let's suppose from the outset that each of you has taught an average of 10 years. Now I know that many of you have been teaching since I was a lad, and I know that some of you are new to the profession. Still, if we each average 10 years of teaching, then together we represent over twenty-five thousand years of experience. Twenty-five thousand years—what can I possibly say in the next two hours that will be of any help? What do I know that hasn't been said before by wiser and keener minds?"

I feel the same way at the outset of this project. How can my educational passions, observations, and discoveries over the last 40-some years make a difference in this field that is so full of proposed practices and theories? My only answer is, "I feel I must." Every time I push this feeling aside and think I should leave this task to others, I hear the deeply emotional voices of devoted, veteran teachers who approach me at the end of a workshop and say, "Why didn't I know this 30 years ago? Think of the difference it could have made."

Hoping that this can make a difference for you, I submit first what many see as a ludicrous notion. It is simply that each of us, in our own way, is an expert teacher. By this, I mean that we are all experts at teaching people who learn exactly the way we do. The simplicity of this notion ends when we have to teach students who learn differently from the way we do.

From our earliest consciousness, we have been the recipients of the teaching efforts of others. Everything we know has been taught to us either by the natural consequences of life's experiences or by the formal and informal teaching of those who have taken their time to pass on what they have previously learned. Our entire life journey is a process of learning. Our brain, through the data-gathering assistance of our other organs, is constantly fed with new information. The acquisition of knowledge is one of the overriding purposes of life and the continuation of our species. Each new rising generation gathers the lessons they have learned from the previous generation and expands their understanding by adding their own personal discovery and insight to what was previously known and shared.

Along this journey of learning, we have observed all types and styles of teaching. We have seen what we consider good and bad, and we have formed well-defined opinions of what appeals to us and what does not. We have gathered a collection of favorite teachers, learning environments, and ways to learn. These observations form the basis from which we evaluate all our learning experiences. From these experiences come our individual preferences as they relate to the gathering and processing of information.

Each of us has a different view on what makes good teaching. But, as different as we are in this area, there is one thing that binds all learners together: We all want the things we are learning to have meaning in our lives. We want learning to be relevant to our existence and to compel us to understand and gain increased mastery of skills and knowledge. We long to be engaged, to have our minds entertained and held captive by new ideas, concepts, and meaning. Because we are all different, we arrive at this place by differing means and avenues. This is why there are so many different opinions on what constitutes good teaching practice.

A careful examination of our most powerful learning experiences reveals that these important educational events have much in common. The truth is that all sound educational theories are correct in their place, but not for every student and not in every situation. Attempts to create an overarching method or set of rules to govern all teaching practice have failed because proponents of such systems do not understand that what works brilliantly for one learner is anathema to another.

To say that we are all experts suggests we have more to learn from each other than we have ever imagined before. It also requires us to accept that each of our students has similar experiences and feelings as they relate to their individual learning preferences. Acknowledging this fact puts teachers and students on a strange and equal footing. It begs us to learn what we can from each other rather than dismissing contrary practices or styles out of hand. Acknowledging this fact would allow our profession to move forward at the speed of our changing technology and to finally stop the educational pendulum from making its predictable 10-year swing. In so doing, we would forever break this cycle that keeps us continually hashing over and revisiting old ideas and past practices.

As educators, we must realistically answer this question: "Will I be more successful if I expect students to change the way they learn to correlate with the way I teach, or will my students be more successful if I learn to modulate my style of teaching to meet their learning needs?" To those who hold the latter half of this question to be correct, I invite you to consider the ideas and principles you will read on the pages that follow and see if they can help you achieve the *Aristotle Effect* in your classroom. The ideas, theories, principles, and practices I discuss are an amalgam of the influence that many great educators have had on my life. They are presented and explored in an effort to help put the fun back in our teaching and help us remember why we entered this profession in the first place. If we can focus on our own wonder and awe for learning, we can find the personal energy and drive to sustain an *awe-based* educational approach in our own teaching environment.

Acknowledgments

Corwin Press gratefully acknowledges the contributions of the following reviewers:

Laura Cumbee
Classroom Teacher
South Central Middle School
Emerson, GA

Dr. Stacey Neuharth-Pritchett
Associate Professor of Elementary Education
University of Georgia
Athens, GA

About the Author

George D. Nelson is a professor, writer, teacher, curriculum designer, director, and educational consultant. His work and influence has been felt in a wide range of institutions and educationally oriented organizations, colleges and universities, state departments of education, state departments of corrections, public schools, corporations, community outreach organizations, and foundations. Curriculum he has created has been used internationally to help teachers and trainers better reach their dramatic learners.

Professor Nelson travels extensively giving workshops, lectures, and inservice training for trainers, teachers, professors, and administrators. He is presently an associate professor at Brigham Young University with a dual appointment in the David O. McKay School of Education and the College of Fine Arts and Communications. He has received numerous teaching awards and has been recognized by the American Alliance for Theatre in Education with the Linn Wright Special Recognition Award for his work with incarcerated dramatic learners.

1

The System

To help us understand the value of the educational journey I would like to take you on, we first need to take a realistic look at the realities that are presently in place. I apologize for beginning in such a traditional fashion, but having a clear understanding of where we stand at the outset is the best way to ensure that we can navigate a course to where we eventually want to be. We are where we are for a reason. Past and present political and educational rhetoric calls for the development of a unified educational system that spans an entire continent. Though the system is to be the main responsibility of state and local control, the goal has been to establish some kind of national uniformity. From the smallest classroom in the most rural area of this country to the inner city megaschool, educational practices are expected to meet the same goals and objectives, and each child is expected to be given the same opportunity.

The reality of this expectation, which exists in our national consciousness, is evident in much of what we say, but it is in little of what we do. Holding to the ideal and not the reality, any failure to meet these expectations runs the risk of meeting criticism from parents, social conscience advocates, or anyone else who has an ax to grind or a finger to point at the system.

This contemplated system must be conducive to the learning needs of inner city children and youth, suburban children and youth, and the children and youth of rural farms and ranches. It must be applicable to the children and youth of every race, language, religion, ethnic group, and socioeconomic background. The contemplated system is expected to house, exercise, transport, nourish, enrich, empower, and educate a population of tens of millions of 5- to 18-year-olds for 6 to 10 hours a day (longer in some cases).

Because of waning parental involvement, this system is expected to motivate the unmotivated; discipline the undisciplined; establish a work ethic; teach and clarify values for those who are confused about what is right and wrong; teach social skills; and provide information on sex, sexuality, and sexually transmitted diseases, and where that fails, provide nursery services and parenting classes for the children of teenage students. Increasing political pressure, from all manner of special interest groups, demands that careful attention be paid to every decision so that nobody will be offended with regard to religious practice, language or innuendo, sexual preference, holiday observance or nonobservance, issues of customs or heredity, treatment of animals, issues of native tongue or dialect, gender, and taste in clothing—just to name a few.

In addition to these essentially noncurricular issues, the system must provide for a bevy of extracurricular activities. Every imaginable sport, club, and organization must be given equal time, place, and support under the umbrella of public education. In addition to the learning needs of children and youth, there is now pressure for the plan to provide adequate remedial education for illiterate, non-English-speaking, and other undereducated adults. In fact, the buildings and all the other resources of the system must accommodate constant use by every imaginable outside group or organization. All facility-related considerations must also encompass strategic planning needs for renovating old and building new facilities.

The system must also provide adequate time and resources for the constant training, updating, enriching, and motivating of faculty and staff. It must have the ability to adjust to and interface with each new technological and learning tool that comes along. This assumes that there is enough flexibility in the overall training plan to ensure that it can allow for successful midstream course adjustments necessary to meet the demands of future changes and developments that have never been considered.

In this increasingly violent society, the educational system is expected to develop policies and procedures for dealing with gangs, lethal weapons, "kids killing kids" and other forms of violence, drugs, extortion, and prostitution on school campuses. These policies need to interface properly with local law-enforcement agencies and officials; provide adequate protection for students, faculty, and staff; and still protect the legal rights and due process of alleged offenders and the rest of the affected population.

Returning to the curricular needs of the system, in addition to these logistical issues, the results achieved in the classroom must be measured against constantly changing national testing standards and university entrance requirements, and they must compete favorably with the educational efforts of other countries. The system must take into consideration new educational requirements for teaching students during this age of information, with all of its new high-tech industries and the ever-increasing need for students who are well prepared in math and the sciences.

It must allow for the needs of an ever-changing job market where employment for those who drop out of the system is becoming increasingly scarce. In addition, it must also instill in successful graduates the desire and skills to compete effectively in some form of postgraduate training in order for them to be marketable in an evolving job market.

Under the weight of all these requirements, and many more that I have not listed, there is one last issue that needs to be addressed: The public education system has no money and little means for generating income of its own volition. Sometimes, those who are the most demanding and critical of the system are the ones least willing to dig into their pockets and pay a fair price for these educational services. Many government officials and citizens alike openly condemn a system that they fail to comprehend and fail to fund fully.

With such an impossible burden to bear, is it any wonder that on every corner we hear that education is failing? Signs of its demise are evident to all who wish to point them out. Purveyors of educational doom use much of this unmet burden to show what is wrong, without acknowledging an ounce of their responsibility or the failure of their own myopic vision.

The worst part of their tirade is that they are flogging a system they don't even understand. Their views are often unrealistic and unfounded, and they tend to do nothing more than demoralize, discourage, and hamstring those who could actually make a difference. Their strident voices and lack of real understanding serve only to further exacerbate the predicament of those individuals whose educational journey is a story of disenchantment and failure.

These critical voices of unknowledgeable outsiders and the disenfranchised students, parents, teachers, and administrators who believe their words are wreaking havoc on our educational system. They breed fear and contempt where hope and awe belong. They turn learning into drudgery, and they turn discovery and personal development into despair. The more we listen to them, the more we risk the loss of the potential of a rising generation. Their voices do nothing more than create an atmosphere of demoralizing fear for students, parents, teachers, and administrators alike.

This debilitating fear is mostly responsible for placing our whole educational system on an apparent verge of collapse. This fear must be replaced with a true and realistic hope. There is much in our system that is exciting, exemplary, and good. Many people who are unable to see this are prepared to dismantle and destroy everything in their attempt to "fix" it. They are treading in dangerous territory. If history is any indicator of the educational future these naysayers hope to build, they will not succeed. We have already been where they want us to go, and in the mirror of time we can still see the failed images of what their unwise efforts have begotten.

When will we as educators learn to steer a steady course to the future rather than going back and forth between competing shores? When will we find a common ground on which to build the foundation of our profession rather than drift in endless circles of dubious practice and rubrics? Is it really that hard to know what to do?

I submit that the answer is simpler than most experts imagine (though many of my colleagues seem to have a tragic disdain for simplicity). We academicians harbor a heroic love for making problems unfathomable, almost as if their continuation is the purpose of our existence. How often are simple answers rejected by the declaration, "Complex problems cannot be solved with simple solutions"? Too often those who are doing the analyzing make the problem complex. They unwittingly create a wall around the problem itself, hedging up the way for any who would offer a viable solution.

The book *Shantung Compound,* by Langdon Gilkey, describes life in a Japanese internment camp in China during the Second World War. In the initial problem-solving meetings held by the camp leadership, Gilkey discovered the following:

> In these nightly meetings I also recognized for the first time the unique character and value of the business mind. The core of its strength was what I might call the "mentality of decision." One or two of these men seated around the table had taken part in academic discussion groups in Peking. There we pondered such abstract issues as peace, international justice, and the relations of ethics or theology to world affairs. I had noted then how strangely silent, though observant, polite, and respectful, these men had been. By contrast, we academicians had fairly flowed with verbiage. And as hour after hour went by with no comment from these business types, I thought to myself in some disappointment and not a little disdain, "Nice responsible men, but hardly bright—surely not able to

> think." Here, however, all was different. The minds of these men accustomed to practical problems, which called for both know-how and decisiveness, clamped onto our situation and dealt with it creatively. What was needed here were concrete answers to technical and organizational problems. (Gilkey, 1966, p. 27)

Often the academic approach to problem solving goes awry because it is based too much in theory and not enough in practical consideration. It focuses on vague similarities and theories that often point to where the problem appears to be, but not where it is in reality. In this context, consider the following problem. Three deer hunters had gone into the forest on their annual hunt. The weather became so threatening that they began to fear for their lives. Their panicked search for shelter proved fruitful when they came across a hunting lodge nestled deep in the woods. Inquiring after a room, they found that there was only one left. They gladly agreed to share. The cost of the room was 30 dollars per night. It seemed a modest price under the circumstances.

Each man contributed 10 dollars, and they retired to their lodgings to sit out the storm. Later that evening, a routine audit revealed to the night manager that these three hunters were overcharged for their room. Their room was on the east side of the lodge, and east-side rooms were only 25 dollars per night. To rectify the problem, the manager called for the bellboy, explained the problem, and handed him a five-dollar bill to refund to the hunters. As the bellboy walked to their room, he decided that it would be hard for the three men to split the five-dollar bill evenly, so he came up with a novel plan.

He knocked on the door, told the hunters that they had been overcharged for their room and gave each man a one-dollar bill from his wallet as a refund. Placing the five dollars in his wallet, he justified keeping the remaining two dollars as a tip. The next morning, after the storm had passed, the hunters continued their hunt feeling good about their warm night's sleep and the seemingly honest treatment they received at the lodge.

This appears to be a very simple story with a rather insignificant and ordinary ending. I hope that a closer inspection will reveal why I have chosen to relate it. Let's begin this inspection by accounting for all the money that was passed around in the story. Following the cash flow, we find that the hunters initially paid 10 dollars apiece for the room, equaling 30 dollars (3 × $10.00 = $30.00). Of that 30-dollar outlay, five dollars was to be refunded to the hunters. Instead, the bellboy kept a two-dollar tip and returned one dollar to each hunter. Having received the one-dollar refund, each hunter now spent only nine dollars on the room ($10.00 – $1.00 = $9.00).

Therefore, 3 hunters × $9.00 = $27.00 (the amount that the hunters actually expended for the room). The bellboy kept the remaining two dollars. By adding the amount that the hunters actually paid (27 dollars) to the amount that the bellboy pocketed (two dollars), you are left with a total of 29 dollars ($27.00 + $2.00 = $29.00). What happened to the remaining one dollar?

Attempting to solve this problem using this kind of logic could lead a person to believe they have discovered a mathematical black hole. Many individuals have contemplated the seemingly mystical nature of this disappearing dollar bill while missing the simple answer. Twenty-five dollars are in the cash drawer of the lodge, one dollar is in the pocket of each hunter, and two dollars are in the wallet of the bellboy ($25.00 + $3.00 + $2.00 = $30.00).

The first approach seems logical because it follows the flow of the money. Quickly the application becomes more complex because it mixes where the money was with where the money is. This past/present conundrum distorts the real picture and leads to the incorrect answer. Only by focusing entirely on where the money actually is can we come up with the right answer.

Granted, this is a simple example, but it illustrates the real problems that exist in trying to solve our educational equation. We are mixing where we appear to be with where we think we are, and we have therefore become lost. In this predicament we have not only become physically disoriented, but, in the fear that this disorientation has caused, many have also lost their vision and hope. In a fearful and hopeless state, we will never find the answers we seek.

Around us, however, are those who have never been lost. Through it all, they have kept their vision and hope. They have discovered the secret, and they quietly create endless strings of small educational successes while the rest of us busily attempt to make our way through our own discouragement. Many of these successful educators find themselves disregarded and even shunned because of resentment and mistrust from their less successful peers. Rather than examining what these teachers are doing, many disgruntled colleagues see these successes as only a greater evidence of their own failure.

Without hope, any problem remains overwhelming and unmanageable. Those of us who have become hopeless seem to find a macabre solace in the overwhelming size of the obstacles we face. This is because the sheer weight of the problem we perceive justifies our overblown and complicated evaluation of the problem. In our educational world, this lack of hope is easily maintained by looking at and recording any possible problem as a failure. Dropout rates are especially attractive in this regard. A view of the problem, failure by failure, will continue to feed the feelings of wholesale panic that plague many teachers and administrators, but to what end? Will it not lead to the actual failure of the system we have dedicated our lives to sustaining and preserving?

What would be the continued cost of maintaining this pessimistic point of view? Which one of us followed the call to teach for fame or fortune? We knew the price we would have to pay when we entered this arena. We knew the realities of low pay and lack of respect and recognition; and yet our enthusiasm and optimism drove us on. We were the true believers, the banner bearers. We knew that any person—every person—who really reached with all their might for the brass ring of learning and seized it firmly would create a lifelong journey of positive personal growth and joy. Many of us chose to teach because of the influence of one beloved mentor who led us to this discovery, and we long to do the same for others. Most of us came on this crusade for the purest of reasons, but we became lost somewhere along the way.

Were we wrong? Were the goals we set out to accomplish misguided, or has the need for quality education and enthusiastic educators passed? No, if ever there were a time and a need for what we once believed, that time is now. We should refocus our questions on what we can do now. What can we do to return to our first dreams? How can we rebuild our splendid optimism? How can we sustain hope in our students, our colleagues, and ourselves? How can we go back to what we once believed? How can we move forward with a constant hope?

Like the lost mariner, we must fix our gaze on the educational North Star. We must return to the foundation of what we do. As there is little agreement in our field about that foundation, let me offer a strong suggestion: Learning, in its purest form, is still the most exciting and invigorating aspect of human life. It is the major element of our journey that expands our hearts and minds and makes life worthwhile. We must identify these pure elements of learning, and we must hold to them with all we are worth. Our focus should be first on the principles of learning and how and why people open their minds. When we fully understand this phenomenon, we will be prepared to discover ways to create an environment that will naturally encourage this kind of pure learning to happen.

2

Dramatic Elements

There is a universal question that parents ask as their children arrive home from school. It has several variations, but its basic form is "What did you do in school today?" Regardless of the exact words that are used, the universal answer children give to cover all the variables is simply "Nothing." This answer is a startling indictment of our learning system, yet it is explained out of hand with statements that range from "It's just laziness on the part of the child to keep them from having to offer a more in-depth answer" to "This is nothing but a lack of respect for the question."

For me, however, it signals a deep problem in our educational system, and it begs another question: "Do students really feel like they're doing nothing in school?" Sadly, the answer is often "yes," not because they aren't doing anything, but because they are usually doing little that is of interest to them. More typically, too, they are often passive observers who watch as the teacher does most of the work of learning.

In contrast, think back on the things you do remember: the books you've read, the music, the songs, the plays, movies, or the lasting positive educational memories you have. There is a strong reason those memories have burned their place in your memory. Dramatic elements were at work in these experiences deepening their value and making them stand out. Of your scholastic memories, if you were asked about what you did on a particularly memorable day, would your answer have been "Nothing"? As you analyze why you remember these kinds of learning experiences, consider the reasons that made them so powerful. What was it about them that causes them to remain so vivid in your memory? Now compare these experiences to the thousands of other run-of-the-mill educational experiences you've had. It's funny how they stand out in the sea of lost learning opportunities and forgotten teachers' faces and names.

Can you make a list of the elements that made these learning events special in your mind? Let's see if I can play the part of the clairvoyant for a moment and list some, if not all, of the elements that made these moments so memorable.

1. You were an active participant in the learning process.
2. There was an overriding activity that was directly related to the curriculum that drove the entire event.
3. You were required, either individually or as a group, to make a report on what you had learned. The report was some kind of a performance made to either the rest of your class, your parents, your school, or some other group.
4. There was some form of costuming involved.
5. You or your group spent much more time on the assignment than you were required to spend.
6. You learned something that you had never realized before.
7. The topic you worked on was or became one of your favorites.
8. You had fun doing it.
9. It was different from what you expected.

10. You felt good about what you did.
11. You thought your teacher and the class were "cool."
12. You were given freedom to explore the assignment in a way that was interesting to you.
13. The grading process was innovative and fair.
14. The learning activity caused you to walk out into unexplored territory, but you felt secure enough to try it.
15. Your teacher was encouraging and demanding but not overbearing.
16. The teacher seemed to be a participant in the learning process.
17. The teacher was as excited as the class was about the process.
18. Food was used in one form or another.
19. You made friends with people you didn't know very well before.
20. You created some form of multimedia presentation for your report.

If you look closely at these 20 elements (and this list is not by any means exhaustive), you may see a common thread tying them together. This list embodies the major principles that foster learning. Each element is necessary to engage learners in powerful and lasting ways. Every great teacher knows these things instinctively. These elements bring learning alive because they are dramatic in nature.

Life without drama is uneventful and dull. So is "dramaless" education. Drama makes things "real." In any subject, drama provides the spark or drive that keeps us interested and willing to keep trying. It is a kind of hope or thrill that gives us joy and leaves us filled with a desire to grow, develop, and improve. William Shakespeare's famous line "All the world's a stage" has been personalized by many successful teachers to read, "Every classroom is a stage." These talented teachers have learned, mostly by intuition, an interesting secret of curricular design and classroom structure. They have learned to adapt dramatic structures into successful classroom practices.

In the environment established by these teachers, students are able to learn in the same fashion they have been learning all of their lives. Teachers do not, for the sake of conformity, place students in a completely unnatural educational state, and ask them to learn in highly uncomfortable ways. Instead, great teachers structure their classes to reflect the life-centered learning that each child has been doing naturally since birth. They employ the same dramatic means to motivate learning and encourage discovery that exists naturally in life.

Most man-made learning environments do not reflect this natural learning phenomenon. Explaining the unnatural state of most classroom structures, Linda Darling-Hammond states:

> The bureaucratic school created at the turn of the twentieth century was not organized to meet these needs for intellectual, social, or personal development. Its mission was not to educate all students well but to process a great many efficiently, selecting and supporting only a few for "thinking work." Strategies for sorting and tracking students were developed to ration the scarce resources of expert teachers and rich curriculum and to justify the standardization of teaching procedures within groups. . . . The rote learning needed for these early twentieth-century objectives still predominates in today's schools, reinforced by top-down prescriptions for teaching practice, mandated curriculum packages, standardized tests that focus on low cognitive skills, and continuing under investment in teacher knowledge. (Darling-Hammond, 1997, p. 45)

Howard Gardner (1991) refers to the educational results of this kind of structure as the "correct answer compromise." According to his theory, expediency replaces real learning, and so we teach students to memorize correct answers to prove that our system is effective. To establish the validity of our work, we turn from measuring the actual understanding of our students as our ultimate outcome to touting their ability to pass standardized tests. This is the case in all drama-less education systems: Real learning is replaced with expedient learning.

Real learning compels an individual to action, and it engenders a lasting change of thought and direction. Real learning goes beyond facts and figures. It measures its success by an individual's actual ability to use knowledge in real-life situations and applications that reach far beyond the classroom. Large educational systems have a hard time making content interesting and compelling to each student. Individuality is sacrificed for the needs of the whole, and, in the process, many learners are left out.

Learners who are disenfranchised by systemic education are most often referred to as *at-risk* learners. So labeled, the system may dismiss their needs as being outside the scope of its mandated responsibility. In this way, the at-risk learner may be blamed for his or her own academic failures. Because the learner is the one with the problem, education as a whole can go on about business as usual. The system can maintain its present course and purpose.

The truth, however, is that these learners are not really as at risk as the label suggests. To save itself, the system has turned on these individuals and branded them with this nefarious title. Institutional education, as a whole, understands that it will be the one that is at risk if it is required to alter itself to meet the learning needs of these individuals. For sheer self-preservation, the system must classify these learners, label them, and set them aside.

The at-risk learner has as much desire to learn as the rest of the student population. If we were to take the time to ask these individuals, they would be more than happy to tell us, in great detail, how they like to learn. For this reason, I am coining a new phrase to describe these nontraditional learners.

The name I propose grows out of the way these individuals prefer to learn. It is positive yet accurate in describing their educational needs. They are *dramatic learners*. They are unmotivated and unexcited by the unnatural drama-less learning environments that have plagued most of their formal educational experiences. They need to feel the relevance of what they are learning before they will fully engage in it. As this relevance is a deep-seated need of all learners, even those learners in the mainstream will benefit greatly by exposure to the techniques that are most successful in reaching these dramatic learners. A quick reference back to the analysis of your most memorable learning experience will give further validity to this point.

As drama gives meaning and purpose to real life, and as dramatic structures seek to represent life, so these same dramatic structures give meaning and purpose to learning. In real life, people must face the actual consequences for their decisions, but within a dramatic structure, individuals may explore the consequences of an action, real or fictional, without having to face any of the negative aspects of real consequences. They are free to explore a world vicariously under the protection of a secure harbor from reality.

For example, an actor can play the role of Lady Macbeth and wrestle with the cold-hearted decisions her character makes to achieve her goal of power and position. The actor can examine the ins and outs of each proposed action and then return safely to the realities of her real world. Though it is true that students in a classroom setting must deal with the consequences of grades, they are still relatively free to explore without having to fear any other kind of real-life consequences.

Dramatic structure, as described by the ancient Greek philosopher Aristotle, is actually simple to understand. In the classical sense, it offers us a way to understand how we must design a dramatic piece that will have lasting and universal appeal to an audience. It is interesting to note that all dramatic pieces, whether traditional or not, contain some elements of the structure that Aristotle outlined several millennia ago. Properly understood, this structure is similar to the structure that exists in all good learning environments.

In this light, many teachers balk at the suggestion that they should be considered entertainers. Interestingly enough, Aristotle taught that individuals are never really learning unless they are being entertained. In his statement, Aristotle's definition of entertainment refers to having one's mind engaged rather than having it filled with mindless amusement.

A close observation of great teachers reveals that they draw heavily, whether they know it or not, on dramatic elements to hold and engage their students. These elements do not take away from the learning process; they are at the very core of what motivates an individual to learn something new. For the sake of this discussion, we will assume that every class of students can be considered an audience. Taking this to the next level, each classroom can therefore be considered the stage, and the teacher then becomes an important character on that stage.

In this all-too-common setting, what happens when the students (the audience) are not compelled by the character (the teacher) they are observing? When this main character doesn't have the ability to relate to the audience, boredom will naturally result and precious learning opportunities will be lost. How many teachers spend hour after hour involved in these dramatic performances without even knowing it? Many have been teaching for years and have never even given a passing thought to how their character is being received by the intended audience.

Regardless whether teachers wish to admit it, they are, in reality, performers or characters in some form of a dramatic presentation. How could it be otherwise? Creation of a sound learning environment requires one to be aware, intuitively or otherwise, that every classroom decision or every interaction with a student or group of students, in any way, causes teachers to enter a world where dramatic laws and principles have a controlling influence. A teacher who ignores this fact would be comparable to a mountain climber who ignores the laws and principles of gravity. The results are deadly.

In fact, teachers would do well to see their role expand far beyond that of a character to that of a director and/or playwright. The compelling nature of each educational performance is completely in the hands of the teacher to compose and direct. Like those of any dramatic performance, the type and style of the production are up to the director and playwright. In a dramatic learning environment, the teacher should be as free as any artist to draw from every possible resource to determine the outcome. Certainly, at the end of each learning day, what is actually put on the educational stage and how compelling it is to the students is virtually in the hands of each individual teacher. Many teachers and administrators might be appalled by this comparison, but before dismissing it out of hand, let us take a close look at the structure and essential elements of Aristotle's dramatic model.

In his aesthetic treatise, *The Poetics,* Aristotle outlines the major dramatic elements in a sound play. Though these writings and observations of theatrical productions are thousands of years old, the principles and elements Aristotle articulated apply today. Literary or dramatic works that do not follow Aristotle's guiding principles lack clarity, depth, and universal appeal. Those that have attempted to depart wholly from the Aristotelian bulwark have often seen their work languish over time.

As I mentioned earlier, Aristotle claims that individuals learn only when they are being entertained. For this reason, a teacher must fully understand the principles of dramatic structure to engage the mind and heart of a student. The elements Aristotle describes are essential in holding interest and creating an atmosphere where individuals are willing to move out of their present situation and stand on higher ground. These are the same principles that a teacher must use in a classroom to move learners from their present plateau to new vistas of understanding. Aristotle describes these major dramatic elements as plot structure, character, thought, style, and spectacle.

Plot Structure

In the dramatic or literary world, plot (or plot structure) is the story line. Good plots are compelling and hold the interest of the audience. Plotting is the art of interweaving the facts and events of a story in such a way that the audience remains involved and entertained from the beginning of the production to the end. Regardless of the medium they use, master storytellers have the ability to hold an audience spellbound as they spool out the events of their yarn. On the other hand, there is nothing so uninteresting as a plot that is too easily figured out or poorly presented.

In the classroom, good plotting refers to the ability of the teacher to create unit and lesson planning materials in a way that fully engages the students. It is the power of creative introduction, of presentation and exploration skillfully fashioned to meet the particular needs of the students. Teachers who gain the skills to create lessons that use dramatic elements find themselves able to draw their students emotionally and physically into the learning process. Speaking of the importance of plot, Aristotle said, "The goal is a certain activity, not a qualitative state. . . . It is in their actions that they achieve, or fail to achieve" (trans. 1987, p. 37). The plotting or, better, the lesson and unit planning of a teacher must ensure that students are compelled to action in the learning process. This action, of course, need not be physical; powerful results can be achieved through emotional and intellectual action as well. More on this element of dramatic structure is explained in the discussion of curriculum development in Chapter 6.

Character

In the dramatic or literary world, character refers to the believability and depth of the individuals that are being portrayed in the work. In Aristotle's world, character was the second element in importance next to plot. It can be argued that in the modern world, character has grown in importance as a dramatic element. In some plays, films, and literary works, character is the driving and unifying force. Compelling and real characters can draw our attention and hold our interest to an equal or greater degree than can an interesting plot.

In the classroom, character refers to the personality of both the teacher and the students. The number-one factor in determining educational success is still the personal interaction between student and teacher. All our advances in technology and information still depend on the teacher to make them accessible to the learner. As touched on earlier, teachers must understand the effect that their "character" (persona/personality) has on the students in the class. They must also have a deep understanding of the learning needs of each of their students to fully answer the character needs as they relate to the educational choices of each student. According to Aristotle, "character is the element which reveals the nature of moral choice" (p. 38). As teachers depend on students to exercise their choice to learn or not, any knowledge we can discover that reveals the nature or means by which individual learners make these important learning decisions is something we should strive to understand. I cover more of this element of dramatic structure in Chapter 3 and in the discussion of learning styles that takes place in the appendix.

THOUGHT

In the dramatic or literary world, the element of thought relates to the ability of a piece to invoke deep introspection on the part of the audience. It is a measure of the intellectual power of work. Thought, as described by Aristotle,

> is the capacity to produce pertinent and appropriate arguments. . . . Thought arises in passages where people show that something is or is not the case, or present some universal proposition. (p. 38)

In the classroom, then, thought is the ability that teachers or curricula have to help students internalize what is being taught. It is the ability of the environment to invoke intrinsic and lasting change. Thought is fostered in the depth of the subject matter, the ownership of the student in the learning process, the power of teacher questioning to engender analytical thinking, and the freedom that students are given to seek for real answers. It is the power that comes from a real search for understanding, rather than from the dampening of thought that results from teaching students only to pass standardized tests.

Style

In the dramatic and literary worlds, style originally referred to "the composition of spoken metres" (Aristotle, trans. 1987, p. 39). Aristotle used this term as it related to the poetic meter that was chosen to express the meaning of the lyric poetry, which was used to tell the story in the ancient Greek plays. Today, style has a broader meaning and use. It refers to all of the individual choices that artists make to produce a unique piece. In Aristotle's mind style was not as weighty an element as the others.

In the classroom, this element refers to the individual style of teachers. As teachers are ultimately responsible for establishing the learning environment, the tone or style of each class reflects a great deal of a teacher's personal philosophy and values. Again, whether teachers are aware of this fact or not, it is a highly visible aspect of all learning environments. It is amazing how the majority of our educational battles are fought over issues of style and taste rather than over the more meaty considerations of pedagogy and curricula.

Spectacle

According to Aristotle, spectacle, the final dramatic element, is the "least important garnishing." He states that "spectacle is emotionally powerful but is the least integral of all" (trans. 1987, p. 38). Many modern plays and movies fall into the trap of being nothing but spectacle. In these pieces, plot and character suffer because all the energy of production is spent on wild chase scenes, gratuitous sex or violence, or massive vistas or sets. Productions that are based on spectacle flash brilliantly in the pan, but then vanish quickly into thin air.

In the classroom, spectacle consists of added elements that create novelty and whimsy. These unexpected elements spice up the learning environment and create much-needed variety and intrigue. As with dramatic pieces that are based on spectacle, educational thrusts that depend on these kinds of glitzy attractions fail to sustain themselves for any length of time. Spectacle in the classroom is the yeast, the spark, and the thrill that lift the whole learning process. It can often fuel amazing growth and discovery, but it is highly flammable and must be handled with care.

In a classroom where all of these elements are used together with extreme care and balance, the most important magic in life occurs. This is the magic of dramatic learning and the expansion of understanding. It is the power of the *Aristotle Effect*. It happens only in a mind and heart that are open and willing to learn. It happens only in a mind and heart that are being entertained and challenged with information, ideas, thoughts, feelings, and new skills that will keep growing and expanding for a lifetime.

3

Character and Education

To create a more dramatic learning environment, we must look more deeply at the major Aristotelian elements as they relate to the classroom than we did in the previous chapter. The most important elements to Aristotle are plot and character. These two elements are examined in their own chapter. The remaining elements, thought, style, and spectacle, are interwoven into these chapters. We begin this examination by looking at the element of character (the personality of the teacher and the students). Many teachers agree with Aristotle and begin their pedagogical design with the curricular (plot-structure) elements. However, where real learning is concerned, the element of character (personality) needs to be placed foremost in our consideration. If we make the curricular (plot) stand preeminent, we lose our bearings and fall back to an environment that is drama-less. If we begin by carefully considering the character (personality) needs of the learner and the establisher of the learning environment, we can build from that foundation to create the most effective plot or curricular structures.

The science of learning is not exact. In reality, those with the deepest understanding of pedagogy acknowledge it is more of an art than a hard science. As an art form, therefore, the lines and rules for what is or isn't good theory, principle, or practice are less rigid and more personal than a strict science. As I have stated before, in many cases what is educationally right or wrong comes down to a question of the Aristotelian element of style or taste. Arguments on these issues can never be won; they simply swirl around and around, causing deeper confusion and divisions, which separate individuals and slow the advancement of our field of study. As the educational camps line up along their chosen battle lines, the shrill voices of dissension create a rift that keeps teachers and teaching from being fully accepted as a profession.

As teachers, we want respect and acceptance, but we will never find it until we are willing to stake out an inclusive common ground of what is good and acceptable teaching practice. We tend to look beyond the mark, or, like sheep, we follow one path or another to the exclusion of all others. We do this in the hope that we can find the educational promised land where all students learn effectively and where all teachers are masters. When will we ever see the clear path of diversity and recognize that learning is an individual process, that people have clear preferences and talents when it comes to their desire and ability to gather and process knowledge?

In the study and advancement of most fields of endeavor, the beginning point for all research and development is gaining an in-depth understanding of all the parts that make up the whole. For example, prospective doctors spend years learning the parts of the body by name, location, and function. This is where they must begin: How else could they prepare to heal others? Is there not an associated educational rigor that should precede the preparation of all prospective teachers? Shouldn't there be some common core of knowledge that all teachers should master as a foundation?

If there were, what would be the anatomy of learning? What core of knowledge should every teacher be expected to know? Certainly those of us who are responsible for teaching or for training teachers should at least have one piece of common ground to use as a binding touchstone from which we could safely depart or to which we could turn for our bearings. The foundation piece that is missing relates directly to the dramatic element of character.

The study of pedagogy should begin from the inside out. We do not teach subject matter, we teach individuals. For this reason, we must first understand how individuals learn before we can understand how to create and use educational structures. The character (personality) of each individual student and teacher is at the heart of all learning. What other explanation can be made? All great teachers see themselves in this light. They are keenly aware of the dramatic nature of their world, and they do all in their power to use every tool of dramatic structure that is available to them. They seek to understand their own character (personality) and the character (personality) of each class member. They realize that these character issues play an important role on the stage of their classroom.

I had a high school chemistry teacher who understood this clearly, even to the point that he developed his own costume. Nowhere but in his classroom did you see him dress and act like the stereotypical scientist. For us, his lab coat, pocket protector, crepe-soled shoes, and safety goggles turned him into the consummate expression of "Chemistry Man." His character became so compelling that we believed he knew every answer to every chemistry-related question that we could ever imagine. In his role as the absent-minded professor, we sincerely looked forward to his antics and explanations. Science became an extension of the character he created, and we all grew to love chemistry because we loved his character.

The goal of all teachers should be to define themselves and their love of the subject they teach in a fashion that resonates positively with their students. Teachers must acknowledge the impact their character has on learning to properly evaluate their ability to reach their students. To bring out the true character of the learner inside each student, teachers must develop the skill of using their own character as a foil. Teachers who understand this secret know their students are the most essential characters in this process, and they must use every tool at their disposal to gain and maintain their students' interest.

Whether we accept it or not, we are what we teach. A teacher cannot escape this fact, because students won't let them. The character of the teacher is so much more provocative than the words that come out of his or her mouth. I remember, as a young child, seeing one of my teachers shopping with her family. This scene was almost beyond my imagination. I had never considered the fact that she had a life outside of the classroom. Surely this can be explained by my lack of emotional development, but there is more to this situation that needs to be uncovered. In my young mind, her character was so incomplete that I somehow believed she was unlike other women I knew. In fact, I was so detached from this individual who was directing a major portion of my day, that I assumed she simply retreated to a closet at the end of the day and awaited our return to school the next morning. This is an extreme example, but it is not too far from a commonly held perception among students that many teachers are flat, one-dimensional characters who exist only to demand, discipline, and extract specific subject matter allegiance.

This present tirade is not a call for all teachers to become their students' friends or peers. Rather, it is a simple reminder that appropriate character connections need to be established to create an effective educational environment. The choices and decisions you are making at present are already forming these character connections. Have you considered how effective you are at creating and projecting the image and power that will make you the best teacher possible? In a true dramatic fashion, when your character (personality) can compel your students' character (personality) to action, they will finally become the true protagonists in the real drama of learning.

As they become engaged in the learning process, students move across the stage of enlightenment, independently interacting with ideas, concepts, and theories. They will seek to collaborate with other similarly engaged learners. As they explore this dramatic stage of the classroom, they can become intimately familiar with facts, figures, texts, places, historical figures, and unimaginable worlds of wonder. The character of the young person invigorated by the love of knowledge should be the goal of all educational endeavors.

In order for teachers to have this kind of educational power, it is essential for them to be deeply familiar with their students' intrinsic needs as learners. A director preparing to mount a dramatic production spends many hours on an in-depth analysis of each character in the script. According to the great stage director William Ball, one of the major reasons for this analysis is to find the "Golden Key" (1984, p. 73) that unlocks the access to understanding the characters in the play. This key is nothing more than finding out what each character in the play really wants. It is an analysis strictly aimed at discovering the intrinsic, driving values or motivations that cause the characters to do what they do.

Thinking again of teachers as directors or playwrights, how much more powerful would the educational process be if they had the ability to understand better the personality (character) and learning preferences of each student? This information is readily available to teachers. There are a number of instruments available to assess a student's learning style or "character issues" painlessly.

This personal information makes it easier to deal effectively with the different personalities in each class. Knowledge of Ball's Golden Key, as it relates to learning, helps in all aspects of a teacher's responsibility. From lesson planning to disciplining, this information holds many secrets that can eradicate failed practices. It can even help an exasperated third-grade teacher to understand why one of her students flies his pencil up and down the aisles of desks every time he finishes his worksheet assignments. It may help solve the riddle of why a shy first grader chooses to bring a knife to school or why a young, bright freshman won't participate in class.

To discover the Golden Key to the character (personality) of my students, I have learned to trust a learning styles instrument. This information, along with information that can be gained from parents and personal observation, helps me immeasurably to understand the character and learning preferences of my students. Their behavioral choices become much clearer as I discover the individual secrets of their intrinsic values and desires. Certainly this information isn't completely predictable, just as no human behavior is, but it goes a long way in helping me stand close to the place where a student really lives and learns.

Without going into an examination of the pros and cons of each learning styles instrument, my research makes me most comfortable using one that is based on the work of Carl Jung. I have found his focus on individual preferences to be highly accurate and reliable. Instruments that are based on other factors tend to be overly prescriptive or unreliable. Jung's seminal examination of psychological types is the basis for the Myers-Briggs Type Indicator, Keirsey Temperament Sorter, and a host of similar instruments.

This body of work examines the preferences that people exercise as they pursue their own personal happiness and determine the meaning of their existence. This personal search for understanding uses the concepts of learning preferences. I find this methodology for determining learning style to be more flexible because it does not attempt to offer a prescription for behavior. It simply explores individual preferences and the role they play in the individual choices people make in all aspects of their lives. This approach is especially helpful in determining how a person prefers to learn, because perceptions are much like perspectives: Everyone has their own.

Many teachers and administrators shy away from instruments that measure learning style or personality because of a concern that the information derived from them will be used only to further label students. This pious position drips with hypocrisy, because educational institutions are guilty of the grossest kinds of labeling. My real-life experience with this issue reveals that labeling only happens when individuals have a limited understanding of learning preferences. Fellow teachers and administrators who fully understand the positive impact of the knowledge of learning styles know that this information provides the truest insight into the heart of an individual. This knowledge can reveal very accurately what a student values.

Teacher knowledge of this individualized value base is the key to creating a successful educational experience for each student.

Personal Paranoia

As a young professor at the University of Texas, I had no understanding of this important ingredient of education. I became distraught with my inability to reach all of my students. Some considered me one of their best teachers, while others held a lesser opinion of my abilities. Here I was, a teacher of teachers, and I clearly had no idea what I was doing right or wrong. As I began to look for an answer, my research led me deep into the world of teaching and learning styles. I was amazed that I had never been fully exposed to this concept before.

It is true that the concept had been lightly brushed by a professor or two, but its mention was only as a passing notion that some theorists on the fringe of sound educational practice espoused. At first blush, I clung to their bias, and my initial research did little to change my outlook. It appeared too simple. How could every learner in the world fall into 3, 4, 6, 7, 8, or even 16 different types?

This opinion is readily held in most educational circles. In my own tenure battle at the university, several colleagues considered my research, curriculum development, and writing in this area to be "spurious at best." This is because most of my colleagues who evaluated my work looked at it through the lens of their own learning and teaching style. David Keirsey explains their skepticism in a unique way as he also explains the views of the majority of educators.

> Neither SJ [his name for a tradition-based teacher or administrator] teachers nor the SJ administrators feel any need to defend their views on instruction or administration, even if it occurred to them to do so. Belonging to so massive a majority, the SJ educators unconsciously assume their views to be the norm and are continuously surprised when colleagues take issue with them on "basics" or "fundamentals." (Keirsey & Bates, 1978, p. 155)

Though many of my colleagues found it difficult to accept my work, they could not argue with the results that were being achieved in the classroom. Some of them seemed almost chagrined by the success that many school systems were experiencing as they adopted elements of my approach. It has saddened me in many ways to see them openly wonder at the results that have been achieved while remaining unwilling to analyze the principles that were used to achieve the results.

My continued research in this area led me to a personal discovery that has changed the way I approach teaching and preparing teachers. As I became more and more convinced that all students have their distinctive preference toward learning, I ran into heavier and heavier opposition concerning my ideas. It caused me a great deal of consternation, especially in light of the fact that I believed I was beginning to understand where many learning problems were based.

As I tried to explain these not-so-new ideas to my colleagues, I began to experience all kinds of opposition. My work was being dismissed with comments such as "That's just a passing fad; it will fade away in time," "It's nothing but another method of labeling," "It's too simple," "You can't expect me to be responsible for the way someone prefers to learn," "I'm the teacher, and if the students want to be successful in my classroom, then they'll have to get used to the way I teach," "That's just another excuse for lazy students," "Do you know what you're saying here?" "What would happen to education if we had to try and teach each student in a different way?" and "This is a lightweight solution to a problem that is too big to solve."

In the face of these comments, my own classroom experiences and those of teachers I was training only served to prove the validity of my findings. I still worried at first, fearing I was out of step with the rest of the educational mainstream. I often felt as if I were standing in the wrong ticket line. You may know the feeling. You want to get tickets to see a show and you stand where you think you should, but your line is so much shorter and seems to be moving so much faster that you begin to worry. You become afraid that you are in the wrong line and that everyone else is right.

This fear is finally behind me because every time I've reached the window, I've been rewarded with the "ticket," the Golden Key I was seeking. I am now confident that I'm in the right line, though my new fear is that it will forever remain short because so many teachers are unwilling to take the same risks they expect their students to take. I sadly believe that many of my educational colleagues are happy to stand in their present line for the simple reason that they are in such abundant company. The fact that the line is not moving and that they have yet to reach their goal seems to have eluded them. They dismiss this shortcoming with such statements as "This is the way it's always been" or "The problems we face are too complex."

Many of us gain great comfort by standing together and believing that the solution will soon appear. Others use the complexity card to defer culpability, as I have mentioned earlier. The logic appears to be that "If we make the dragon big enough, nobody will expect us to slay it." What if, however, the problem is not that difficult? What if the major problem we face has a solution that most of us simply ignore? What if an increased understanding of the character of our students as it relates to their learning styles is an important part of the answer?

Come and stand in this shorter line for a minute, and see how simple the pedagogical process can become when we start with the premise that maximum learning occurs when we focus on the dramatic element of character (personality) and adapt our teaching to the learning style of the student. Using learning styles as the base, an educator begins to understand teaching and learning from the perspectives of the individual teaching preference of the teacher and the individual learning preference of the student.

The process begins by developing an understanding of an individual's preference along four different scales as conceived by Jung. This research into the character of the teacher and the students helps us to harness the power of the rest of the dramatic elements. All curricular design should begin with an understanding of the student; otherwise, there is an extremely high likelihood our planning will be met with a bevy of relevancy problems.

Interaction Scale

The first Jungian preference scale seeks to establish individuals' preferences for the way in which they like to interact with other people. Because learning is a person-to-person process, this information is vital to understand.

Introversion and Extroversion

Some people have a clear preference toward working with others and learning in the company of many companions and friends. Jung designates these individuals as those who prefer *extroversion*. Conversely, those who prefer *introversion* typically prefer learning in ways that are more isolated. These two individuals represent each end of this interaction scale. The major difference between the two is how they prefer to gain energy or interact with others. Again, simply put, those who prefer introversion tend to seek opportunities to work in isolation and be alone in their educational endeavors, while those who prefer extroversion seek the constant association and encouragement of others.

The important thing to remember about these scales is that they are infinite in nature. There is clearly room on the continuum for every person's preference as it relates to introversion and extroversion. Most people tend to score in the midrange of this scale rather than at either extreme. Following the typical bell curve, these midrange scores mean that preferences are often less extreme in most individuals. This allows them to operate as needed in either area even though they have a definite preference toward extroversion or introversion.

Thinking of your own preference between extroversion (E) and introversion (I), where would you place yourself on the following scale?

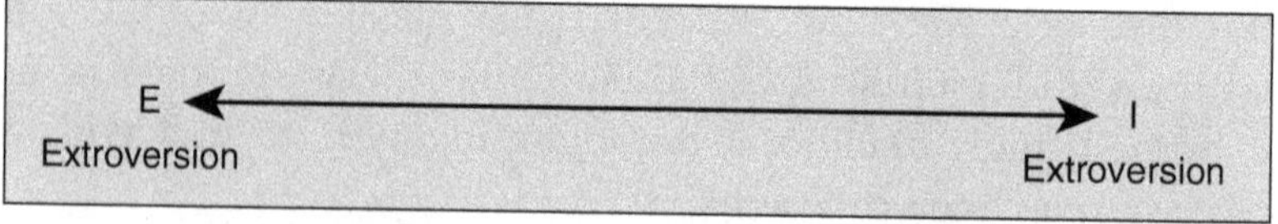

As I previously mentioned, some people have no clear preference and are equally comfortable in either arena. Such individuals would find themselves moving back and forth along this scale, depending on the given situation. Individuals with a clear preference typically find it more difficult to operate in the opposite world. This does not mean, however, that people cannot move out of their preference. Certainly, as mature adults, we realize that the demands of life require that we function well in many different situations, regardless of our preferences. The true indicator of preference comes when these individuals are free to do as they choose. Those who prefer introversion, who have spent many hours interacting with others, will typically seize the first available opportunity to be alone to recharge their personal batteries. Those with an extroversion preference, who must spend long hours working in isolation, will usually seek the first opportunity to recharge by interacting with others.

Introversion in learning is exhibited by an individual's desire to work alone and at his or her own pace. This preference becomes evident in their true desire to achieve the joy of individualized accomplishments. Although others may view this solitary existence as problematic, a true introvert is rarely lonely. Introverts often want to figure things out for themselves, without interference by a teacher or anyone else. They see a teacher as simply another resource to use when they need to expand their world of understanding. Like any resource they may find inadequate, introverted learners have little value for teachers who they esteem to be incompetent.

Introverted learners are often observed working off by themselves or exploring things on their own. They are typically the most self-motivated of all learners. The problem is that they prefer to learn what and when they want. Unless they are motivated intrinsically, they feel that learning something that has merely been assigned is nothing but busywork. For these reasons, introverted learners often fail in a traditional school setting. The failure does not occur because of a lack of ability, but rather because of a lack of relevance and personal interest.

Extroverted learning is the opposite of introverted learning in almost every way. School is a fun place for extroverts to be because it's filled with lots of other people. Extroverts typically thrive in a gregarious environment that offers plenty of interpersonal stimulation. They love to learn with and from others. To them group projects are often the most exciting.

In many cases, extroverted learners will be happy just to pursue the same educational path the rest of their friends travel. In this regard, I quizzed my extroverted daughter one day about her reason for taking French when Spanish seemed to be a more practical language in our community. Her response was a clear indication of her preference: "Daddy, all my friends are taking French." The language that was being taught clearly wasn't the focus of her decision; her decision was based on who would be there rather than what was to be learned.

For this reason, the extrovert's individual success is often greatly influenced by peer groups. Those who have prosocial friends find school a challenging and rewarding place. However, those whose peer group has gravitated to another set of values struggle to excel. When extroverted students are forced to work in isolation for an extended period, they tend to lose interest in what is assigned, and they can begin to exhibit highly off-task behavior. Because they thrive on human interaction and attention from others, extroverts will often compensate for feelings of isolation by behaving in ways that draw attention to themselves. They often like to take leadership roles in the class. This can take the form of simply handing out books, or can be as elaborate as serving as a teacher's aide. Their need to interact with others will be filled either at your expense though negative, attention-seeking behavior or as part of your plan for creating a more fulfilling learning environment.

Educators who attempt to reach students without an understanding of their preference toward extroversion or introversion can sorely miss the mark, regardless of their level of sincerity or desire. Picture an extroverted teacher working in the lunchroom. She sees a child sitting all alone, off in a corner, reading a book. What does she assume? Typically, "because of the student's personal preference toward extroversion," the teacher will assume that the individual is lonely, sad, and in need of a friend. Her immediate reaction will likely be to attempt to reach this "lonely" student.

If the student is an extrovert, the teacher may be on the right track. But if the student is an introvert, the chances are that he or she has taken this seat as a matter of choice and is engaged in an activity that is more personally rewarding than the other available choices. In this case, the teacher's attempt to reach the student in need may be seen as nothing more than an invasion of privacy. Let's play out this very scenario with the teacher and student.

Teacher: (Enters the cafeteria and notices a student off by herself reading a book) Hello.

Student: (Looking up from her book) Hi.

Teacher: I noticed that you were all alone here and I just wanted to . . .

Student: Am I bothering anyone?

Teacher: Of course not, but I thought I'd check and see . . .

Student: I'm fine really. Now, would you please leave me alone?

Teacher: I was only trying to help.

Student: In that case, why don't you go over to that table and ask those guys to keep it down.

Teacher: Has anyone ever taught you how to respect your . . .

Student: Has anyone ever taught you to mind your own business?

However exaggerated this example is, it illustrates what happens so often in our world. This teacher's sincere attempt to help a student turns into a confrontation that was never intended by either party. How will this teacher ever know what she should do? The answer, of course, is that unless she can read the mind of the child, she will never know for sure. Short of this impossibility, knowing the learning preference of the student is a great place to begin when trying to determine what the most appropriate action should be.

Let's replay this little scenario with the teacher and student. This time, the teacher will apply her knowledge of learning preferences as they relate to interaction. The teacher is still an extrovert, and the student is still an introvert who has chosen to sit alone.

Teacher: (Enters the cafeteria and notices a student off by herself reading a book. Crosses over and sits at the table with the student, but not too close) Hello.

Student: (Looking up from her book) Hi.

Teacher: Looks like you've found the quietest spot in the place.

Student: It's all there was.

Teacher: Sorry to bother you. I just wanted to make sure you were sitting here by choice.

Student: I can think of a million places I'd rather be.

Teacher: You're not alone there. Sorry I bothered you. I'll let you get back to what you were doing.

Student: Thanks.

Teacher: If you need me for anything, you know where to find me.

See the difference? This knowledge helps the teacher because it allows her to make decisions from a knowledge base rather than merely guessing. Certainly there is no way to predict human behavior. This information about preference, however, allows a teacher to act like the manager of a stock fund, who relies on the knowledge of market and financial trends and proclivity to make educated guesses in an uncertain world. In the same fashion, a teacher who understands the preferences of students will be more successful in predicting the right course to take in the long run. At the very least, a teacher can enter into a difficult situation aware of several different exit strategies. Because most teachers do not have a frame of reference for these preferences, they have no clear idea of where to begin or where to retreat should things go the wrong way.

Without a clear understanding of preference, as in our first scenario, a problem occurs from the point of view of the student as well as the teacher. The student feels that nobody understands her needs, and the teacher feels unappreciated for her efforts. Both were sincerely following their preferences, but neither received what they wanted in return. The gift that the teacher offered in trying to help the student not feel lonely was seen by the student as nothing but an intrusion. Neither person was edified. Both left the situation unsatisfied.

This is the major problem in most human interaction. It happens even under the most well-meaning circumstances because we tend to give others what we think they need, based on our own evaluation of the situation. The reason we give unwanted gifts is that we usually read the needs of others through the lens of our own perspective. If the person we are interacting with has the same preferences as we do, then we will naturally be more correct in the decisions we make as we deal with them. When students have different preferences, as is usually the case, we often find ourselves way off base. A good rule of thumb to follow when interacting with others is to try to give the gift the other person wants to receive rather than the one we would prefer to receive. This also works well in every interaction we have with other people inside and outside the classroom.

For example, on a particular anniversary, I decided to surprise my wife with a diamond ring. I planned for weeks how I would afford it and then spent a considerable amount of time finding what I thought would be the perfect ring. As you can imagine, I had a particular response in mind when I gave her my gift. The gift I gave her and the response I received did not meet the expectation of either one of us. Her idea of what the ideal anniversary gift should have been was very different from what I had chosen. Much like the first cafeteria scenario, what was intended was not achieved. Gifts offered, whether from the heart or the wallet, are best received when given with a knowledge of the preference of the person receiving the gift. This works in relation to all of the scales we will discuss.

Gathering Scale

The next Jungian scale relates to the way in which individuals prefer to gather information. Gathering is the first process that students must go through before they can learn anything new. As mentioned before, this and all other Jungian scales are infinite. The student's gathering preference is a choice on a continuum between sensory and intuitive gathering.

Sensory gatherers are individuals who prefer to gather information in very concrete or tactile ways. They like to touch, see, smell, taste, hear, and experience everything with their physical senses before they tend to assign it real value or importance. They see themselves as very practical gatherers. However, intuitive gatherers use a more abstract process for gathering information. They are adept at using their vast sense of intuition or foresight to gather important ideas, concepts, and information that have particular personal value without having to actually experience it through their tactile senses.

Some individuals clearly have a strong preference at either end of this spectrum, whereas others find it hard to choose which process they prefer most. Effective teachers must know how individuals prefer to gather information before they will have the ability to package information in a way that will be attractive to a student. It is important to remember that learners only gather information that they perceive to be valuable. For verification of this fact, just think of all the information that you disregard simply because it appears, on the surface, to lack value.

Sensory Gatherers

Sensory (concrete) gatherers prefer to interact with knowledge, ideas, concepts, facts, or information in the present. Information that is not immediately relevant, quantifiable, malleable, and usable is passed over as worthless to these learners. Unless something new immediately stimulates their senses, they usually leave it behind. These students often like to physicalize ideas and concepts, by counting on their fingers, for example, or acting them out, or rephrasing them in terms that make the concepts more familiar. They tend to look for the bottom line in everything by using one or all of the following resources: charts and graphs, agendas, timetables, deadlines, syllabi, and schematics that show clearly how things work together.

Sensory gatherers are often driven by a desire to obtain closure. They tend to deal with one item or project at a time, finish it, set it aside, and then move on. They can often appear almost robotic in the way they can focus on a single task at the exclusion of everything else. For some of these gatherers, to be finished with something does not mean to complete it, as much as it means to be done with it in terms of "I'm ready to move on now." These particular sensory learners spend time doing something until they are bored, and that becomes reason enough for moving on to something else. To their counterparts, to be finished does mean complete, and they love to finish things so they can check them off their to-do lists. This need for closure can cause the sensory gatherer to pass over anything that cannot be understood in terms of what is already known, what can be immediately applied, what is stimulating to the senses, and/or what should be in terms of rules, laws, or precedent.

Intuitive Gatherers

On the opposite end of the scale, intuitive gatherers are typically seeking understanding and meaning by gathering things that cannot be manipulated in a physical fashion. Rather than looking for closure or immediate understanding like the sensory gatherer, those with the intuitive preference look for ideas that expand thinking and understanding in a global sense. They like to gather without hands the ideas and concepts that take them outside the present boundaries of their understanding so they can discover the true purpose of life or comprehend the ethereal mysteries of existence. Unlike the sensory (concrete) gatherer, the intuitive gatherer constantly makes connections—personal or otherwise—and seeks new ideas, vistas, theories, postulates, or concepts to explore.

Some unique differences within this preference alter the focus of what they desire to gather. Some people have a tendency toward issues of fact, worldly theory, and scientific discovery. Other people have a focus that is related to people, relationships, and the pursuit of happiness. In gathering, as well as in all the other scales, it is important to understand that even though individuals may share the same preference, they still have deep differences, within these preferences, that make them unique and individual. There are as many differences among the same preference as there are between preferences.

Thinking of your own preference between sensory (S) and intuitive (N) gathering, where would you place yourself on the following scale?

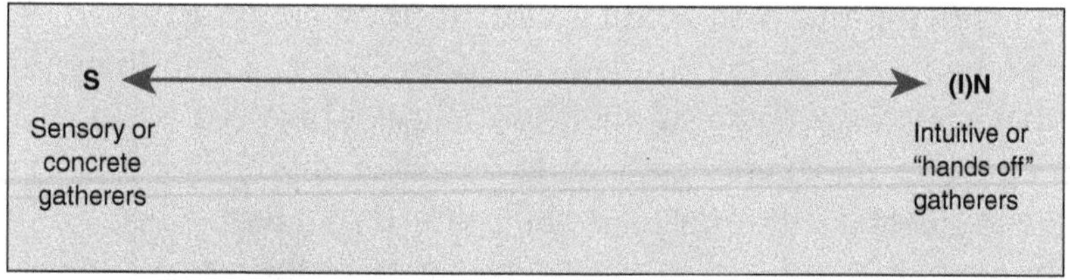

Here, as before, the preference is an individual one. There may be a clear choice between the two extremes, or one could be comfortable gathering information either way. The problem again arises in education when students with a clear preference are only presented information or knowledge in a manner that does not relate to the way they prefer to gather. Teachers who know how to present material to only those students who gather information the same way they do cut off many of their other students from gathering new information.

Think of a teacher who is so excited by an idea or concept that he analyzes it for his class from every possible angle without grounding the analysis in something relevant in the lives of his students. Those students who are intrinsically interested in his idea or concept, or who share his method of gathering information, will be enthralled with this approach. However, those who gather in a more sensory or concrete fashion will be frustrated as they struggle to see his point. In fact, they may eventually, politely or impolitely, ask him to get to his point.

Information or knowledge that a learner does not gather cannot be mastered. It lies on the ground like unharvested fruit. When teachers learn how to modify or package a given subject to meet the multiple gathering needs of their students, then they have essentially mastered an important step in making a learning message accessible to learners of different styles. It is not a particularly difficult task, but it is one that few teachers have been trained to address in their classrooms. It is one that seems more complex and overwhelming than it really is.

Using another example with my daughter, one night we were together at a wedding reception. The buffet that was prepared for the guests was one of the most delectable assortments of seafood dishes that could be assembled in one place. As we scanned the table, it quickly became obvious that we had a different perspective on the spread. As I "gathered" with great gusto from the delicacies, my plate wasn't big enough to hold all I desired. She, on the other hand, only gathered a roll, a few croutons, and a drink. Noticing my judgmental look at her plate, she replied, "I hate it when there's nothing to eat."

Our gathering activities at the buffet table reflected our individual preferences. We were each inwardly critical of the other because we could not understand the other's selection process. She would not have been happy had she been forced to live with what I gathered, and vice versa. The same is true in learning. We gather what we deem to be valuable and important, and we leave the rest to others.

What one person may step over, another may treasure. Again, anything that is not gathered cannot be understood. Teachers must understand the importance of this gathering process. We cannot be smug in this respect and expect students to change their preference to fit the picture of what they deem to be important. It is our job as educators, the professionals, to discover the preferences of our students and to alter what we offer to resonate with their gathering preferences.

Returning to my food analogy, this is not to say that my daughter shouldn't learn to enjoy other foods. She is the one that is being limited by her own lack of vision. She should reach out and expand her world by trying new things. That change, however, will never happen by force, and especially not when the other wedding guests are looking on. In her case and in the case of our students, these kinds of changes happen only over time as individuals gain confidence in themselves and the one that is trying to help foster their change in attitude, outlook, and behavior.

Once students learn to trust a teacher's desire to help them gather in their preferred way, they will expand their horizons and follow the teacher's lead in gathering things that previously seemed unimportant. This does not mean that they will change their gathering preference; it simply means they will begin to expand their vision of what is important to gather.

I once observed a group of restless second graders sitting at their desks while the teacher, whom I knew to be dedicated and experienced, tried to teach them the difference between man-made and natural resources. The children had a worksheet in front of them with two columns on the page. One column had the heading "Man-Made Items" and the other column had the heading "Natural Resources." The teacher called out the name of an item, held up the item, or held up a picture of the item, and the students were then asked to write the name of the item in the appropriate column on their worksheets.

It was interesting to watch the frustration rise in both the students, who were getting confused, and the teacher. The students kept getting hung up on how they should number the items rather than focusing on which column each item should be listed under. The teacher didn't really care about the numbering, but she couldn't find a way around the problem. Rather than stopping to clear up the obvious gathering problem, the teacher plunged ahead, hoping to keep her lesson on track. The results were disastrous.

The next day, after an evaluation of the lesson and a discussion about the gathering preferences of her students, this teacher and I redesigned the lesson. The results startled her, despite her experience. We used the same worksheets, but instead of working at their desks, the students were asked to go outside to participate in a learning activity. The items or pictures to be classified were distributed in a limited geographic area. Each one was clearly numbered and spread out in the search area to give enough room for the students to work.

Before the activity began, the teacher led them through a discussion in which they created common definitions for the terms "man-made" and "natural resources," and learned how to distinguish one from another. They were then given instructions to enter the area and identify and classify each of the 20 items, according to these definitions, whether they were man-made or natural resources. Their findings were to be recorded on the worksheets. When they completed the assignment, they were to report to the classroom within a given time limit. Finally, they were given the option to work in teams or alone. With these instructions carefully in place, they were set loose to solve the problem.

In essence, the lesson hadn't changed. It was simply modified to allow students of all gathering preferences to have access to the information. The sensory gatherers could roam through the space with their clipboards and personally examine each item as much as they needed to come to the right conclusion. The intuitive gathers could use their intuitive skills as they wished and even rely on their tactile skills if they wanted.

The discussion and comparison activity that followed was remarkable. Each child or group was willing to stand up and defend his or her results. The depth of their understanding of the subject exceeded the expectations of the teacher. She was quite surprised that this could happen when all she did was set up the learning environment and then serve as a discussion leader and a fixer of mistaken ideas. (It is important to note that the younger the children are, regardless of their actual preference, their developmental stage will often be more sensory than intuitive.)

Thinking and Feeling Processors

The final two scales measure the way in which a person prefers to process the information that he or she has gathered. These scales, in conjunction with the others previously discussed, reveal the full learning preference of an individual. The two processing scales are also infinite and present two clearly opposite preferences. The first processing scale focuses on the internal method an individual uses to sort information and stimuli. It measures a learner's preference between the categories of thinking and feeling. The second processing scale focuses on the external method used to understand the world and measures a learner's preference between judging and perceiving.

Students who are thinking processors pass all gathered information through their brains. The head is their organ of decision. They typically trust their own intellect. To these learners, anything that doesn't have enough supportive facts certainly doesn't deserve serious consideration. The more facts the better, the more resources the better, and, of course, the more time that is available the more the student can process and analyze the information to come up with the right conclusion.

Students who are feeling processors go about this essential learning task in quite the opposite fashion. They are more comfortable processing information in the heart. For them, information or knowledge is not valuable unless it improves the human condition and provides a way for people to live more happy and fulfilled lives. Where thinking processors are often obsessed with facts, those who prefer feeling-based processing often see facts as misrepresenting the most important aspects of any decision: how it affects others. These individuals have developed a deep trust in their ability to determine what is really important and true in life. Their feelings provide them with a safe network or filter for determining how to prioritize things in their lives.

In evaluating the effectiveness of a teacher, the feeling processor typically follows the old, clichéd phrase, "I don't care how much you know until I know how much you care." The thinking processors' spin on this phrase shows their real difference. To them the phrase would read, "I don't care how much you care until I know how much you know." Those with a preference toward the thinking side of the scale usually enjoy a quiet atmosphere to work in while processing the information they have gathered. Those with the feeling preference often gravitate toward an atmosphere that allows them to be with and use others as a sounding board during the processing time.

Judging and Perceiving Processors

The final preference continuum relates to those processors who gravitate toward judging or perceiving as their method of processing information. Judging processors rely on their deep sense of how things should be to give value to that which they are learning. For these individuals, information is processed by comparing what they newly encounter with the things they already understand. Everything new is judged against what they perceive to be historical, traditional, or right. These individuals are looking to put everything they have gathered into its logical order or proper place. They gain great satisfaction by creating a world in which everything has an order or proper place where it belongs. When new information can be processed through this filter and put carefully away, these individuals are typically very happy. Life is a satisfying process of comparing and judging one thing against another to determine where everything belongs and where it fits together.

Like the thinking processor, these individuals typically prefer a more quiet and orderly atmosphere in which to work. Beyond quiet, they typically seek a neat and organized place. They often feel stressed and uncomfortable in any space that lacks structure and order. This kind of processor typically feels most at home in the traditional educational setting because their style matches the way the majority of teachers teach. Their logical-sequential outlook is evident in this preference.

The final processors we will discuss are those that Jung called perceivers. These individuals prefer to process information according to how it strikes them in the present. Their organ of decision would be their gut. They trust their impulses and use them to determine the value of anything they gather. First impressions are ever so important because these individuals live in the present. How they feel here and now about something is typically their first line of processing. History, facts, or feelings have little to do with how this group processes information. They immediately perceive the personal value of something new and act accordingly. For better or worse, their highly developed impulses often determine what they will do with the things they have gathered in their educational pursuits.

Perceivers like to process in a stimulating environment. Often they are most happy working with laughter, talking, music, and other sounds in the room. They like to be in a place where a lot of things happen at once. This type of processor is the most likely to fail in our present educational system. Because the present value of information and first impressions are so important to them, they place little value in learning for learning's sake. Lecture-formatted classes and traditional arguments about why they should learn provide little that they see as valuable in their present life.

Looking at these four distinct processing preferences we have just discussed, where would you place yourself along these two continua?

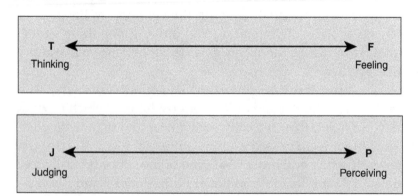

When we gain an understanding of these four scales and how they interrelate, we can start to put together an amazing puzzle that reveals a relatively clear anatomy of each individual learner. Say, for example, that an individual has a clear preference for introversion as her method of interaction, her preference for gathering is intuition, and her preferences for processing are judging and thinking.

This individual would place herself on these four different continua as follows:

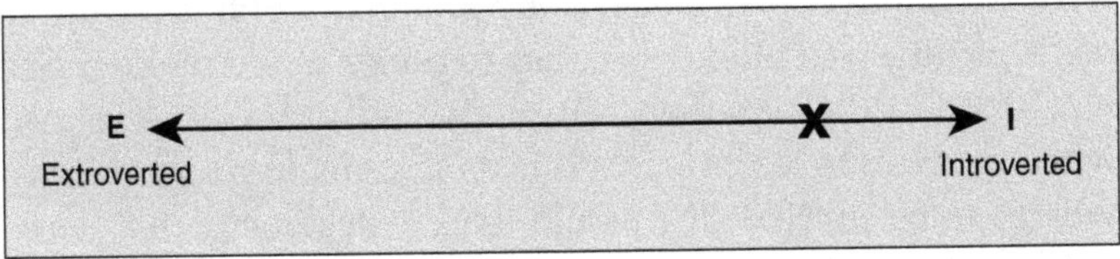

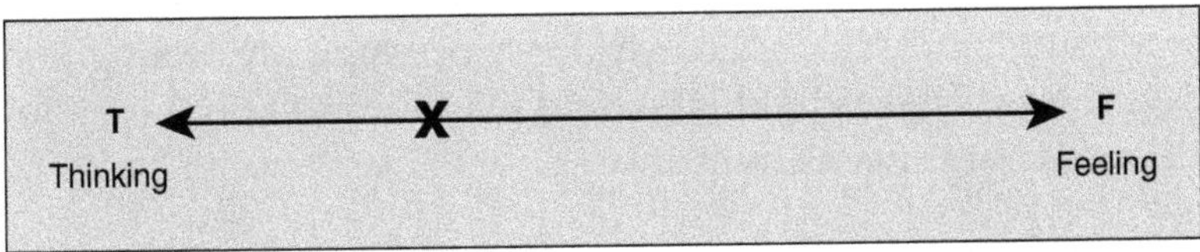

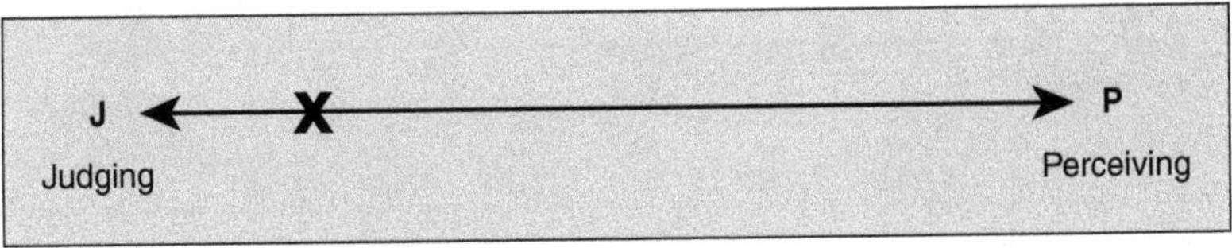

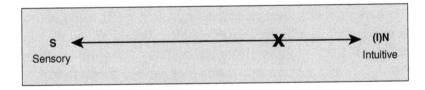

According to the Myers-Briggs Type Indicator, our subject would be designated an INTJ. Under the simplified notion of temperament theory, developed by David Keirsey, this same individual would be called an NT. According to the Clime International instrument, this person would be considered an Inward Green with Gold. Regardless of the name or label given to this learner, a teacher who knew this information about a student would have a marvelous starting point for understanding how to reach this individual.

Reviewing what we know about each of these scales and putting the whole picture together, let's draw a brief portrait of what we might expect the learning preference of this person to be. Typically, we could expect her to prefer to learn alone. She would tend to be extremely self-motivated and self-disciplined when it comes to learning, as long as she saw intrinsic value in what is to be studied. She would tend to become highly bored with routine tasks and rote exercises and want to learn outside the walls of the classroom. She would often thrive on using imaginable and unimaginable resources. She would tend to get lost in details and minutiae and often need to be gently reminded of deadlines and timetables. Before she would be willing to learn anything from her teachers, she would usually need to perceive them to be knowledgeable and competent.

Using another example, let's examine what this can tell us about an individual who has a slight preference for extroversion as his method of interaction, his preference for gathering is sensing, and his preferences for processing are feeling and perceiving. This individual would place himself on these four different continua as follows:

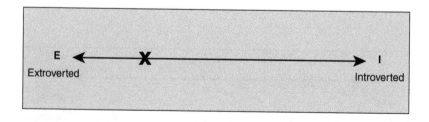

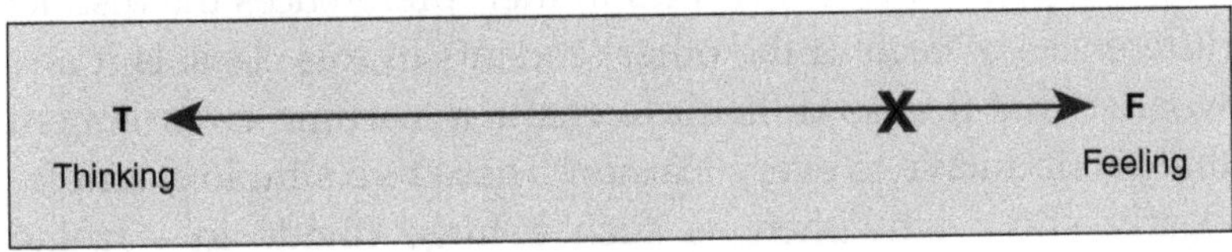

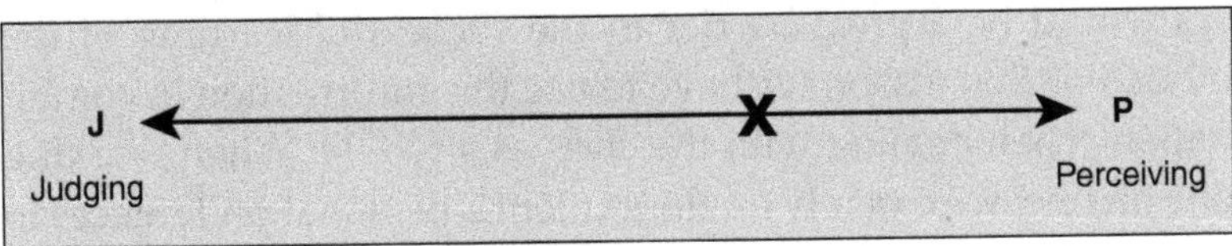

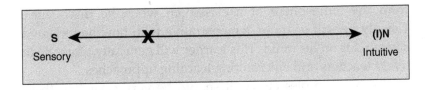

According to the Myers-Briggs Type Indicator, our sample person would be designated an ESFP. David Keirsey would call him an SP. The Clime International instrument would designate this person an Outward Orange with Blue.

Because this learner tends to be more of a people-centered person, we could typically expect him to prefer to learn in groups. Group projects and discussions would usually be more appealing than individualized work. He would tend to put off work in order to enjoy his present needs, and therefore he would not be the most self-motivated learner. Concrete reminders are often necessary in order for deadlines to be met.

As a learner, he would tend to become easily bored and seek a variety of learning experiences. He would tend to be most comfortable with hands-on learning and highly relevant lessons. When inspired, he can be a great leader and motivator of the rest of the class. On the other hand, he can greatly distract from the atmosphere of a classroom when he disengages. Usually he will be quite demonstrative with how he feels and say what is on his mind. This learner will generally gravitate to lively teachers and entertaining learning approaches.

In the examples above, it should be very clear that these individuals have very different needs when it comes to their learning preferences. Now add to their preferences the distinct differences of each of the other students in this class. Is it any wonder that it is so difficult to create a learning environment that is conducive to every learner? These two simple examples clearly show why there is such a huge divide in learning theories, principles, and practices. One size does not fit all. What would be the perfect environment for one of these learners would be a great barrier to the successful learning of the other. For this reason we have to use this information in combination when dealing with the class as a whole. When working one on one, we can rely on the student's personal preferences to better inform our decisions.

It is essential that I make one final point before leaving this discussion of preference. Every individual has the ability to step outside of his or her own preference and learn things that are not presented in their preferred style. Maturity is the natural process of growth and adaptation. Your goal in this process should not be to keep students from ever having to deal with learning preferences that do not mesh with their own. It should be to manage the learning environment in your classroom so that all students feel that time and respect is being given to the way they prefer to learn. When they gain this confidence in you as their teacher, and as they experience this kind of respect and understanding in their educational world, they will naturally begin to expand the limits of their own preferences and increase the scope of their abilities. In the supportive environment of a balanced educational experience, students demonstrate a remarkable skill for adaptation and change. Walls that once kept them out become windows of opportunity and awe.

As with all the preferences I have briefly described, each of the other types of learners have clearly identifiable patterns for learning. It is important to point out again that these preferences are only indicators that give us important insights into the way a person likes to learn. This information cannot predict human behavior. Its purpose is to help us communicate and educate in a way that creates intrinsic value.

Understanding the individual learning anatomy of students provides teachers and administrators with an important foundation on which they can measure the success of their efforts to effectively reach their students. This information should be used as the basis for modifying curricular approaches and assessment tools. It should be used as a compass to give general direction and not as a shovel to heap all learners into a manageable pile. Used properly, it will help us navigate an educational course that caters to the needs of all learners.

This Aristotelian element, character, must not be ignored. In the classroom as well as in the dramatic world, the value we place on understanding characters and individuals naturally reaps rewards and consequences. Those who apply this essential element properly will grow and develop into remarkable teachers. Those who do not will remain where they are. Sadly, some are content with such a fate. Teachers who learn to respect the individual character considerations of their students will create an effect that will play itself out in the lives of individuals for generations to come. Those who do not will fade into oblivion with the rest of the teachers of our past who failed to lift and inspire our hearts and minds. Individual respect, or respect to character (individual learning style and personality), is the first step we must take if we truly desire to reach the dramatic learner. After all, this is who the student really is. When our teaching can reach inside and touch this part of all individual learners, then our efforts will have an impact in their lives long after they leave our classroom.

A detailed summary of the preferences of each of these Jungian-based learning styles and their different designations are outlined in the appendix. I strongly suggest that you jump to the appendix now if you are not already familiar with these terms and concepts. The following chapters are written with the assumption that the reader is at least remotely conversant with this body of knowledge.

4

The Profile of a Dramatic Learner

Dramatic learners come in all ages, shapes, sizes, races, and religions. They are also found in surprisingly equal numbers in each gender. On the surface, they are hard to distinguish from other learners. This is because the truth is that there are elements of the dramatic learner in every one of us. Few learners, given a choice, would choose to learn in a completely nondramatic fashion. We are each driven, in our own way, to search for meaning and purpose in life through the things that we learn. In the natural world, learning is a function of growth and development. It is necessary for survival.

As I mentioned before, my use of the term *dramatic learner* is meant to describe those learners who are presently referred to as "at-risk learners" in the educational world. This extremely negative label connotes that these individuals have something wrong with them that puts them at a greater risk to fail than their peers. It presupposes that they are not good or willing learners, and it brands them as individuals who do not naturally seek to expand their knowledge base. Nothing could be further from the truth. Before examining how they prefer to learn, let's first delineate how they do not like to learn. This exercise will reveal a great deal about the origins of the term *at-risk learner*.

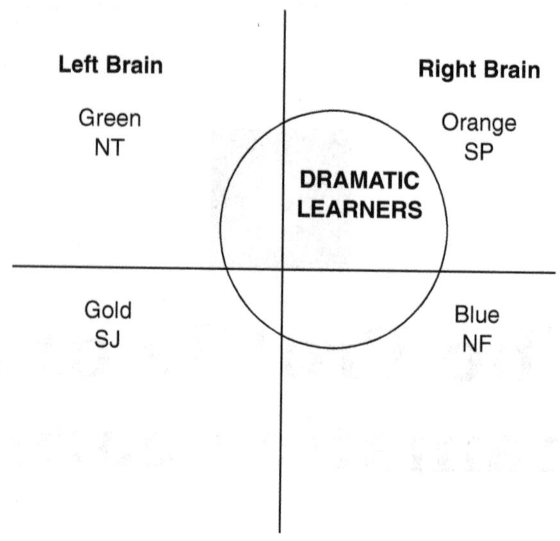

We can refer to the Jungian-based chart in the appendix to diagram the predominant learning styles of these individuals. The majority of them are typically SP (sensory perceiver), followed by NT (intuitive thinker), NF (intuitive feeler), and then last, the SJ (sensory judger).

The reason for this distribution is relatively straightforward. Schoolteachers and administrators are predominately SJ and NF. This means that the structure of our educational institutions closely reflects their learning preferences. Though the NTs are highly motivated learners, they are more interested in learning things that are important to them than in following the curricular restrictions that are placed on their shoulders by their teachers. People who are SP have little natural interest in a formal education that is designed to provide order and structure. There are just too many more exciting things to learn and do that are fun.

Dramatic learners do not usually thrive in the traditional classroom. The neat and orderly structure, where the teacher presides over the learning process as a lecturer/instructor, may work well for other students, but not for them. They grow restless and bored very quickly in a world of set routine and strict, meaningless (to them) rules. The details of learning, such as turning in homework assignments, returning books, or coming to class prepared to work, that are easily mastered by other students, are not second nature to the dramatic learner.

Dramatic learners are not naturally motivated by a need to fit in and conform to expected behavioral norms. They often see those who do conform as "teacher pleasers" or "kiss-ups." Report cards, degrees, and diplomas are not their natural motivators. They see these traditional items as pieces of paper they need to obtain to get other people to leave them alone. In this light, they often see the educational process as a series of mindless hoops that they have to jump through to fill requirements that are important to somebody else. Honor roll membership, National Honor Society membership, certificates of merit, and other outward labels of academic achievement often have no real value to them except for what it might get them in the eyes of other people. These typical awards are certainly not the motivating factors behind what they do. They often seek these forms of recognition only to play the game.

They do not fare well in an educational environment where learning takes the form of a clear, chronological, and rote recitation of facts, opinions, concepts, and ideas. Highly organized agendas and syllabi often cause contempt rather than educational comfort. Deadlines are seen as roadblocks, lectures as educational dribble, worksheets as busywork, and diagrams, maps, and charts as containing more than they want to know about anything.

They do not want to learn by a set of prescriptions or procedures. The more specific an assignment, the more they dread it. The minute a teacher begins to list the number of pages a report has to be, along with the margin width, font size, and other MLA requirements, the less valuable the assignment becomes. They see these kinds of requirements as capricious and teacher centered. To the dramatic learner, they are only further evidence that formal education is nothing more than learning to play the game by someone else's silly rules.

They do not thrive in a classroom where they are expected to sit quietly and take notes while a teacher passes on information. Overheads, Power Point presentations, and board work are measured as the deepest evidence of a poor teacher. Classrooms where there are strict rules for behavior and participation often stifle any desire they might have to become involved. The more efficient, structured, or predictable the learning process is, the more inaccessible it is to this kind of learner.

Learning environments that are overly intimate have little appeal to dramatic learners. They have a deep need to make a connection with other people, but only on their own terms. Many of them look at learning as a very independent journey. They question everything and have little patience for ideas, procedures, and people who can't stand up to heavy scrutiny. Teachers who become highly emotional under this constant onslaught or who rigidly hold to indefensible positions are viewed with deep concern and suspicion. The simple question "why?" is often the first thing out of these students' mouths when they are given something new to do. This usually begins as a sincere and searching query that seeks to justify the requested expenditure of time and energy. It can quickly turn into a power struggle when teachers mistake this natural questioning as a challenge to their authority or a doubting of their own knowledge and understanding. Teachers who respond inappropriately to the sincere questions of a dramatic learner will soon find themselves deluged with queries that become the very undermining influence the teachers feared.

In the same regard, teachers who seem to deliver only pat answers and black-and-white perspectives immediately lose credibility with these students. These students do not accept the fact that there is only one right way to do something or that there is only one right answer. When they are required to do an assignment the "right way," they often rebel passively or aggressively—depending on their nature. Regardless of their response, they lose all respect for a teacher who would mark them down for coming up with the right answer in an unconventional way. Their attitudinal reaction to this kind of attempted teacher interference is often, "You do it your way, and I'll do it mine." Because many of these students do not think in strictly linear ways, they follow their own unique path to a conclusion that others may not even understand. Thinking outside the box is a real value to these learners, and those who demand that they color inside the lines are seen as enemies and the destroyers of individuality and independent thought.

Dramatic learners often have little use for existing rules or instructions. In fact, they typically see the rules and procedures that are in place throughout the entire school and in the individual classrooms as up for grabs. Their own independent and self-directed nature runs contrary to the idea of following some previously designed path or order. Unless they can see a personal connection, these learners often see rules that are held as strict guidelines by other learners as mere suggestions of what should be done. They might acknowledge the rules as applying to others and still not recognize that they actually apply to themselves. They seem to have no clear understanding of what the word "no" means. To their way of thinking, "no" is a temporary and arbitrary hurdle they have to get over or around to get what they want.

Their opinion of rules carries over to their view of authority figures. Therefore, they are not naturally prone to respect the authority of teachers, administrators, or other adults. In fact, they often see themselves on equal footing with adults. Where other learners may respect the position another person holds, dramatic learners respect it only when they feel the person in the position has earned it. Those teachers who are seen as too rigid, too boring, too stupid, too easy, or too anything are dismissed as nothing more than an obstacle in the way of doing what they want.

Where other learners are drawn to the security, structure, clear direction, and personal interaction that formal educational settings offer, the dramatic learner sees this environment as uncomfortable, unnatural, and stifling. This world that may be motivating and inviting to many learners often doesn't even recognize the needs of those students who are more comfortable learning outside this limited scope. Sadly, the very pillars on which most educational institutions are founded are anathema to the way a dramatic learner prefers to learn.

Is it any wonder that this system has labeled these individuals "at-risk"? Looking at this situation from our view as educators, that term certainly appears to be an apt title for these students. If we reverse our view and look at it from the perspective of the learner, we certainly have sufficient evidence to conclude that it is actually the system and not the student who is at risk. It could reasonably be concluded that the system is not designed to meet their needs, and is therefore at risk of failing to help these individuals achieve academic success.

Rather than pointing fingers and attempting to assign blame, let's attempt to solve this dilemma through a minor paradigm shift. Such a shift can be put into motion easily enough by first implementing the name change I proposed in Chapter 2. This simple alteration in nomenclature moves us immediately from a negative footing to a positive one. It allows us to accept the fact that dramatic learners have a positive desire to learn. It recognizes and values their particular learning preferences. It may even give us the personal insight to acknowledge that they have just as deep a desire to learn as any other student does, when they are taught in a manner that favors their learning preference. With this perspective, we are now ready to examine the ways that dramatic learners prefer to learn.

Let's begin with the qualities they prefer in a teacher. To effectively teach dramatic learners, they must perceive that we possess personal integrity, high competence, passion for the subject matter, and the ability to engage them intellectually and emotionally. Though this may sound overwhelming at first glance, isn't this the goal of every sincere person who ever entered the teaching profession? Are there any teachers who do not want to be viewed in this manner by their students? If we follow this logic to its proper conclusion, we will increase our ability to reach the dramatic learner and become better teachers overall.

How does one become this super teacher? First, you need to know a little secret: Dramatic learners don't really care what other teachers or administrators think of you. Once they have been won over, they will become highly loyal and motivated students. Sadly, I often notice that those teachers who are gifted in their ability to work with these students are viewed as second-class citizens by many of their fellow teachers and administrators. This is a strange reality, especially in light of the fact that teachers who have developed the skills to reach dramatic learners are better at teaching all other students as well.

It really doesn't take a lot to gain the trust of a dramatic learner. Generally, trust is gained by teachers' willingness to take a chance and try something new. It seems like a logical trade-off to these learners: "I'll put myself into a position to try something new if you'll be willing to experiment along with me." For many of us, this will mean that we need to take a dreaded journey out of our comfort zone. Before we panic too much, it should be reassuring to know that we don't have to venture too far out into this wilderness to be effective. Things have to change just a little bit to be perceived as different to these students. The fun they demand of their teachers is not the kind that comes from teacher frivolity, though a little doesn't hurt. It comes from finally being respected and understood as learners. It is also the natural reaction that comes from getting excited about learning something new and becoming motivated to expend precious energy to master a new skill or subject.

All we need do to be successful teachers of dramatic learners is to respect the way they learn and to modulate the way we teach to take that into account. We need not abandon everything we've done throughout our careers. By moving only a few degrees from where we are, we can step into a magical place I call the learning nexus and open up our teaching styles to include these students.

This learning nexus is the point at which all learning styles intersect. It is common ground, the connecting point all learners share. This nexus area becomes the place of compromise and a foundational reference for curricular design. The next figure illustrates exactly where the nexus resides. When we can learn to focus our teaching in this area, we can be confident that our teaching is going to reach the learning style of each of our students at least some time in our lesson.

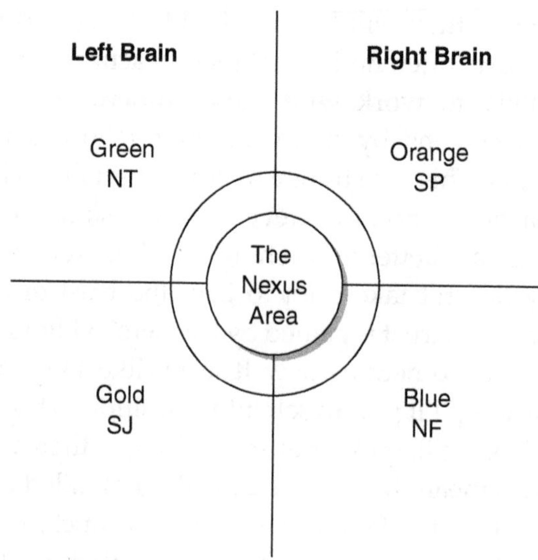

Let's turn our focus now to the classroom environment. The first rule of thumb I follow is that dramatic learners learn best in any environment that caters to their specific learning needs. If I were to provide a prescriptive list of what this environment is like, it would include qualities such as cognitively challenging, hands-on, competitive, independent, mentally and physically active, high-energy, humorous, stimulating, quiet at times, and noisy at times.

The thought of creating an environment like this is usually too overwhelming for a teacher to consider; therefore, to keep it simple, *dramatic learners prefer variety in the classroom.* This doesn't mean they need all the previously mentioned aspects going on at the same time; it means they are looking for an array of learning activities and a modicum of individuality. They can conform nicely to structures they don't prefer, as long as there is the hope they will be rewarded for their patience with something more to their liking in the near future.

For example, dramatic learners will happily work alone at their desks to master a concept or skill they know they will be able to apply later in a more rewarding and hands-on fashion. They will dogmatically follow rules they have had a hand in making. They are highly motivating leaders when given the direction and the confidence of others. They will sit quietly and listen to a lecture when they are convinced it will benefit them personally. They will spend hours fulfilling an assignment when it has been made relevant to their lives. They will happily work with others when they know they will have time to go off and work on their own. They will work alone when they know there will be time later to share ideas. They will dramatically defend your rights as a teacher when you have defended theirs as a student.

As long as there is a variety and balance of approaches, the dramatic learner can be at home in any learning environment. It is faulty thinking to believe that teachers must completely adapt their learning environment to fully cater to every whim of their dramatic learners. In so doing, teachers rob these individuals of the opportunity to develop the skills they need to fit into a diverse world. Their education would not be complete without instilling in them the need to compromise and adapt as needed to different situations. In addition to these concerns, teaching only to the dramatic learner destroys the balance that is created by teaching to the nexus, and it leaves out the students who do not prefer to learn in this fashion. This practice would create a reverse discrimination situation for the nondramatic learner.

Dramatic learners are motivated by the thrill of independently overcoming an obstacle. They love to use their talents to do something better than anyone else. When they latch onto something that fascinates them, they will pursue it almost compulsively until they have mastered it. Some are driven to solve educational dilemmas through deep, logical pursuits, while others prefer to use their physical prowess. All of them, in their own preferred way, desire to play an active role in the learning process rather than being a spectator. They will engage in learning only when it appeals to them, not when others say it is important. Their engagement in the learning process is often hard to evaluate by traditional means. Supervisors or teachers who look for only one acceptable form of interaction will entirely miss the learning efforts of these individuals. Dramatic learners will often engage in their own way and then become discouraged and turned off if those who are evaluating their work do not recognize their efforts or deem them appropriate.

Recently, I observed a student teacher who was faced with such a dilemma. She had assigned her eighth graders to work in particular groups to fulfill an assignment. Most of the groups seemed to come together rather quickly in their ability to reach a compromise on how to proceed with the assignment. One particular group, however, simply could not come to consensus. The teacher watched with concern, as the group seemed to flounder. Finally, two of the group members came to her with the suggestion that since they couldn't reach a consensus in their group, might they be given permission to break their original group into two smaller groups? As I watched this teacher deal with the situation, I knew she was worried about what I might think if she allowed the kids to change the group size from what she had originally assigned. To her credit, she allowed them to complete the project as they had suggested.

When the class was over, she approached me expecting to be upbraided for altering her lesson plan. Instead, I congratulated her for her ability to evaluate the situation properly and respond to their request appropriately. When she was still puzzled by my response, I asked the following questions:

- What was the goal of your lesson?
- Did your decision to allow them to form two smaller groups help or assist them in meeting the objective of the lesson?
- Did your choice show respect for the individual learning needs of the students?
- Did your choice in any way take away or diminish the work of the other students in the class?
- Did your choice undermine or strengthen the respect your students have for your ability to deal with their individual needs?

In essence, I was trying to point out to her that the wrong choice would have been to hold fast to the arbitrary rules she had established for the class. Her rigid adherence to them would have sent the wrong message to her dramatic learners. They probably would have turned their attention from fulfilling the assignment to finding reasons why they couldn't work together in the groups she had assigned. The vast energy they spent to solve the problem would have been rendered useless by not allowing them to fulfill the assignment in a little different fashion than she had originally mapped out. (If the objective of the lesson had been to teach them how to reach a consensus in a group, then the change would have been counterproductive and inappropriate.)

Dramatic learners can lose interest in a subject just as quickly as they engage. This is one of the most frustrating aspects you will face as you try teaching them. There are little secrets that can be employed to reduce this problem. In the case of the previously mentioned example, the students kept their interest in the assignment because they were allowed a little flexibility in coming to their own acceptable solution. Here are some of the reasons dramatic learners lose interest so fast:

- Frustration with their inability to master the subject
- Boredom and routine
- Lack of time
- Lack of sufficient resources
- Loss of respect for a teacher or for a teacher's decision
- An interest in something new
- No tangible reason at all

Their fickle interest often leads them from one uncompleted project to another. Those who observe this behavioral trait are often annoyed by it, but it causes little or no concern to them. Often the greatest challenges for a teacher who works with these students is learning how to motivate them to stay with a project until it is complete, thereby helping them to feel the satisfaction that comes from actually finishing a task.

Dramatic learners love to play and pretend. They can be highly motivated by learning activities that require simulation and other forms of role-play. They thrive on learning games and competition. If they consider an activity worthwhile and fun, they will easily engage. If they don't consider it that way, getting them involved in the learning process is a hard sell.

Many dramatic learners perceive formal education as nothing more than a litany of very negative experiences. Their penchant for excitement and their unconventional learning preferences have earned them one of many other negative labels, such as ADD (attention deficit disorder), ADHD (attention deficit hyperactivity disorder), LD (learning disability), and BD (behavior disorder). Their natural drive to learn in their optimum style has made many of them regulars in the principal's office or in special education classes. More likely than not, when they will not submit to the demands of nondramatic learning structures, they are subdued with all manners of needless institutional interventions, not the least of which are Ritalin and other mood-altering drugs.

Many individuals need these chemical interventions. However, a high percentage of dramatic learners are misdiagnosed simply because of the way they prefer to learn. In many cases, their learning preferences are so radically different from those of their parents and teachers that they raise alarms. This is especially true when they become scholastically bored and unmotivated. Their subsequent actions can easily cause teachers or parents to become impatient. This is most often the case when these teachers and parents know nothing about learning styles. All too often, chemical solutions have become the quick-fix method of controlling the behavior of these students.

An examination of the main symptoms of ADHD reveals a remarkable resemblance to the temperament of a dramatic learner. It is true that some dramatic learners are ADD or ADHD, or that they will exhibit the symptoms of other identifiable learning disabilities. However, the practice of lumping these learners into this same pile is all too common. This is the direct result of the fact that ADHD is often comorbid with other disorders. Many consider it one of the most common neuro-behavioral disorders in children. It is frightening to note that some child psychologists diagnose this condition in as high as 50% to 75% of their clients. The truth is that the symptoms are highly confusing, and they create numerous challenges when trying to form a proper diagnosis. Of the 14 symptoms of ADHD that have been determined, it is startling to note that six of the major ones match the particular learning style preferences of the dramatic learner. These major symptoms are impulsivity, inattention, motor hyperactivity, difficult temperament, deficient social skills, and academic underachievement. These symptoms contain many of the same common descriptors that are classically used to describe dramatic learners. Sadly, these traits become more pronounced when these individuals are forced to spend the majority of their daylight hours in a highly nondramatic environment.

Please do not mistake what I am saying as a denouncement of proper psychological diagnoses. Many dramatic learners suffer from the disabilities related to ADHD, ADD, and many other conditions. I fully agree that, properly diagnosed and prescribed, Ritalin can have positive effects on a child's academic and social success. I am only stating that in a rush to create conformity and subdue behavior, many teachers, doctors, psychologists, and parents are turning too quickly to this last-resort position as their first form of intervention.

Think of the wasted potential being perpetrated on the vast group of bright, creative, and overly active learners in an attempt to get them to quickly submit to the tyranny of the non-dramatic educational world. How different would our lives be today if the major innovators and creative minds of our modern era had been subdued by mood-altering drugs rather than being allowed to explore the world in a way they preferred. A closer examination of these creative and innovative individuals will reveal that they are almost exclusively dramatic learners.

There is much to celebrate in dramatic learners. Though highly challenging, when they are enlightened, inspired, and allowed to find their own voice and direction, they often become the movers and shakers of our world. They possess an innate ability to take physical, emotional, and intellectual risks that don't even enter into the imagination of many other individuals. It is their very dissatisfaction with the way things are which serves as the catalyst for the change and forward motion in every advance of mankind. As educators, if we can learn to harness this dissatisfaction and use our talents and abilities as mentors and directors, we can perform modern-day miracles. Our work in this area will not only positively affect the learning environment for our dramatic learner, but when we create a learning environment inclusive of the needs of the dramatic learner, it will also enrich the learning experience of all students.

5

The Structure of Dramatic Learning

Now that we have looked at how the Aristotelian element of character (personality and learning styles) relates to learning and have a better understanding of the specific profile of the dramatic learner, we can begin to apply this knowledge to curricular design. As promised before, when we begin to master the skills of creating dramatic educational experiences that effectively reach our dramatic learners, we find that it simultaneously increases our ability to reach all students, regardless of specific learning preferences. Though this may seem like an impossible task, once understood it can become a highly rewarding and simple road to follow. In fact, it may change forever your outlook on your role as a teacher and the way you approach learning in general.

One of the best young student teachers I have ever had in my program frankly and emotionally shared his disappointment at discovering he didn't want to be a teacher anymore. After years of preparing for a position he loved, the realities of the classroom had usurped his lifelong dream. As I observed his work, it was apparent to me that he had fallen into the teaching pattern of his cooperating teacher. We discussed this at length, and then I made him a promise. It is the same promise I make to anyone who is presently in the classroom or who desires to be a teacher. It is simply this: If you learn to harness the power of dramatic structure in your teaching, your job will become fun and rewarding again. Your students will fill you with energy and delight, instead of draining your spirit.

This particular student teacher took me at my word and began to apply the principles he had been taught in his lesson and unit planning. Within a few short weeks, we both could clearly see the positive evidence of his efforts. He was happy, and so were his students. After a day of observing his work, he shared a wonderful discovery he had made. He said,

> I now know when I've been a good teacher and when I haven't. When I haven't, I come home at the end of the day tired and beaten. When I have, I come home excited and renewed. The difference is always in what I have done. If I do the students' work for them, it always drains me; but when I allow them to work and learn and discover, we are both filled.

His remarks, and the work I continued to observe in his classroom, convinced me that he had learned how to move his teaching into the nexus area I discussed in Chapter 4. Once he understood and accepted the different learning needs of his students, he began to create curricula that employed learning elements related to all of his students. This design approach allowed him to include as many students as possible in his teaching plans. This power comes from using dramatic structure and teaching in the nexus area. The first figure again illustrates where lessons and units must be focused in order for them to have this added educational and dramatic power. For the sake of clarity, I have added the color nomenclature as set forth in the Clime International Instrument. By placing these styles into a quadrant chart, we can clearly see where the nexus area is.

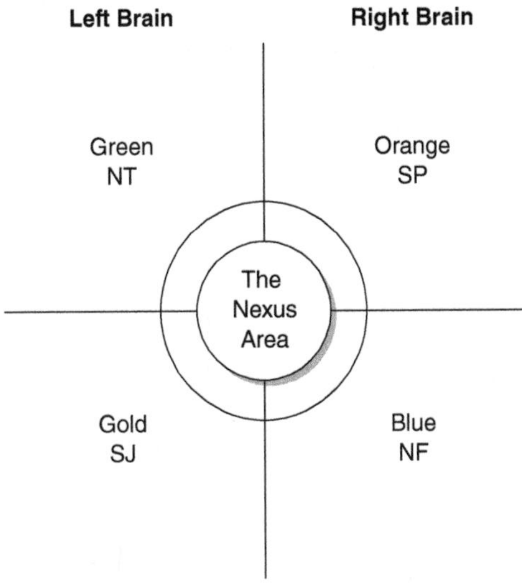

We can use this figure to emphasize the value of teaching in the nexus. If we were to plot all the learning preferences for a class of 30 students on this matrix, the overlapping area would reveal the natural learning nexus that exists for this class. It is interesting to note that this class's learning nexus correlates directly to the teaching nexus represented in the first figure. Every learner has a natural stake in an educational process that sinks its roots down deeply in this foundational common ground. Here is where all learning preferences intersect and share common values. Here, all learners can find a measure of comfort in a learning experience. Teachers who gain the skills to center a lesson in this nexus become free to move back and forth across either axis to visit and explore the outer reaches of each preference without excluding any of their students. With this centrist base, they can feel certain that something in any given lesson or unit plan will have the ability to resonate with each student in the class.

Let's return to the example of the man-made/natural resource classification lesson introduced in Chapter 3 as an example of this practice. If we were to plot the learning preference used in the first pedagogical approach it would look like this.

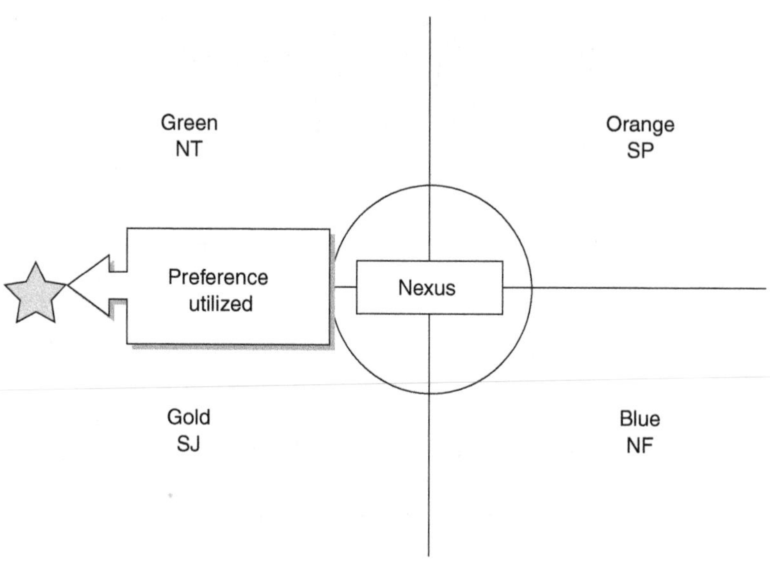

This lesson is structured and taught clearly outside of the nexus area. The figure illustrates that the lesson clearly favors the learning preferences of the SJ and NT learners. This is typical of most nondramatic-learning structures. If you recall from this example lesson, the students were passive participants; they were sitting quietly in rows and expected to focus their attention on a worksheet while the teacher directed the process. They worked individually with little interaction with the rest of the class.

Now compare the plotting of the first version of the lesson in the previous figure to the way the lesson was taught the second time in the next figure.

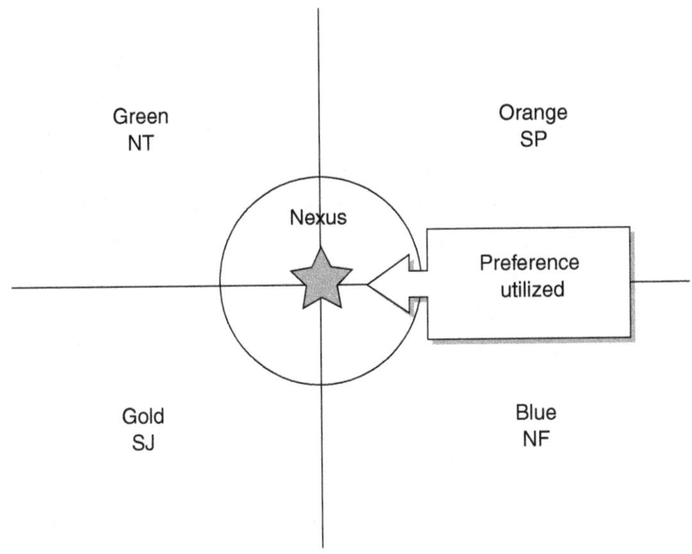

This lesson is clearly taught in the nexus area because it simultaneously uses elements from each of the learning preferences. The students in this learning structure are now active participants, even though (1) much of the lesson remains the same, and (2) they still use the same worksheet. They can work individually or in teams. They are free to employ their learning preference. The teacher is not at the center of the lesson, but serves as a resource. The children are free to leave their desks, but the area in which they can wander and the time they have to complete the process are limited. Though the structure has changed and is more dramatic, their answers are still evaluated, and an assessment of subject mastery is given.

In this lesson, careful attention is given in the planning phase to ensure that elements from every preference are present. Teaching to the nexus changes the role of the teacher to that of a director or playwright. Teachers that work in the nexus plan the outcome and carefully construct a learning process that leads the class on an educational journey. It is dramatic learning because the educational process now becomes a structure of action. The very involvement of the student immediately thrusts the lesson into the nexus.

To help us understand how to construct learning experiences that allow us to teach in this dramatic fashion, we need to discuss the requirements for effective plot structures. We also need to examine how effective plot structures relate to learning. Those individuals who are familiar with the classical elements of plotting—exposition, inciting event, rising action, climax, and dénouement—understand how important they are to the success of a dramatic or literary piece.

Exposition

The first element of plotting is called *exposition*. In a play or a book, exposition is often called the "background story." It is the part of the story that fills the audience in on what happened before the present action occurred.

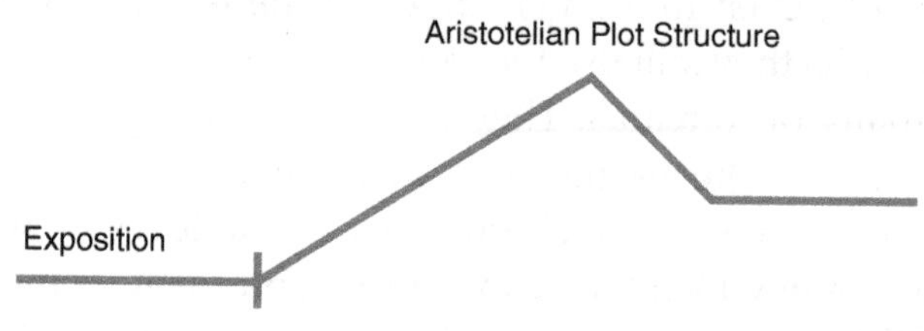

In ancient Greek theater, the chorus would come onstage and chant, in unison, a lyrical speech to tell this exposition to the audience and ensure that they knew all the important background information that took place before the play began. Today in the plays or the films we are familiar with, we have a very different kind of exposition. If we're watching a movie, the exposition is usually created in a very visual fashion. For example, we'll often see some kind of aerial shot that zooms through the streets just above the city in which the movie is set. It proceeds down the streets until it zooms in on a particular residence. Then it cuts to an interior shot where we see the main characters, let's call them Mary and John, in their "real" world.

This visual exposition reveals (1) who the stars will be, (2) the socioeconomic level of this couple, (3) where they live, (4) something of their background, and (5) the environment in which they live. All that information becomes extremely important as the story proceeds. In the modern dramatic and literary worlds, the audience learns the exposition in a piecemeal fashion through speeches, visuals, or other subtle ways. Without exposition, a dramatic or literary piece lacks context and clarity.

Too much exposition, however, causes the audience to lose interest. How long are we interested in observing what we already know about the plot or the characters before we are ready to move on? In the classic Spielberg film *Raiders of the Lost Ark,* for example, how long would an audience be willing to watch Indiana Jones and his expedition team trek aimlessly through the jungles of South America without finding a sign that they had reached their desired destination? Patience for protracted exposition is quite short in our modern world.

Let's return to the example of our movie starring John and Mary. Through an exterior shot (seen through a window into their bedroom), we see them in bed together. They have obviously been married for some time because they are sleeping in rather old, worn, and unsexy sleepwear. By the side of the bed on John's side, lies a pile of clothes. We hear the alarm clock ring, and John quickly reaches up and shuts it off. Mary doesn't move. John carefully slips out of bed and makes his way to the kitchen. In a highly routine fashion, we see a montage of shots from different camera angles as he goes through a ritual of making coffee, showering, dressing, and heading out the door. It becomes even more obvious through this process that he's been involved in this routine for a long time. As John leaves the house, we see a shot of Mary still sleeping.

Inciting Event

How long would this movie keep our interest? Not long, right? Once the exposition or background story is established, good plotting requires the introduction of the second element: the inciting event or incident. The *inciting event* is the moment in which the exposition ends and the status quo of the play is altered. Its purpose is to smash the equilibrium that has been established in the exposition and begin the forward advancement of the plot. This is done because the disruption of the equilibrium naturally introduces a series of problems into the mix. Relationships become altered, situations escalate, and the initial conflicts of the plot begin to appear. In the process, we hope things begin to become more and more interesting as the story line begins to unravel.

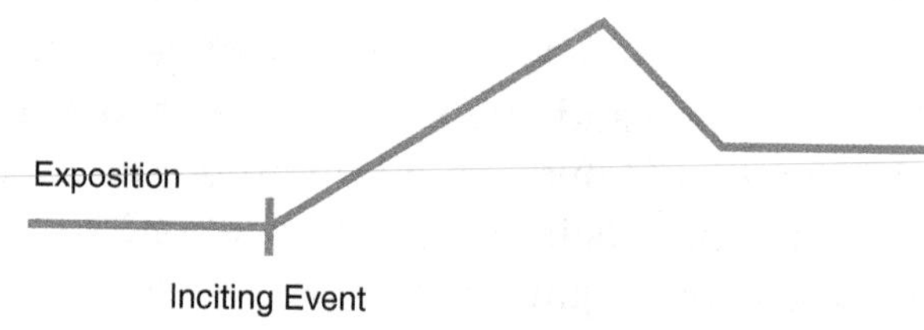

In our movie example, after John leaves for work, the camera cuts to a close-up of the alarm clock on the headboard. The room is now lighter, as it is 8:00 a.m. Mary rises slowly and goes through her morning routine, which includes making the bed and putting away the pile of clothes John left on the floor. In her actions, it is apparent that this is a sore spot in their relationship.

As she picks up his clothes off the floor, a close-up shot reveals a note falling out of the pocket of John's pants. The note lands on the floor, and, in deeper disgust, Mary places the clothing on the bed and reaches down to pick up the note. She opens the note and begins to read what it says. What she reads causes her to collapse on the bed in tears. We cut to a close-up of the partially crumpled note in her hand. We can read what it says: "John, Thanks for the wonderful time last weekend. Love, Sally. PS: Let's do it again, okay?"

Do you think our story has reached its inciting event? One good way to judge this is to determine if the event has altered forever the way things were in the story before the inciting event happened. I think it is fair to say that the appearance of the note and Mary's reaction qualify. In your mind, I'm sure you can begin to imagine the number of problems that have been introduced into our little movie. The stakes have been raised, and the equilibrium that once existed is forever shattered. At this point in the story, we are ready to move to the next plot stage. To repeat, without this inciting event, the plot languishes in a boring rehash of what is already known by the audience.

Rising Action

The third element of a sound plot is the *rising action*. It is in this stage that the plot begins to thicken. The story is driven forward as the characters attempt to solve the problems introduced by the inciting event. As an audience, we expect a plot that draws us along and keeps us in suspense. When the rising action is too predictable or too disjointed, we quickly lose interest.

The plot development that occurs during rising action is naturally altered from other similar story lines by the individual style of the author and its genre. For this reason, very similar plots can appear completely different, simply because of the way the elements are organized. The same is true in the development of dramatic lessons. Though a similar structure

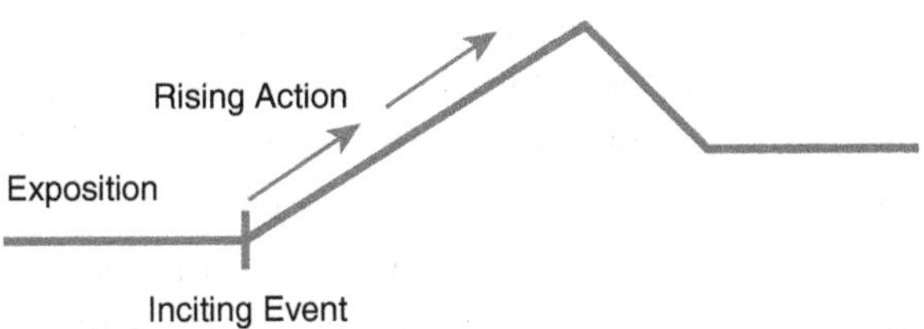

is used each time, the variety of choices available to the teacher can make each lesson look unique.

The more unpredictable the rising action is, the deeper the appeal of the piece. Returning to our example, we find Mary still on the bed, holding the crumpled note found in John's pants. We know that something is about to happen, but we are not quite sure what it will be. We may be able to gain a few clues from Mary's emotional state, but in a good rising action, we just have to hold on to our seats and watch it unravel.

Proposed plot 1: Mary picks herself up off the bed and resolutely goes into the bathroom. We see a close-up of her talking to herself in the mirror as she splashes water on her face. She tells herself that what is good for the goose is good for the gander. She proceeds to dress herself to the nines and prepares to go out and paint the town red.

Proposed plot 2: Mary gets up from the bed, goes to the closet, and removes a huge duffel bag from a secret compartment. She throws the bag on the bed and begins to rifle through its contents. She finds the small box she is looking for. We see her walk to the bathroom, open the box, take out camouflage makeup, and begin to apply it to her face.

Proposed plot 3: Mary slowly reaches for the phone on the side of the bed and dials a number. We cut to a shot of a phone ringing in the seedy back room of a nightclub. A huge bodyguard character answers the phone in a gangster's voice. Mary asks to talk to her daddy. Her "daddy," a godfather-type character, asks her what's wrong. She begins to weep and tell him that John has been cheating on her.

Proposed plot 4: Still an emotional wreck, Mary stumbles to the bathroom and opens the medicine chest. She desperately searches through the pill bottles, toothbrushes, and hairspray. In her rage, she flings the contents of the cabinet throughout the room until she finds the bottle she is looking for. She takes it back to the bed, opens it, and pours the contents into her hand.

She considers what she's doing for a moment, and then she pours the pills that are in her hand into her mouth. She grabs the glass of water on the nightstand and washes the pills down. Then calmly, she makes a phone call, leaves a message on John's voicemail, gets back under the covers, and goes to sleep.

These are four of the endless number of plot options that could grow out of our inciting event. Each one could be the logical next step in the story. Each would lead us down a very different path. Using any one of these options, if our plot is a tragedy, Mary, John, the writer of John's note, or everyone in the surrounding six states could die as the story unfolds. If the plot is a comedy, Mary could go through all kinds of gyrations to get even with John and then find out it was all a mistake. However the story ends, the purpose of the rising action is to build the conflict and interest by following a plausible path to overcome the problems that were introduced by the inciting event. These very same dramatic elements must be used to increase the interest of our students in what we are teaching.

As we think of ways to apply these dramatic choices to our teaching, it is apparent that endless options are available to us. For example, if we had covered a particular subject and wanted to further drill our students to increase their skills and accuracy, we could give them a written quiz or other assignment—but how dramatic is that? How could we be more creative? We could create some kind of game for that purpose. Creating a new game takes a lot of work; therefore, I like to use an existing game. When I do, I know that I already have an existing structure of proven rules and precedent to draw on. My favorite classroom game is Baseball. I have used it to teach and/or review everything from physics to current events.

I break the class into two teams and set them to work creating the "pitches" that will be thrown at the other team. These pitches are nothing more than questions they create to try to stump the other team. The teams create the questions by researching the material. As they focus on stumping the other team, these dramatic elements come into play, and the students get caught up in the hunt and forget that they are learning as they go. It's hard to create a question without first discovering the answer. The more a team researches the topic, the more they are prepared for the questions that will be hurled at them, and the more likely it becomes that they will be able to stump the other team. The challenge of the game becomes their inciting event, and their search for their pitches is the rising action. Like our plot options for John and Mary, from this basic beginning, I can alter the game in genre and style in any number of ways. For example, I might

- Allow them to answer questions as a team
- Allow them three strikes or guesses before they are called out
- Require each team member to answer alone
- Allow them to use their references
- Increase or reduce the numbers of outs per inning
- Introduce my own questions
- Settle disputes as the umpire
- Change the subject being reviewed
- Bring in outside people as resources
- Allow them to pitch questions to me
- Reduce or extend the preparation time
- Take the class outside and play the game on a baseball diamond

This is an example of the dramatic options available for one simple learning activity. With a little thought, these dramatic principles can be applied across the curriculum to add variety and power to your lessons. By using the other elements of dramatic structure to expand the options, teachers can virtually increase their teaching repertoire and move their lesson into the nexus with relatively little additional prep time.

Returning to our discussion of dramatic structure, the conflict of the play increases in direct proportion to the amount of personal risk in which the characters are placed as they seek to resolve the problems that have resulted from the action of the play. The most effective use of the rising action is to engage the audience completely in the struggles of the characters. The simpler the rising action is in a plot, the easier it is to figure out. This is problematic because once the suspense of the audience is lost, much of the draw of a piece is diminished. The more complex a plot is, as it twists and turns with unexpected obstacles, the more an audience gets involved. When this involvement and interest is achieved, the audience becomes willing to suspend their disbelief and accept the make-believe world created in the dramatic or literary work. Just as there is a problem with plots that are too simple, plots that are too abstract or convoluted also have difficulty holding the interest of their audience.

Returning to our Baseball activity, the dramatic elements of risk, struggle, and suspense are all part of the preparation and playing of the game. The twists and turns of the questions and answers propel the action along and engage the learner. Even those students who are waiting for their turn to bat or who are symbolically playing the field are learning as they are listening.

Climax

When the plot reaches its highest emotional state and the problems of the story come to a logical conclusion, we have the *climax*. Every development in rising action moves the plot along its way to the climax. Whether it is personal conflict, plot reversals, physical obstacles, complications, or accomplishments, each element of plot development works together with the others to drive the structure to a natural and satisfying ending point. An effective climax is the ultimate objective of every dramatic or literary piece. It is often the final measurement of success or failure. In a dramatic production, every effort of the entire production team is focused on bringing about a satisfying conclusion.

A possible climax for our John and Mary story might be Mary's sentence to the electric chair for the torching deaths of John and his lover in their love nest. It might be Mary going through a long and messy divorce and winning custody of their two children. It might even be her discovery that Sally was

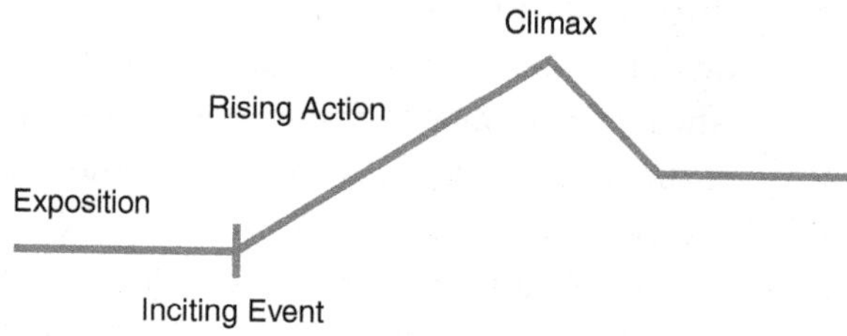

really John's 90-year-old aunt whom he took out for dinner on his last business trip. Whatever it is, the climax must be logical and consistent with the rest of the plot. The natural conclusion to our Baseball example is the final out of the final inning. If played right, it will dramatically hold the students' interest until the end.

DÉNOUEMENT

Once this dramatic climax is reached, the driving action slows down, and the elements of the piece begin to come together to create some kind of conclusion. This is the final element of plot, the *dénouement*. It is a time for the story to resolve and for the lives of the characters to return to some kind of normal plane. In our example of Mary and John, the dénouement after Mary's execution could be John and Mary's children getting together to reconcile the fate of their parents and to decide to bury Mary beside their father. In the divorce ending, Mary could establish a new routine for her life and go on without John. In the Aunt Sally ending, Mary could realize that she had the greatest husband in the world and feel so sorry for doubting him that she never complains about picking up his clothes again.

In the educational world, this dénouement is a time of sorting and synthesizing what has been learned. It is often a personal time for the student to individually put all the pieces of what has been learned in place. It is where wise teachers draw together what has been taught and help their students to see and articulate the value that the new skill or knowledge

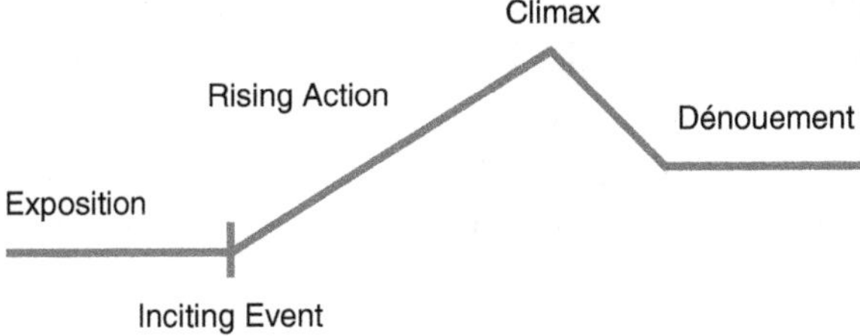

will have in the rest of their lives. In our Baseball example, it could simply be a discussion about what the students learned that will help them the next time they review a subject in this manner.

Not every dramatic piece follows this plot structure to the letter. Though it is not necessary for every element to be present in a successful plot, those that completely ignore the elements of classical structure are doomed to failure. Every great and enduring plot draws heavily on these elements and uses them effectively to engage and enthrall its audience.

Turning to real life for a moment, how many students would rather sit and watch a film than listen to a lecture? Even though they understand that nothing is real and that artists have contrived every nuance, they still are completely drawn into it. As I mentioned before, a story with a strong and compelling plot structure has the ability to transport the audience and let them enter and enjoy a completely contrived world. This is the true power of dramatic structure at work. When used correctly, it has an awesome power over its audience. We are just beginning to understand the powerful learning tool this medium can be for good and ill.

In its own hypocritical way, the media sells advertisers commercial time with the promise that people who watch their promotion will be influenced to buy their product. These same individuals, who promote the power of their influence on changing people's buying decisions, refuse to admit that the same tool can influence individuals to use drugs or alcohol, to be violent, or to act in other ways that are unproductive. They can't have it both ways. If dramatic elements can be used to influence an individual's behavior in one way, they can certainly be used just as effectively to influence it in another way. Using the same logic, if they can be used successfully to get people to see things differently in one environment, why can't they be used in another?

If we understand dramatic structure correctly, we can learn to use it in our classrooms with great success. We can learn to harness its power to entertain and engage young minds. We can use it to reach dramatic learners and help them understand the power and thrill of learning. We can get them to willingly suspend their disbelief and move to areas of discovery that they never thought possible. To do this, we must be able to recognize how close dramatic structure matches the structure of learning. Just as drama mimics life, so does formal education. My father, who never completed a formal education, jokes that his degrees are from the school of hard knocks. He's right. At age 16, he became responsible for helping his widowed mother care for the physical and financial needs of her large family. At 19, he was married; and so goes the story of his life. The lessons he learned about life were not from a textbook. They were not theory- or concept-based. If he made a mistake, he couldn't sit around and ponder the theoretical ramifications of other choices. He had to deal with the real-life consequences. Without the umbrella of a formal educational setting, he learned as he went.

Formal education isn't reality. It is a world apart with its own set of rules and conventions. All of its requirements, deadlines, and outcomes are arbitrarily set. It exists in the no-man's land between childhood and adulthood, and has been established to prepare a rising generation to take their places in the real world. Certainly one could argue that the importance of receiving good grades makes formal education real, but I disagree. Assigning a letter grade has never been an accurate measure of what someone has learned. In fact, quite often the reverse is true: Many honest students will testify that lower grades are typically earned in the classes that engendered the greatest amount of learning. In truth, people never really know how much they have actually learned until they are required to use it in reality. Sadly, it is often in the light of real-world application where we see the glaring error in our educational system.

My argument that formal education is not real does not mean that it's not important. I realize how fortunate most of the modern western world is to be heir to an almost universal educational dream. Rather, I make this statement in an attempt to illustrate how similar the formal educational and dramatic worlds really are. Each is intended to open up our minds and expand our understanding of others and the realities of the world we share. Each has the power to wield an ever-expanding influence for good and evil. Each can create a cataclysmic atmosphere of change. And each is the function of a man-made structure that has been designed to simulate reality. Because of this close connection and its bearing on personal growth and enlightenment, we would be derelict in our duty as educators to ignore the existence of these two parallel worlds without gaining an understanding of how they relate.

To help bring these two worlds together, it may be helpful to examine the research that is summarized in Edgar Dale's Pyramid of Experience. It aptly illustrates the vast overlap in these two worlds. It is hard not to see the direct correlation among teaching methodologies that are used and the impact they have on learning and retention. Dale's pyramid demonstrates that the more dramatic the learning process, the more a student retains and learns.

Notice that the most common learning activities, which are the backbone of the majority of formal educational strategies, are also the least effective. The more dramatic the learning experience is, the more likely the student will retain what is being taught. While teaching at the University of Texas at Austin, I was hired to help create a more conducive learning environment in a Title I school. As the principal oriented me to the particular needs of the school, we passed a classroom where the teacher was showing a video. The principal was very quick

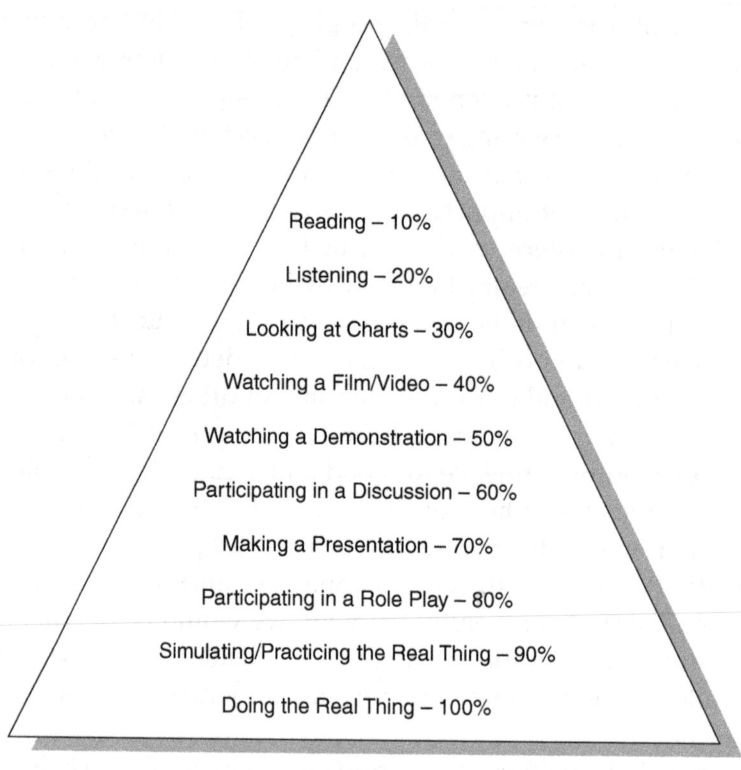

to point out her disapproval of videos in the classroom, and she expressed her concerns about the work ethic of this particular teacher. As I grew more acquainted with the school, its principal, and this teacher in particular, the principal's assessment of this teacher couldn't have been more mistaken.

What this principal labeled as "lazy teaching" turned out to be anything that used even the slightest dramatic element. To accomplish what I was hired to do, I would have had to turn every teacher in the school into a lazy teacher. Even as this principal watched her failing students begin to excel under these lazy teaching methods, she could never understand what was going on. In her mind, learning wasn't meant to happen unless the student was either reading, listening, taking notes, or taking a test. She was entirely unable to see that teachers who properly enriched their curriculum with dramatic elements such as supportive learning activities, videos, demonstrations, discussions, oral presentations, creative projects, role-play, or simulation are two to five times more effective than a teacher who only lectures.

The experience I had in this school isn't an educational anomaly; it still prevails as the dominant attitude in many learning environments. It is an overwhelming reality in the majority of the courses and programs designed to train future teachers. This educational outlook is a direct result of the failure of most educators to recognize the relationship between learning and dramatic structure. It has led to the development of many highly unnatural pedagogical practices that ignore preformal learning practices of every human being. Real-life or natural learning is always dramatic. It is only in the formal classroom that the two are separated for the sake of uniformity. When the dramatic structure is removed from learning, it no longer has a true connection to life. Learning becomes a cold and meaningless pursuit of facts and figures, and it loses its lure, real purpose, and thrill. It becomes a shell of what it should be.

Without the dramatic spark that exists in natural learning situations, education loses all relevance. It flounders for want of a purpose, and seeks to substantiate its worth with arbitrary measures and required practice that supposedly give an accurate assessment of what has been learned. Teaching, in this drama-less world, is relegated to a dead or dying practice. It has the form but not the substance. It is driven by method and rules that fetter and bind, rather than by the principles that elevate and expand.

Educational Model

To ensure that we add the natural element of drama to our teaching efforts, we need to compare the structure of learning with the dramatic structure we have just covered. A careful comparison exposes a striking similarity and reveals just how much they overlap. Notice that in the accompanying figure, in the educational version of this model, that exposition has been labeled as normal life. This represents the normal life of the learners before they participate in a particular learning experience. As with exposition in the dramatic model, it is essential that the educational model begin with knowledge of background story. The difference here is that it now consists of an in-depth knowledge of the students and their background, values, and needs as learners. How can one hope to create an effective learning environment without knowledge of where students are and where they have come from?

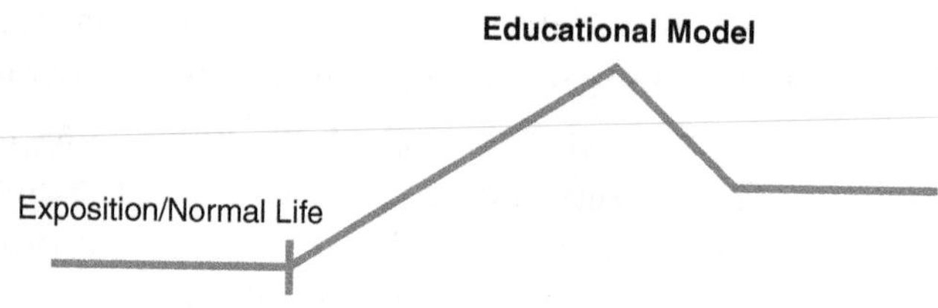

Exposition/Normal Life

Students, like the rest of humanity, are doing all they can to avoid making any changes in their lives. Change, for most of them, is not a positive process. It is usually viewed as a time of loss or deprivation, so most students expend an inordinate amount of energy trying to avoid it. As teachers, we need to understand the problem of inertia that this represents, because when students need to change the most, they are typically most resistant. As we move to introduce new knowledge and skills into the lives of our students, we have to realize that what we are offering will have to replace something that is already important. We have to view everything in this fashion and consider what we are asking our students to give up. Only when they realize that what we have to offer is sufficiently valuable to warrant a change will they exert the energy necessary to assimilate the new information into their lives.

If there is not a cost-benefit ratio that favors the new knowledge of skills we are introducing, we have often lost before we have begun. Without this positive benefit, why should our students be willing to proceed? These issues are some of the most important and first considerations we should examine before beginning to design educational experiences (lesson and unit plans) to facilitate learning. Most students adequately maintain their normal life by doing as little as possible in school. Typically, unless our students are intrinsically motivated in a particular subject area, they attempt to get out of a class by expending as little effort as possible. If, however, they experience an educational inciting event, their normal life can be changed forever. As a dramatic plot is forever altered by the introduction of an inciting event, in a similar manner our students' educational lives can be completely transformed when they experience an event that has sufficient power to propel them past their fear of change.

Inciting Event/Hook

In the educational world, the inciting event has been given different labels. Madeline Hunter refers to it as an "anticipatory set." I call it a "hook." The hook has the same purpose as the inciting event in the dramatic structure. It is created by teachers as an element of curricular design to alter the normal life of their learners and to purposefully disrupt their equilibrium.

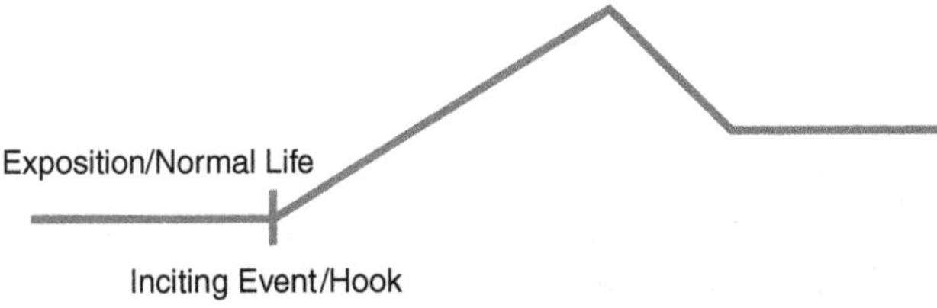

It serves to attract the students' attention and open their horizons. Much of what I see teachers doing in this regard is not dramatic at all. For the most part, the anticipatory set practice I have observed is relegated to the teacher showing the class a visual. One recent example is a teacher's introduction of the Civil War by showing a picture of the Confederate flag. Surely, this flag is one of the enduring symbols of that conflict. To some people it carries a message of hope. To others it represents shattered dreams or oppression. But to many it has little intrinsic connection. To those who do not have a connection to this symbol, and even to those who do, what power does a picture of the flag have to invoke a change in a student who doesn't already have an intrinsic desire to learn more about this pivotal struggle in American history?

In order for a hook to have the power to disrupt the normal life of our students, it must hit them in their heads and in their hearts and it must challenge how they have looked at a particular subject in the past. Then it must move them to mental, emotional, or physical action. An effective hook will provoke learners to experience embryonic stirrings of an intrinsic value for what is being examined. It poses purposeful questions, perplexes, and strictly avoids giving quick answers. A hook need not be complex; in fact, many of the most effective hooks I have seen have been sweetly simple.

If we return to our story of John and Mary, the mere discovery of a simple note changed their lives forever. So it can be with learning. My outlook on math was forever changed by a simple question from Mr. Russell, my sixth-grade teacher: "Who can I count on to make me look good?" He was looking for tutors to work with students in the lower grades and help them with their math. He explained that he would send only those students who would make the other teachers think he knew what he was doing. A simple hook, carefully baited and worked by a master teacher, changed my whole outlook on learning math.

The right hook can create interest and respect for an area of study that students, in their normal lives, see as boring and worthless. Teachers armed with the knowledge of the learning preferences of their students, combined with their understanding of how their students feel toward the subject matter, can quickly learn to develop simple hooks that will incite students to action. Returning to our Civil War example, if we use the Confederate flag, not a picture of it, as the beginning point of our hook, some exciting things can happen. For example, we could display the flag, put the students in groups, and ask them to think about the feeling this flag might engender in different groups of people. Assign one group to look at it as people in a small town in Pennsylvania would while seeing an army coming toward them. Ask another to look at the flag as a group of slaves living on a plantation in the South. Another group might explore the feelings of a trapped Confederate platoon caught behind enemy lines, or as Union soldiers standing to face a Confederate cavalry charge.

It becomes quickly apparent that the difference in these two hooks (anticipatory sets) is vast. One is merely for show; whereas the other requires the students to explore the real human issues that were at the core of the Civil War. It should also be clear that the difference in what was required of the teacher in each of these examples is relatively small. The more dramatic approach is not that different from the nondramatic one. The real difference is created by what the hook requires of the students. Remember, it must engage their hearts and minds. To do that, we must begin at the exposition or normal life of our students and then design an experience or inciting event that causes them not only to stop and pay attention for a few seconds, but also to invest a little of their time and energy. As with any kind of personal change or growth, your willingness to try something new and practice it until you've become proficient is the key to adding this dramatic element to your teaching skills.

The best thing I have discovered to help when developing effective hooks is to ask myself one simple question: "How would my class best like to be introduced to this topic?" Beginning the process this way gives me an instant filter that allows my knowledge of my educational goals and objectives and of the needs of my class members to help me create an engaging but very simple hook. In our example of the man-made/ natural resource lesson, this question was used to create the new lesson format. It became immediately obvious that these particular children would rather experience this lesson than be taught it in the traditional way. The hook that I helped develop was a minor variation of the plan the teacher had already created. As far as teacher preparation went, the only additional work required was making the numbered signs and placing the items outside. This additional effort was more than compensated for by the fact that the teacher did not have to spend 30 minutes lecturing on the subject. I want to be as clear as I can that this is a simplifying process. It is not intended to make work for already overworked teachers. In this example, once the students were instructed on how to conduct the scavenger hunt, the rest of the lesson was like pedaling downhill. The lesson was sustained by the students' energy and excitement to learn, and not only by the teacher's.

Rising Action/Body of the Lesson

Once the hook (inciting event) is set, we are ready to move into the body of our educational structure. On the dramatic model, this is called the rising action. Here in the educational world, I refer to it as the body of the lesson. The body of the lesson is a step-by-step process designed to lead students to the heart or objective of the lesson. It is a carefully constructed set of learning experiences that are designed to mesh in such a way that students are drawn into a challenging yet friendly exploration of the subject matter.

The body of the lesson needs to be designed with the same meticulous attention to detail that is used in the fabrication of any good plot. It must be logical. It must engage and hold interest. It must grow from one point to another while bringing along an interested audience of students. It must allow for students to interact with the material intellectually, physically, and emotionally. And finally, it must continue to move their

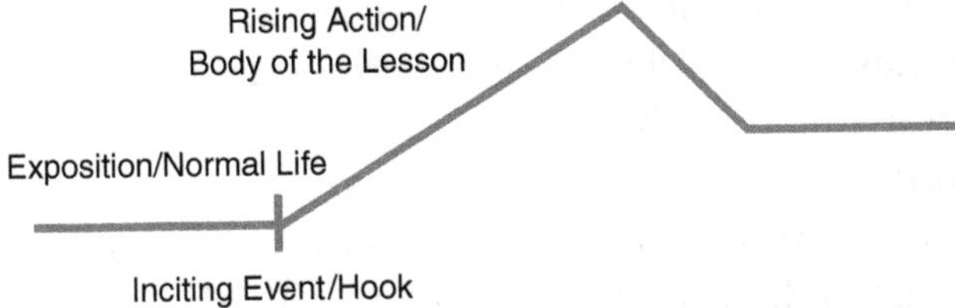

interest forward by taking them from one carefully structured success to another.

A lesson plan that doesn't follow this dramatic structure in its body will often start out with great promise and then fizzle in its ability to hold the interest of the learner. Compare the structures in the following figures to gain a clearer understanding of how important adherence to these principles is in educational design.

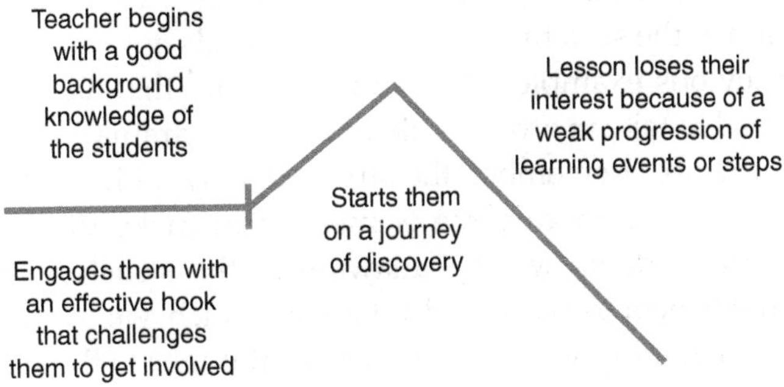

If we modify our example of the man-made/natural resource lesson from Chapter 3, we can demonstrate this particular structure. Let's assume that the lesson begins with instructions for the students to go outside, examine the items, and record their answers. The effective hook and lesson progression to this point fill the students with excitement and energy because of their participation in the learning process. If we now make a drastic change in approach, we will effectively kill everything we have tried to establish in the beginning of the lesson. We might do this by escorting the students back into the classroom and requiring them to sit at their desks and work individually, while the teacher lectures and evaluates their findings.

Let's say, instead of allowing them to share the answers they discovered, the teacher had them individually check their answers against an overhead transparency. The teacher's efforts to lecture them at this point through each one of the items on the overhead would completely violate sound principles of dramatic structure.

However, a properly designed lesson body begins with the engaging hook and then is carefully structured to hold the students' interest. Reexamining the modified man-made/natural resource lesson, we can see that this dramatic lesson has the structure necessary to pique and hold the interest of the students through the whole lesson. This lesson structure is simple to implement because the students begin to teach themselves once they get involved in the process. A close examination of the structure of this lesson reveals how it differs from the previous example. This is the structure that all of our lessons need to take in order for them to have a dramatic impact on our audience. Remember, the structure may look the same to you, but as you modify the elements that make up your lessons, your students will be unaware of the structure at all. How many people who read books or watch well-made dramatic presentations give one moment of thought to the structure that is being employed to engage their attention? It is only when the structure doesn't work that it is even brought into question.

A simpler example of this would be to look at the old Wile E. Coyote cartoons. Here, the poor coyote endlessly struggles to catch Road Runner. This silly cartoon uses dramatic structure perfectly. In fact, a close examination reveals important secrets that would immediately increase the dramatic value of our teaching and show us why many of our lessons lack the structure to hold the interest of our students. These cartoons are quite adept at holding the interest of the audience even when they know that the coyote will never win. This is very

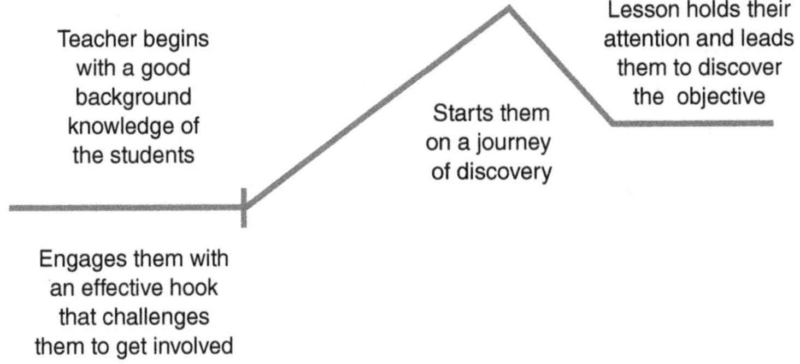

simple to explain. Each time Wile E. fails to catch his dinner, he resorts to a more elaborate and hair-brained scheme. The appetite of any audience always demands something more. Wile E. never disappoints. His futile efforts go from fake stop signs to lead-laced birdseed. From there, he advances through one failed effort after another until he is strapped to the top of an atomic-powered rocket.

In an ever-escalating progression, Wile E. advances through each attempted pursuit by constantly increasing the risk to Road Runner and to himself. Each failure is more spectacular than the last; each attempt is calculated to raise the stakes. To do otherwise would spell dramatic disaster. Think how ridiculous it would be to expect an audience to follow Wile E. through a reverse progression. If he goes from a larger attempt to a smaller one, the risk would reduce each time, and so would our interest in following his struggle. Lesson progression must play by these same rules of economy. It must follow a sound progression to hold interest and increase involvement.

As the teacher, you are in control of every aspect of the lesson. There are many ways to teach any concept, and you must design the process so that it will be most compatible with the learning needs of your students. You control the amount of conflict or risk your students will experience as they are subjected to the learning process. You have to carefully balance your ability to keep and hold their interest, while at the same time make sure they are mastering the subject. The two must be carefully orchestrated together, because a student who is lost quickly loses interest in the subject. Examine the accompanying figure for a moment and notice the angle of the line that rises up from the hook.

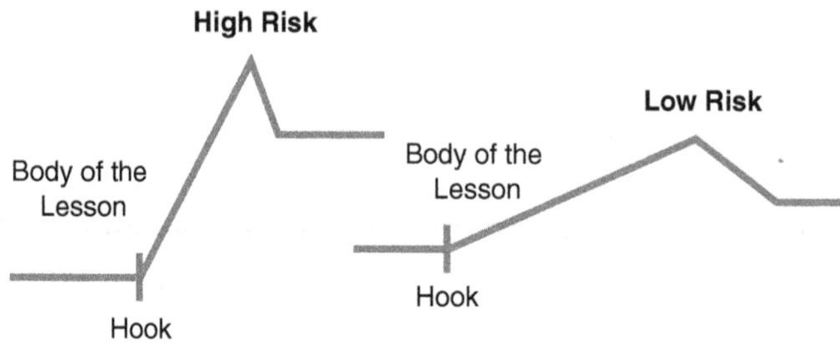

The slant in the line that represents the body of the lesson determines the risk level that is required of students. The steeper the incline of the line, the more the teacher is requiring of the students. Careful lesson and unit planning with attention to this risk factor can pay great dividends. We must be reasonable in what we ask of our students, and at the same time, we must push them to grow and excel. The more we are aware of this element of our lesson planning, the better we will be at making midstream adjustments which increase or decrease the risk factor we are imposing on our learners.

Climax/Objective

The rise of the line that denotes the body of the lesson must continue upward until it reaches its highest point. In the dramatic model, it is the climax. In the lesson represented in the following figure, we refer to the climax as the objective. It's the point in which the "Aha!" happens and a person gains mastery of a skill or concept. In the highest forms of learning, it is the point where the learner internalizes or understands something new and recognizes its intrinsic value. At this point in the learning process, it is usually necessary for some kind of assessment to be given so that the teacher and the learners can realize and celebrate the success that has been achieved.

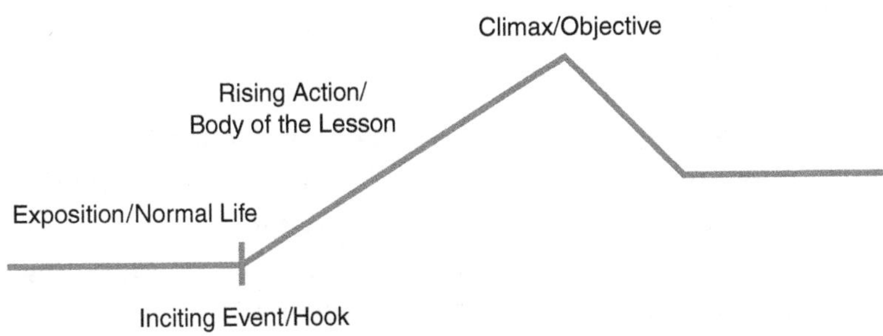

Once the assessment has occurred, the learning process must begin to recycle in order to reinforce the concepts and ideas that have been taught. This necessary repetition serves to ensure the longevity of what has been learned. In his book *The Unschooled Mind,* Howard Gardner discusses the need for deeper learning aimed at helping the student gain understanding. He refers to the need for educators to not only present students with new ideas and ways of thinking, but also to approach learning from as many points of view as possible. If we do not, he warns, our attempts to educate will fail because we have created a learning environment without the power to overcome students' previously held view of the world.

According to Gardner, when the new ideas, information, or theories we have taught our students come in contact with a problem or phenomenon outside the realm of the limited learning environment in which they were introduced, the previously held views, or "primitives," of the students will overshadow anything new. This reverting to behavioral patterns or knowledge that were learned in the past occurs because the new subject matter has not been learned with enough power to replace the old ideas.

Dénouement/New Life Pattern

Gardner contends that unless these new models are reinforced sufficiently, real learning and student understanding will not be achieved.

> This state of affairs—an enhanced understanding—can come to pass only if the students become familiar with the new models, understand the reasons for them, perceive why they are more appropriate than the older, competing ones, which may well have retained their attractiveness. . . . (1991, p. 157)

In the educational model, this becomes the new life pattern rather than the dénouement of the dramatic model.

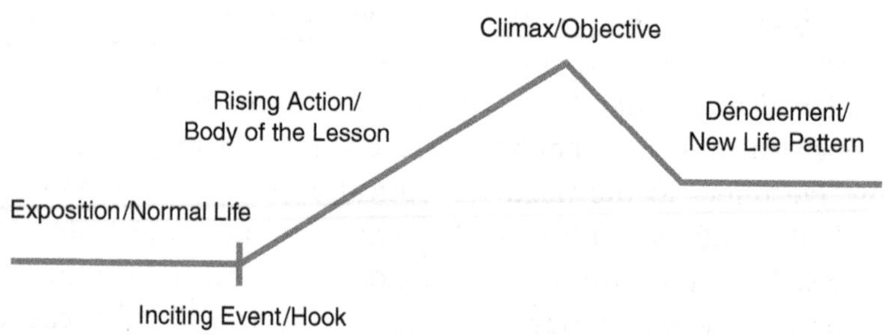

The new life segment of a lesson or unit plan is the real measure of the power of the learning experience. It is the difference between being satisfied with students who can regurgitate the right answer on a test and having students who truly understand and can apply what they have learned in their daily lives. It is what should happen in education when we do our job right. If a new life pattern doesn't emerge from an educational experience, what good is it? In fact, what good is any learning or knowledge that is not used?

The best evidence that real learning has taken place is what it does in the life of the learner. If we go back to the first element on our model, look at the normal life pattern of our learners, and compare it with their life after the lesson or unit, we should be able to see some proof of individual change. If what we've done has no impact on the life of the learners when they are out of our presence, then we have failed. If that is the case, our inciting event and learning structure did not have the power to create or alter the equilibrium that already exists in the life of the learner.

Please don't think that this change needs to be drastic or life-altering to prove effective. It doesn't. It merely needs to open vision, alter expectations, enhance fundamentals, or provide the slightest change of heart and mind. The real power comes in the cumulative effect of the incidental changes on the individual over time. Remember that change is the personal journey that turns a series of small, seemingly insignificant successes into overwhelming personal progress.

By using this dramatic structure in our classrooms, we create a powerful learning environment. We can incite learning and excite young minds and hearts to open up to new ideas and understanding. By reintroducing dramatic elements to the structure of learning, we open so many doors that have been closed to whole populations of learners. We blend the natural learning abilities of all students with the curricular pressures of modern educational realities. This is the secret to returning the fun and the thrill of learning for teachers as well as students. In retrospect, isn't this what drew us to education in the first place?

6

Curriculum Design

The design elements for a curriculum (plot) that will best meet the learning needs of dramatic learners are not much different from those elements typically used for traditional lesson and unit planning. Teachers and administrators who have developed sound curriculum-designing skills should have no problems making the adjustments necessary to create learning experiences that are better targeted to reach their dramatic learners. In reality, we need to understand and master just a few simple keys to make the planning process more successful. Though they may seem like minor adjustments to standard lesson planning practices, these keys are essential to use when working with this particular population of learners.

It doesn't matter how we have fared with other learners. We must change what we are doing so it appeals to the learning preferences of the dramatic learner. In fact, we have to move out of our own comfort zones as teachers to be able to reach them. This is hard for many teachers to do because it asks them to take risks they simply are not willing to take. In response to those concerns, I have to reiterate a question posed earlier: Is it more likely that success will come from these learners changing the way they learn to meet the way we teach, or will we find more success if we learn to modulate the way we teach to better fit their style of learning? The correct answer is all too obvious.

We do not need to abandon all we know about teaching to be successful in reaching the dramatic learner. We simply need to combine the knowledge we have gained about our target audience with our previous teaching experience to create a hybrid approach that will assure the highest likelihood of achieving better results. In practical terms, to help us make the proper modifications in our own teaching practice, we must first alter our lesson- and unit-planning skills. As mentioned before, this alteration is not radically different from traditional curriculum design techniques. Learning experiences aimed at reaching the dramatic learner must first pass a relevancy muster. To do so, the experiences must contain several elements and adhere to key principles that will give them the power to draw and maintain the students' interest.

A simple way to determine if a lesson or unit meets these criteria is by using a four-question assessment. Each question focuses on the key elements that engage dramatic learners. Apply them to the units and lessons you have already developed and see where you stand. You may be pleased to discover that your most successful lessons already pass this muster. Once you understand this process, you can easily modify the rest of your lessons and units if you choose.

Question 1: Is the lesson fun and different? Before you dismiss this question out of hand, let's define what I mean by *fun*. The fun I allude to in this context is any activity that is enjoyable, enlightening, and keeps and holds the interest of a learner. Referring back to Aristotle, it is that which engages, enlightens, and entertains the mind.

As I introduced this question in a workshop, a teacher emphatically raised her hand and vehemently objected to the idea that teachers have a responsibility to make learning fun. She stated, "My job is to teach, not to entertain children all day long. They get enough of that already." I watched as she braced herself for an argument. She and the rest of the teachers in the room who shared her point of view sat poised and dared me to take them on. Instead, I asked her to keep her concern on the table as I asked the rest of the participants to answer a related question: "When are you having fun?"

As teachers pondered the question and shared their answers, I returned to her question for clarification. The teacher's answers included "I'm having fun when I'm interacting with others," "when I finally learn to do something I could never do before," "when I do something new," "when I'm recognized for something I've done well," "when I'm actively engaged in something important," "when I'm not bored," "when I'm accepted," "when I discover something new," and "when I come up with a solution." As each of these answers was voiced, I turned to the woman and asked her if these elements are important in a successful learning environment. She quickly agreed they were, and immediately realized our disagreement had been only a matter of semantics. She had been defining fun in a very narrow way. In the vernacular of this text, remember, fun means that which we enjoy, that which holds our interest and causes us to search for greater meaning, understanding, or mastery.

Question 2: Is the lesson engaging? Does the lesson clearly capture the interest of the learner and hold it throughout the allotted class time? Is there power in the lesson and its associated learning activities to progressively involve students in the process of educational discovery? Is there a layering of activities that constantly deepens the interest, involvement, and understanding of the student? This engagement must occur at many different levels because students are attracted to learning by varying factors. The key here is a strong balance between intellectual, physical, and emotional elements. This balance will create an atmosphere that is accessible to the highest majority of learners. If the students can find something that engages their curiosity, they will be more apt to spend the time necessary to explore, master, and internalize the subject matter being introduced.

Question 3: Is it theirs? This question relates to our understanding of where the burden of learning lies. Does the lesson place the ownership of learning on the students, or does the teacher carry it? Do the students actually get to earn an increased understanding or skill in the subject area because they are required to do the work of learning? To make a lesson belong to the students, one must actively involve them in the learning process. This means it must be hands-on and/or brains-on. Students cannot be passive participants in the learning process.

Question 4: Is it value based? This question relates again to our awareness of where the curriculum has its focus. Are we sure the lessons and units are clearly aimed at the values of the individual learners? Is it something that is important to them, or are we focusing our efforts on making it important? Have we considered the interacting, gathering, and processing needs of our learners? It is not possible to prepare properly unless we know what their values and learning needs are in the first place.

If these four questions are answered in the affirmative, then the rest of the planning process is relatively easy. Educators who will learn to use this simple, four-question filter can easily modify teaching units and lessons that do not meet these criteria. These questions help to modify our design of curriculum simply because they make us look outside of our selves and consider more fully the needs of our target audience.

Most traditional teaching units and lesson plans contain a clear teaching objective or benchmark, and some form of outline or step-by-step process to follow to reach the stated goal. The following is an example of a lesson plan format similar to many that are commonly used in classrooms across the nation. This one formalizes the man-made/natural resource lesson. Let's analyze it for effectiveness in reaching dramatic learners by using the four-question test: (1) Is it fun and different? (2) Is it engaging? (3) Is it theirs? (4) Is it value based?

SAMPLE LESSON PLAN #1

Identifying Natural Resources

Educational Objective: Students will gain an understanding of the difference between man-made and natural resources.

Prep:

1. Gather different items or pictures of items that represent a good cross-section of objects that are either man-made or natural resources. Examples might be a fish, a brick, a rock, a pop can, a tree, a newspaper, a toothbrush, a stick of chewing gum, a pitcher of water, a picture of a deer, and a picture of a log cabin. You will need 20 items in all. Make sure you have a good mix of the man-made and the natural items.

2. Have a piece of paper and a pencil available for each student.

3. Create a worksheet.

Procedure:

Step 1: State the objective to the class.

Step 2: Ask the class if they know the difference between a natural resource and a man-made object. Listen to the answers and help students come up with a working definition of each term. Write the answer on the board so they can see it. The answer should read something like this: A natural resource is something that exists in nature without the interference of men. A man-made object is something that has been changed or altered from its natural state by man.

Step 3: Once you have the definitions, ask students to clear off their desks, and then pass out a worksheet to each student. Make sure they each have pencil or pen to use to fill out the sheet, as you direct.

Natural Resources	*Man-Made Objects*
1.	1.
2.	2.
3.	3.
4.	4.
5.	5.
6.	6.
7.	7.
8.	8.
9.	9.
10.	10.
11.	11.
12.	12.
13.	13.
14.	14.
15.	15.
16.	16.
17.	17.
18.	18.
19.	19.
20.	20.

Step 4: Instruct the class that you will be showing them different objects, pictures of different objects, or simply stating the name of the object. When you do, students are to use the definitions on the board to determine whether the item is

man-made or natural. If it is man-made, they are to write the name of the item under the proper heading on their sheet next to the corresponding number. For example, if item number 4 is a waffle, they would fill out their worksheet like this:

Natural Resources	*Man-Made Objects*
4.	4. Waffle

Have them follow this same pattern for all of the objects.

Step 5: Go through each item with the class to make sure students have the right answers. Ask for volunteers to give you the right answer for item 1. If the answer is right, ask another child to explain why that is the right answer. If the answer is wrong, ask another child to explain why it is the wrong answer. Establish a pattern for checking all the answers. Have the students write in the correct answers where they have made a mistake.

Step 6: Review for the students what they have learned by restating the definition of each of the categories and reviewing how they can determine if an object is man-made or natural.

A quick reading of this lesson reveals that it is well organized and that it has a clear objective. It may work fine for many students, especially those with the judging processing preference. Though these elements are important, their presence in a lesson doesn't necessarily mean that it will meet the relevancy muster required for teaching dramatic learners. Remember, we are looking for dramatic elements that will engage this particular target population in the learning process. Let's explore why this well-planned lesson falls short.

Question 1: Is it fun and different? Not really. What is different in this lesson from all the other lessons the student will experience on any given day? As the lesson outlines, the teacher is to state the topic and begin the lesson by explaining what the students are meant to learn. Though this is the standard approach required by a majority of standard teacher-effectiveness evaluations, what does a typical statement of the lesson's objective do to instill in the student the desire to search for meaning, understanding, or mastery of the given subject? The truth of the matter is that whenever we clearly state our objective for the class, we put them in a position where they naturally make an immediate value judgment on the subject we are presenting. How many students are intrinsically interested in learning their required course material?

Which creates more interest: a lesson where the outcome has already been revealed or a lesson that creates a feeling of suspense and then offers the academic freedom, in a supportive educational environment, to discover the path that has been delineated? Let's return to our dramatic model for a moment. How much do we hate it when a person tells us the ending of the movie? The reason for our disdain is clear; it takes away the entire thrill by disengaging our own sense of discovery and wonder. For the dramatic learners, this is one of the quickest ways to remove the fun from learning. Remember, they are constantly looking for a challenge they can master and for information that has particular meaning to them.

This concept doesn't mean that the teacher shouldn't develop clear objectives for each lesson; objectives are more essential than ever when working with this population. The difference is that when you are working with the dramatic learner, you need to ensure that your objectives are used to direct *your* efforts rather than the efforts of the learners. The objective is there simply to help the teacher keep focused and directed while the student experiences the satisfying work of learning. What good is a stated objective if it becomes a stumbling block?

In another training I conducted, the principal became very alarmed when I mentioned this concept. He asked, "How will

I know the teachers' objectives if they don't state them for me?" With a little coaching from others and me, he soon realized there were a myriad of acceptable ways that this could be accomplished. The suggestions that were given included having teachers give their evaluators a copy of their lesson plans, having teachers write the objective on the evaluation form before they are evaluated, and simply having teachers tell their objective to the evaluators before class.

When teachers use objectives as *their* tool to direct learning, they make the learning process more fun for the student. They create an educational experience that allows the learner to believe that he or she has discovered the purpose of the lesson. Just a little side comment: Never tell a dramatic learner that you are going to do a "fun" activity. It's the surest way to promote failure. When a learning activity is fun for them, they'll be the first to let you know. Your desire to label it as fun doesn't make it so.

Question 2: Is it engaging? Not really. The lesson calls for the students to sit at their desks, as passive listeners, and keep notes on what the teacher says. If they are intrinsically interested in the lesson, the students might naturally engage, but for those who have no interest in the subject matter, the lesson does nothing to get them involved in the process of learning. Certainly, a teacher must spend some class time teaching things that the students don't already know, but there are other ways to do this that will engage the students more in the process.

This lesson assumes that the students have no previous knowledge in the subject matter. On the surface this may be true, but somewhere in their past experience, there is a thread of life-learning experience that is similar to the task of comparison that this lesson is asking them to make. When a teacher can draw on what students already know, learning reverts to its most natural form. The connection becomes very easy for students to make. It gives students a leveraging context from which they can use what they already know as the fulcrum to gain power to master new material. The ability to find this connection is one of the greatest tools for engaging dramatic learners.

This lesson draws only on the knowledge and activity of the teacher. The only place where a student can really engage is by being interested enough to raise a hand and ask a question or offer an answer. Even then, the structure allows only one student at a time to participate. Experience reveals that this format typically creates a situation where one or two students participate by answering questions while the others passively sit and watch. How can students be expected to engage in a process that doesn't really encourage or involve their full and active participation?

Question 3: Is it theirs? Again, the answer is no. The lesson is completely teacher centered. The job of the students is to watch as audience members. There is no place for them to gain ownership of the process or the information. In each step, the learning process is heavily dependent on the teacher being able to pass the information on in a meaningful manner while the students quietly observe the process.

Without ownership, learning is only temporary. Think of your own practices as a student. How many times did you throw away your class papers and notes immediately upon taking the last test in the class? You did the work because you had to, but it wasn't for you; it was for the teacher and the grade. It was merely a right of passage rather than anything educationally significant. The learning process was external, and so the information had no personal connection to your life. Therefore, once you received the grade, you had no need for the information, and you immediately forgot it.

This lesson falls into the same trap. It doesn't really engage the mind or the body. There is no attempt to help the student see why it's important to know the difference between man-made and natural resources. When we work with dramatic learners, this perspective is essential. If they don't see the immediate value in learning something, they will often pass it by and never engage. Learning activities that allow the student to interact with the material create a learning bridge over the gap that often separates the dramatic learner from the subject matter. The ability to connect in a physical, emotional, or intellectual way brings information into the world of the student and makes it important. When this happens for a student, it gives school a whole new meaning and turns it into a place where the dramatic learner feels he or she belongs.

Question 4: Is it value based? No, the lesson is being taught from the point of view of the teacher and the school district. In essence, the message of the lesson is clearly, "You have to learn this because we (the teacher, the principal, the school board, etc.) think it's important." There is no attempt to tailor the subject matter in such a way that the student's own set of values perceives it as something important.

When the students see learning as the key to attaining the things they desire, everything changes. School changes from an activity they have to participate in to one they get to explore. Lessons and units designed to reach the values of the learner require interaction and individual involvement. Without the ability to reach the values of learners, education will forever be something that is done to them. This lesson is missing an element designed to create a personal connection and an understanding of its personal value to the student. This lesson is typical of most of the instruction that is being practiced in our schools across the country. Is it any wonder that we are losing the battle with the dramatic learners?

This analysis reveals that many of our educational failures are not happening by accident. In fact, many happen according to plan. What is even more alarming is that we are going to keep making this same mistake until we learn to plan a curriculum aimed at our target audience. Until we understand how to design the right kind of learning environment, structures, and activities for these students, we will continue to sow the seeds of failure in our design phase. A successful result can never be achieved from a faulty plan, and following a faulty plan perfectly leads only to perfect failure.

Let's consider an alternative approach to lesson planning that takes into consideration the learning needs of the dramatic learner. As mentioned before, this approach will not be that different from traditional approaches. It will, however, be the source of much educational success, if used properly. The exciting thing about creating lessons and units that meet the learning needs of dramatic learners is that in so doing teachers are also creating learning experiences that are more fun and engaging and, therefore, more accessible to all types of learners. Every type of learner does better when learning is made enjoyable.

To modify this sample lesson, or any other lesson, to better meet the needs of dramatic learners, the first key to remember is that it must be aimed at their learning style and must be skill- and activity-based. The addition of kinesthetic elements often brings immediate relevancy to the subject matter and transforms it in the mind of these learners. The lesson objective itself needs to reflect this focus. It is not enough just to identify the objective as in traditional lessons. It is essential to clearly identify the skill that the student will practice and an activity that the student can successfully complete to demonstrate mastery of the identified objective. This focus immediately moves the lesson from passive to experiential. It changes the focus for teachers as well, because it gives them a clear and demonstrable objective or benchmark to evaluate the knowledge and skills the students have gained. It also allows teachers to readily evaluate the effectiveness of the lesson and their own efforts in assisting the students to master the new material. This type of an objective forces the teacher to assess for skill enhancement, knowledge application, and increased understanding, rather than just focusing on whether a student can recite back the right answer to a given question. It places the emphasis on seeking to ascertain evidence of true learning, rather than solely relying on test scores.

Lessons that have a strong activity base have an increased ability to involve students in the learning process. These lessons have a built-in demonstration phase that forces students to display whether they fully understand the material they are supposed to be mastering. The learning activity that is identified in the objective of these lessons serves as the final step of the lesson. It becomes the culminating activity of the lesson and a focus for all preceding steps. It assures greater adherence to the dramatic structure by requiring that an ever-escalating series of learning events be designed to help the students demonstrate the level of their mastery. It forces teachers to plan all these necessary steps that will prepare the students to fully demonstrate their newly acquired knowledge and skills.

Therefore, the objective from the example lesson, "Students will gain an understanding of the difference between man-made and natural resources," may simply be modified to read "The students will increase their understanding of the difference between man-made and natural resources by successfully completing a scavenger hunt."

The difference between these two objectives seems slight, but by tying the objective to a clear learning activity, the whole emphasis of the lesson changes. As mentioned before, these changes will not negatively impede the lesson from reaching other types of learners. Instead, it will also help them to engage more deeply in the learning process.

Let's rewrite the whole sample lesson using this objective as the starting point. We'll then compare the differences using the four-question analysis.

Sample Lesson Plan #2

Identifying Natural Resources

Educational Objective: The students will increase their understanding of the difference between man-made and natural resources by successfully completing a scavenger hunt.

Prep:

1. Gather different items or pictures of items that represent a good cross-section of things that are either man-made or natural resources. Examples might be a fish, a brick, a rock, a pop can, a tree, a newspaper, a toothbrush, a stick of chewing gum, a pitcher of water, a picture of a deer, and a picture of a log cabin. (You will need 20 items in all. Make sure you have a good mix of the man-made and the natural items.)

2. Go outside or to a large open indoor room and spread the items out so that groups of students can examine each one individually. Make sure to place the corresponding number next to the item.

3. Make sure you have a piece of paper and a pencil available for each student.

4. Create a worksheet (the same worksheet illustrated previously in Sample Lesson Plan #1).

Step 1: Pass out a clipboard or other hard writing surface to each student and make sure each person has a pen or pencil.

Step 2: Ask the class to bring their writing surface and writing instrument and follow you. Take the class to the space where you have laid out the items.

Step 3: Once you are in the work area, pass out the worksheet to the class. Instruct students that their job is to go throughout the designated space and examine each of the 20 items that have been laid out. Tell them that when they have determined if the object is a natural resource or man-made, they are to record their findings by writing the name of the object next to its corresponding number under the proper heading. For example, if item number 4 is a waffle, they would fill out their worksheet like this:

Natural Resources	*Man-Made Objects*
4.	4. Waffle

Once they understand how to fill out the sheet, ask students if they have any ideas how they might tell if an item is natural or man-made. Listen to their answers and see if the class can come up with a method or protocol for telling the difference. (Make sure everyone understands how to tell the difference by using an example, such as holding up an item and asking several of them to tell you if the item is man-made or natural and why.)

Step 4: Once they are clear about the task, allow them to work in groups no larger than four. (Give them the opportunity to work alone if they prefer.) Tell them that you will be available as a resource if they have any questions. Give them a reasonable time limit, and have them report to you when they are finished. Set them free to fulfill the assignment. (If appropriate for your class, you can turn it into a race to see which group can finish first.)

Step 5: While the class is working on the assignment, circulate throughout the space and monitor its progress. Observe the groups as they work to determine if they are applying the protocol that was developed. Ask questions that will help them with the process and that will help you to see if they understand how to determine the difference between man-made and natural resources. Be careful not to intrude on their learning or to give answers. Help with time management by reminding the groups how much time they have left and making sure the groups that finish first don't interfere with those that are still working.

Step 6: Assign each group or individual to be responsible for reporting the findings for certain items. Have them gather up their items and numbers and prepare to report to the class. Gather the class together in their groups and review the answers. Call out a group number at random and have that group give its answer and explain how they came to a conclusion. If another group has a different answer, have its members explain how they came to their conclusion. Direct the conversation so that the entire class can see how the right answer was derived. Don't give the answer outright if someone has a wrong answer, but continue to ask questions until class members can apply the proper skills to determine the difference on their own. Have the students change their answers as necessary to correct their mistakes. Make sure they aren't just changing answers, but that they know why they were wrong in their first conclusion.

Step 7: Have students restate the keys they have discovered that will help them distinguish the difference between man-made and natural resources. Instruct them to record on their worksheets the keys that are discussed.

Step 8: Spot check for understanding by calling on different students to examine a new item using the class keys and see if they can determine if it is man-made or natural. If necessary, allow the individuals to be assisted by a classmate when a question is posed.

Step 9: (Optional) Take the class back into the classroom and give a formal quiz. (Allow students to handle the items if they want during the quiz.)

A quick reading of this altered lesson should reveal that it is not that different from the original. It too has a clear objective and a well-organized, step-by-step process. The real difference is that it has been modified to reflect the learning needs of the target audience. Dramatic elements are used throughout to allow for maximum student participation.

Question 1: Is it fun and different? Yes. The students are taken, without explanation, out of the normal classroom setting. The teacher spends little time in a formal teaching role but rather serves as a learning facilitator and resource. The natural curiosity of the students is used, and the teacher hopes they will respond positively by experimenting with the lesson. By presenting the lesson in a different yet natural learning environment, many students who are not intrinsically interested in the subject matter will be motivated to at least give it a second look.

The interest this lesson creates is accomplished by using the element of suspense. Suspense naturally draws a learner down a path to discovery. It creates a sense of thrill and engages the student's own natural sense of discovery and wonder. It is the quickest way to reinsert fun into learning. This lesson creates a natural learning environment that challenges students' intellect and feelings. It sparks in them a desire to master the task and decipher its meaning.

The clear, activity-based objective for this lesson enables the teacher to create an atmosphere of freedom and individual exploration while still maintaining a strong control over the situation. The actual structure of the lesson creates a transparent discipline model that binds the student's attention through active participation in a serious learning exercise. The objective keeps the learning process on track, but it is totally transparent to the learner. It is designed to help the teacher keep focused and to direct the students back on track when their interest strays. The fun that the process creates covers up the real fact that they are involved in a deeply important learning process.

Question 2: Is it engaging? Again, the answer is yes. The lesson moves the students out of their desks and out of the classroom. They are no longer asked to be passive listeners, but are transformed into actual scientists probing their environment for answers. They are not merely keeping notes; they are recording scientific discoveries and applying theories. What the teacher says appears to have a secondary importance; the students' own observations and answers to questions are given the greatest weight.

Some teachers may be threatened by this notion. If, however, we want students to take more control of their own learning, we have to be willing to give up some of our control. The fear is that once given, the control will disappear. The converse is actually true. The more control you are willing to give to your students in the learning process, the more they will be willing to be controlled by you. Their trust in you and their desire to learn will repay anything you feel you might be giving up. In a more practical way, think of the freedom it will give you if you don't have to be the one who knows all the answers all the time.

This lesson attempts to work from the inside out to create an intrinsic interest in the subject matter. If it is successful, students will naturally engage, even if they have no natural interest in the subject matter. The learning environment accomplishes this by employing the Socratic method of asking questions, drawing out answers, and forging connections with other things that the student already knows.

This lesson draws heavily on the previous knowledge the students have in related subject areas. By drawing on their acquired knowledge, the connection to natural learning deepens the experience and makes it more meaningful and lasting in the memory. By using what they already know, dramatic learners feel a rush of confidence from standing on familiar and firm ground. It is always easier for them to forge out into unfamiliar territory when they feel like they know how to get back to where they started. This linkage of past and present knowledge helps the learners believe they already possess the skills needed to be successful.

This lesson puts the students, not the teacher, in the center of the learning process simply by requiring active participation. Their involvement is not restricted to raising their hands or asking questions. The very structure of the lesson demands their full and active engagement. They are required to engage at many different levels because, to accomplish the assignment, they must get involved emotionally as they interact and work with other students, physically as they move from site to site, and intellectually as they develop and test their protocols and scientific methodologies.

The ego of the teacher needs to be set aside here for the sake of the learner. We have to remember that we already know these things and that we are not teaching them for our benefit. We've already done the work of learning; now it's our turn to get our students involved.

Question 3: Is it theirs? Again, the answer is yes. The lesson is completely student centered. In this reversal of roles, it is the job of each student to actively participate in the learning experience. The job of the teacher is to monitor progress and act as a resource. If the students participate to any degree, they will be successful. Any effort they put forth will naturally result in a gained ownership of the process and the subject matter.

A close inspection of this lesson will reveal that each step of the learning process is heavily dependent on the student. They must decide what protocols to test, whether to work alone or in groups, how to record their findings, when to ask for help, how to report on their findings, and so on. Those who choose to work in groups will be practicing other tangential skills, such as peer tutoring, compromising, listening, consensus building, and review. The teacher's involvement in the students' efforts will occur only if they covertly ask for it by getting off task or if they directly request assistance. Though the teacher is constantly monitoring their efforts to ensure that they are on task, he or she is not overtly controlling their activities. Thus, the students feel the ownership of the learning because they perceive that they are in control of the situation. Remember, without ownership, learning is only temporary.

Question 4: Is it value based? Again, the answer is yes. The lesson is no longer being taught from the point of view of the curriculum, teacher, or school district. There is a concerted effort to tailor the subject matter to meet the values of the students. Every effort is made in the planning phase to develop a learning environment that encourages learners to explore the subject from their own frame of reference. This approach increases the likelihood that as each student discovers his or her own solution to the problem at hand, he or she will begin to develop a personal theory for why it's important to know the difference between man-made and natural resources.

When we work with dramatic learners, this perspective is essential. Remember, their in-the-moment perspective on life makes it essential for a learning experience to provide immediate relevancy. If they don't see the immediate value in what they are learning, they have a hard time spending the time necessary to properly engage in and master the subject. For this reason, the learning activities, purposely designed into this lesson, force them to interact with the material. This deliberate design approach creates the necessary learning bridge to connect the dramatic learner to the subject matter. This physical connection to the information brings it naturally into the world of the student, and it makes the subject important. Thusly structured, learning takes on a whole new meaning and turns the classroom into a place where dramatic learners feel they belong.

This approach to any subject will alter learning in the mind of the student. It moves the subject out of the world of drudgery and boredom, and helps each individual begin to see learning as the most important key to personal growth and change. The personal interaction and individual involvement required in this lesson carefully shifts the focus from the extrinsic values of the teacher and the school to something that has personal value for the learners. The process of discovery now becomes something they can participate in rather than something that is done to them.

To deepen our understanding of this process, let's examine several lesson plans side-by-side using our four key questions. The purpose of this examination is to illustrate how simple it is to alter standard lessons to meet the needs of the dramatic learner. It will take some time to get used to the concept, but the rewards for teachers and students alike will be well worth the effort.

Sample Lesson Plan #3

Increasing Vocabulary Skills

Educational Objective: Students will gain an understanding of the meaning of selected vocabulary words.

Prep:

1. Prepare a vocabulary sheet for the following words: *abrupt, advance, alter, assess, allowance, affection, affordable, amicable, ardent,* and *afflict* (see Table 6.1).
2. Make sure you have a dictionary and a pencil available for each student.
3. Create a worksheet.

Step 1: State the objective for the class. Ask students to clear off their desks, and then pass out a worksheet to each student. Make sure they each have pencil or pen to use to fill out the sheet, as you will direct.

Step 2: Pass out the vocabulary sheet to each member of the class and ask if any of them think they know the meaning of any of the words on the list. Have them put down a check next to each word they think they know. (Give them a few minutes to go over the list.) Ask the class members to tell what words they think they know.

Step 3: Instruct them to write down a definition in their own words for each of the words they have checked.

Step 4: Once they have written down their definition for the words they think they know, instruct them to go to the

Table 6.1 Example Vocabulary Sheet

Word	Definitions
1. Abrupt	a) Own Words b) Dictionary
2. Advance	a) Own Words b) Dictionary
3. Alter	a) Own Words b) Dictionary
4. Assess	a) Own Words b) Dictionary
5. Allowance	a) Own Words b) Dictionary
6. Affection	a) Own Words b) Dictionary
7. Affordable	a) Own Words b) Dictionary
8. Amicable	a) Own Words b) Dictionary
9. Ardent	a) Own Words b) Dictionary
10. Afflict	a) Own Words b) Dictionary

dictionary and write down the definition the dictionary gives for each of the words, even for the words they think they know.

Step 5: Have them compare their definitions with the ones that they found in the dictionary. If they find that the definition they wrote for a word isn't correct, have them erase it. Now instruct them to write a definition in their own words for each of the words they did not check. (When you have finished this step, each word should have two definitions, one from the dictionary and one in their own words.)

Step 6: Instruct students to turn the worksheet over and write a sentence for each word to show that they can use the word in its proper context.

Step 7: Have them share some of their sentences with the rest of the class. Correct those examples that do not show a clear understanding of the meaning and context of the word.

Step 8: Have the class members put away their worksheets. Pass out a new copy of the worksheet and have them take a quiz, from memory, by writing a definition for each of the words on the worksheet.

Step 9: Go over their answers and have them keep track of their scores. Instruct the class that this was a practice quiz and that they should study the worksheet as homework to help them prepare for the real quiz on Friday.

This lesson is well organized, and it has a clear objective like the first man-made/natural resource example. It too doesn't meet the relevancy muster required for teaching to this target audience because the answer to each of the four key questions is no.

Is it fun and different? No! It is nothing more than a worksheet exercise. *Is it engaging?* No! The students spend the whole lesson sitting at their desks, as passive listeners, readers, and note keepers. *Is it theirs?* No! The learning process is heavily dependent on the teacher's ability to get the students to quietly sit and complete the worksheet assignment. *Is it value based?* No! There is no attempt to make these vocabulary words important to the students except for the value they place on the quiz.

Let's rewrite the whole lesson so that the answer to each of the four key questions can be yes. Notice again that the change to the lesson will be relatively small. It will be the same lesson with minor adjustments aimed at the dramatic learner. I will point out the changes in the lesson by using brackets to identify each.

SAMPLE LESSON PLAN #4

Increasing Vocabulary Skills (Modified for the Dramatic Learner)

Educational Objective: Students will demonstrate a working knowledge of the definitions of selected vocabulary words by writing and performing a short play. [*Addition of a learning activity to the objective.*]

Prep:

1. Prepare a vocabulary sheet for the following words: *abrupt, advance, alter, assess, allowance, affection, affordable, amicable, ardent,* and *afflict.*
2. Make sure you have a vocabulary sheet, a dictionary, and a pencil available for each student.
3. Have the instructions for the assignment written on the board or flip chart, but cover them up until you want to show them to the class. (They could also be on an overhead or computer screen ready to be shown when needed.) The rules for the play are that (a) the show must be a family series, (b) it must have at least four main characters, (c) it must introduce the theme of the series, (d) the sample script must properly use all the words from an assigned list, and (e) sample skits cannot last longer than three minutes. Add any other rules that are appropriate to your situation. [*Preparing the rules for the activity.*]
4. Prepare a flash card for each of the words on the list. [*Preparation of the flash cards.*]
5. Create a worksheet.

Step 1: Tell the students that they have been assigned to come up with the pilot for a new television series. They are responsible for writing and producing a short skit that introduces the concept for the series. However, they must follow a few guidelines. Show them the list of guidelines and go over the rules so they completely understand what is expected. Tell the students that you will be available as a script consultant if they need assistance. [*No statement of objective.*]

Step 2: Form the class into small groups that will best spread out the talent and leadership skills. (Use as many groups as necessary, trying to keep the size to about four or five students.) Pass out the word sheet (vocabulary sheet; see Table 6. 2) to each student. Show the students where they can find the dictionaries or other resources, and give them a reasonable time limit to write the script and prepare for the performance. [*Establishing the perimeters of the learning activity.*]

Step 3: As they are working, go from group to group and tell the students that before they perform their skits, each one of them will have to have the word list filled out with a definition for each word in his or her own words and in the dictionary's language. Tell the students they will also need to demonstrate understanding of the meaning and contextual use of each of the words on the list. Monitor each group without interfering with its work to make sure students are complying with the requirements of the assignment. [*Layering in of responsibilities.*]

Step 4: Once they have finished their skits, have the students get ready to perform for the rest of the class. Make sure you leave enough time for each skit to be performed. [*Allowing practice time.*]

Step 5: Before they perform, tell them you forgot one additional requirement. The forgotten requirement is that every time they say one of the words from the list, someone in their group must hold up the corresponding flash card, and the person who said the word must give its definition, as an aside,

Table 6.2 Required Word List

Word	
1. Abrupt	a) Own Words b) Dictionary
2. Advance	a) Own Words b) Dictionary
3. Alter	a) Own Words b) Dictionary
4. Assess	a) Own Words b) Dictionary
5. Allowance	a) Own Words b) Dictionary
6. Affection	a) Own Words b) Dictionary
7. Affordable	a) Own Words b) Dictionary
8. Amicable	a) Own Words b) Dictionary
9. Ardent	a) Own Words b) Dictionary
10. Afflict	a) Own Words b) Dictionary

to the audience. (An aside is where the actor turns directly to the audience and tells them something. It is often done by lowering the voice to a stage whisper while bringing a hand to the mouth.) [*Layering in of responsibilities.*]

Step 6: Instruct the class that they are to check the definitions from their lists against the ones given by the performing group. If the performing group gives a wrong definition, the class members should raise their hands.

Step 7: Have them share their performances with the class. Make sure they use every word and correct any definitions that are not right. After the performances, ask if there is any word the students don't understand.

Step 8: Have the class members return to their desks. Tell them to make sure their desks are clear and that they have a pen or pencil to write with. Pass out a new copy of the word list and have them take a quiz, from memory, by writing a definition for each of the words on the worksheet.

Step 9: Go over their answers and have them keep track of their scores. Instruct the class that this was a practice quiz and that they should study their worksheet as homework to help them prepare for the real quiz on Friday.

This lesson uses the same worksheet, requires the students to seek out the definitions of the words in the dictionary, and ends with the same quiz that was used in the previous lesson. It is also well organized and has a clear objective, but that is about all the lessons have in common. Using the key questions as our basis, let's examine why these modifications to the vocabulary lesson make it more accessible to the dramatic learner. Notice how the dramatic elements create an environment that encourages maximum student participation.

Is it fun and different? Yes. The students are given a chance to master the new vocabulary words by using them in a fun and different context. They aren't even told they are doing a vocabulary lesson, though they will quickly figure it out for themselves. They are simply asked to write a pilot script for a television show using certain designated words. This will help create a useful context and engage the students' own natural sense of discovery and wonder. It makes learning fun.

Is it engaging? Yes. The lesson thrusts the student into an active role of having to find the meaning of words and then immediately use them to sell a concept. There is an implied sense of competition because the natural expectation is that only one of the pilots will be accepted. The very structure of the lesson demands students' full and active participation.

Is it theirs? Yes. The lesson is completely student centered because the learning process is totally dependent on student involvement. The teacher constantly monitors their efforts, but it is the students who feel the ownership of the learning. They are the ones determining how to properly use the words.

Is it value based? Yes. It creates an immediate reason and value for knowing and using these words. It forces them to interact with each other to simulate a real-life context for these particular words. Not only do they have to learn the words to complete this activity, they have to apply them in a valuable and realistic way.

Let's look at one more example and then compare the changes in these lessons side by side to see how simple the process can really be.

Sample Lesson Plan #5

Calculating Averages

Educational Objective: Students will gain an understanding of how to calculate average numbers.

Prep:

1. Prepare or obtain an averaging worksheet (see Table 6.3) and make sure you have a pencil available for each student.

Step 1: State the objective for the class. Ask the students to clear off their desks and take out a pencil.

Step 2: Pass out the worksheet to each member of the class and have them work through the sample problem with you while you do it on the board or overhead.

Table 6.3 Example Averaging Worksheet

Sample problem:

Find the average of the following numbers:

8, 6, 10, 3, 9, and 4.

Step 1: Add together the amount of each number to get a total sum.

$$8 + 6 + 10 + 3 + 9 + 4 = 40$$

Step 2: Count the number of numbers you have added together to get a total.

6

Step 3: Divide the sum of all your numbers by the total number of numbers you have.

$$40 \div 6 = 6.66$$

Follow the same process to solve the rest of the problems.

1. 5, 10, 12, 16, 3, 6
2. 18, 25, 6, 12, 15, 22
3. 2, 4, 7, 9, 10, 23, 6
4. 6, 16, 17, 5, 8, 10, 22, 23, 21
5. 78, 71, 75, 80, 71, 72, 77, 68
6. 5, 7, 8, 9, 4, 7, 5, 8, 11
7. 15, 18, 12, 16, 17, 19, 13, 14
8. 22, 26, 25, 27, 28, 22, 21, 2
9. 36, 47, 32, 28, 56, 12, 15, 18, 44
10. 32, 25, 35, 6, 17, 88, 43, 65, 22

Step 3: Review the steps of the process with the class by putting another example problem on the board or overhead and going over it with the class. You can ask for a volunteer to come to the front of the class and do the problem for everyone else to see. (Do several other example problems until you are certain that the class understands the process.) Suggested samples: 41, 23, 15, 33, 17, 6 or 18, 15, 33, 15, 9, 71, 55, 4 or any other you choose.

Step 4: When you feel they understand the process, have students work on their own to complete the worksheet.

Step 5: When they have completed the worksheet, go over the answers with the class, making sure that they understand where they failed to arrive at the correct answer.

Step 6: Instruct students to turn the worksheet over and write a series of numbers of their own.

Step 7: Have them find the average of their numbers. Have them share some of their answers with the class.

Step 8: Instruct the class members to put away their worksheets. Pass out a different worksheet and have them take a quiz.

Step 9: Go over their answers and have them keep track of their scores. Instruct the class that this was a practice quiz. Assign the homework pages from the textbook as practice, and tell students they will have a quiz on this next Wednesday.

This lesson is also well organized and objective driven. But, like the other nondramatic lesson, it doesn't meet the relevancy muster. The lesson is not fun and different, it is not engaging, it is not theirs, and it is not value based. Once more, the learning process is heavily dependent on teacher instruction. There is no attempt to connect the process of averaging with what the students already know or to make it relevant to their life.

Let's examine the following rewrite and see how simple it is to change the lesson and make it more dramatic. Notice again that the change to the lesson will be relatively small.

Sample Lesson Plan #6

Calculating Averages

Educational Objective: Students will demonstrate their ability to average numbers by correctly computing batting averages. [*Addition of a learning activity to the objective.*]

Prep:

1. Prepare an averaging worksheet (same as original lesson) and a baseball averages worksheet. For the baseball sheet, come up with numbers on four or five other fictional players. (You may use statistics from real players.) [*Alter the worksheet as shown below.*]
2. Make sure you have a piece of paper and a pencil available for each student.

Step 1: Show a video clip of a baseball player up to bat in a crucial place in a game. As you show it, tell students that it is the last out of the ninth inning of the last World Series game for this year. (The final at bat showing the young man in *For the Love of the Game* would work.) [*Don't state the object, just place the class in a different frame of mind.*]

Step 2: Tell the students that they are owners of the team and it's their job to decide which player to send up to bat. [*Set up the scenario.*]

Step 3: Pass out the baseball worksheet to each student and tell them they must figure out the batting average of each player and decide which player will be most likely to get the winning hit based on his batting average.

Sample of Player Info Worksheet

Jamal Jefferson

Bats	Outs	Walks	Singles	Doubles	Triples	HRs
500*	299	46	48	63	35	20

Scott Hampton

Bats	Outs	Walks	Singles	Doubles	Triples	HRs
624	314	50	170	80	45	15

James Stewart

Bats	Outs	Walks	Singles	Doubles	Triples	HRs
318	100	20	100	50	30	18

Jesus Vasques

Bats	Outs	Walks	Singles	Doubles	Triples	HRs
544	354	35	100	30	20	5

Freddy Rodriguez

Bats	Outs	Walks	Singles	Doubles	Triples	HRs
156	50	15	25	27	33	6

Bobby Jones

Bats	Outs	Walks	Singles	Doubles	Triples	HRs
485	261	100	66	19	15	24

Edgar Funk

Bats	Outs	Walks	Singles	Doubles	Triples	HRs
643	212	160	201	30	23	17

Oscar De Palma

Bats	Outs	Walks	Singles	Doubles	Triples	HRs
385	178	55	58	42	35	17

Troy Badger						
Bats	Outs	Walks	Singles	Doubles	Triples	HRs
495	299	57	55	45	29	10
Marshall Broomfield						
Bats	Outs	Walks	Singles	Doubles	Triples	HRs
532	250	100	82	45	35	20

* All numbers can be reduced to help younger students grasp the concept more quickly.

Step 4: Ask the class if anyone knows how to figure out a batting average. If a student knows how to do it, let him or her teach the rest of the class. If not, lead the class through the process asking questions that will help to solve the problem. Use the first batter on the worksheet as the sample problem.

Here are some questions you might use to lead students through the process: (1) Where would we start to figure out the average of Jamal Jefferson? (2) How many times was he up to bat? (3) What number do we need to know in relation to the numbers of at bats before we can figure the batting average? (4) What other averages can we calculate using the numbers we have been given? (5) Can you walk me through the process of finding his batting average? [*You rely on the students to teach each other or you lead them through a discovery process.*]

Step 5: Have students, individually or in groups, work on the problem and come up with the solutions. [*Possible use of groups.*]

Step 6: Have the students share the findings with the class as well as the way they determined their conclusions. Make sure they explain clearly why they chose the player they did.

Step 7: Put the following list of numbers on the board and ask the students how they would go about finding the average of the numbers on the board: 7, 23, 56, 19, 22, 6, 30, 67.

Step 8: Have them share their findings with the rest of the class. As they do, make sure they see the correlation between figuring batting averages and finding the average of a series of numbers.

Step 9: Instruct the class to turn the worksheet over and write a series of numbers of their own.

Step 10: Have them find the average of their numbers. Have them share some of their answers with the class.

Step 11: Instruct the class members to put away their baseball worksheets. Pass out the averaging worksheet (same as previous lesson) and have them take a quiz.

Averaging Worksheet

Find the average of the following numbers:

1. 5, 10, 12, 16, 3, 6
2. 18, 25, 6, 12, 15, 22
3. 2, 4, 7, 9, 10, 23, 6
4. 6, 16, 17, 5, 8, 10, 22, 23, 21
5. 78, 71, 75, 80, 71, 72, 77, 68
6. 5, 7, 8, 9, 4, 7, 5, 8, 11
7. 15, 18, 12, 16, 17, 19, 13, 14
8. 22, 26, 25, 27, 28, 22, 21, 23
9. 36, 47, 32, 28, 56, 12, 15, 18, 44
10. 32, 25, 35, 6, 17, 88, 43, 65, 22

Step 12: Go over their answers and have them keep track of their scores. Instruct students that this was a practice quiz. Assign them the homework pages from the textbook as practice, and tell them they will have a quiz on this next Wednesday.

This lesson uses the same worksheet as the other lesson, but it prepares the students to do it in a completely different fashion. It starts from a place of common knowledge and experience, and it allows the students to use what they already know as a link to the new subject matter. It is also well organized and has a clear objective. Notice again how the dramatic elements create an environment that encourages maximum student participation.

Is it fun and different? Yes. The students have to use what they know to solve a dramatic problem. They may not be aware that they are involved in a math lesson until they want to find the answer to the questions that are posed in the lesson's inciting event. This creates a feeling of intrigue that will engage the student's own natural sense of discovery and wonder. It makes learning fun.

Is it engaging? Yes. The lesson thrusts the student into an active role of having to figure out who would be the batter most likely to get the hit that would win the ball game. The drive to find the right answer creates an immediate relevance in the problem. The very structure of the lesson again thrusts the student into a situation where full and active participation becomes the only logical course of action.

Is it theirs? Yes. The lesson centers on the students and requires that they discover how to solve each problem. The teacher takes the role of coach by constantly monitoring their efforts and giving hints and suggestions for how they can move to the next level. The students, however, are the ones who must take ownership of the learning.

Is it value based? Yes. It is tied to a part of the students' world. Even if they are not into baseball, they have a value of winning and making the proper decision to make victory possible. The lesson allows the students to learn a concept in an area of interest and value to them, and then, once they have mastered the skill, it allows them to transfer this knowledge to another set of variables. By basing their first application on something they value, there is a higher likelihood that their value will be transferred to the new set of variables. By building one success on another, this transfer of value from one subject to another is easily made in the mind of the student without much effort on the part of the teacher.

SIDE-BY-SIDE LESSON COMPARISONS

The following side-by-side comparisons demonstrate just how easy it is to make a traditional lesson more successful for dramatic learners.

The Man-Made/Natural Resource Lesson

Natural Resources Lesson #1	*Natural Resources Lesson #2*	*Difference in Lessons*
Objective: Students will gain an understanding of the difference between man-made and natural resources.	**Objective:** The students will demonstrate their knowledge of the difference between man-made and natural resources by successfully completing a scavenger hunt.	**Objective: The educational objective contains a skill to be demonstrated as well as a method for the students to show their increased abilities.**
Preparation Steps:	**Preparation Steps:**	**Preparation Steps:**
1. Gather different items.	1. Gather different items.	**Same.**
	2. Create number cards 1–20.	**Create number cards 1–20.**
	3. Spread the items out so that groups of students can examine each item individually.	**Placing and numbering the items for the students to go and handle and explore.**

Natural Resources Lesson #1	*Natural Resources Lesson #2*	*Difference in Lessons*
2. Make sure you have a piece of paper and a pencil available for each student.	4. Make sure you have a piece of paper and a pencil available for each student.	**Same.**
3. Create a worksheet.	5. Create a worksheet.	**Same.**
Process:	**Process:**	**Process:**
Step 1: State the objective for the class.	Step 1: Pass out a clipboard or other hard writing surface to each student and make sure each person has a pen or pencil.	**Don't state the objective; just make sure students have the tools they need to participate in the lesson.**
Step 2: Ask the class if they know the difference between a natural resource and a man-made object.	Step 2: Take them to the space where you have laid out the items.	**Don't begin with a lecture; take them to where the objects are laid out.**
Step 3: Ask the class to clear off their desks.	Step 3: Instruct them that their job is . . .	**Teacher helps the students understand the assignment.**
Step 4: Show them different objects.	Step 4: Give them the opportunity to work.	**Teacher doesn't lecture.**
Step 5: Go through each item with the class to make sure that they have the right answers.	Step 5: Observe the groups as they work to determine if they are applying the protocol.	**Teacher monitors without lecture.**

(Continued)

(Continued)

Natural Resources Lesson #1	*Natural Resources Lesson #2*	*Difference in Lessons*
Step 6: Review for the students what they have learned by restating the definition.	Step 6: Assign each group or individual to be responsible for reporting their findings for certain items.	**Students report findings as the teacher listens and asks questions.**
	Step 7: Have the class restate the keys they have discovered.	**Students state what they have learned.**
	Step 8: Spot-check for understanding.	**Additional time for one-on-one evaluation of how each student is doing.**
	Step 9: (Optional) Take the class back into the classroom and give them a formal quiz. (Allow them to handle the items if they want during the quiz.)	**Optional step.**

The Vocabulary Lesson

Vocabulary Lesson #1	*Vocabulary Lesson #2*	*Difference in Lessons*
Objective: Students will gain an understanding of the meaning of selected vocabulary words.	**Objective:** Students will demonstrate a working knowledge of the definitions of selected vocabulary words by writing and performing a short play.	**Objective: The educational objective contains a skill to be demonstrated as well as a method for the students to show their increased abilities.**

Vocabulary Lesson #1	*Vocabulary Lesson #2*	*Difference in Lessons*
Preparation Steps:	**Preparation Steps:**	**Preparation Steps:**
1. Prepare a vocabulary sheet for the following words: *abrupt, advance, alter, assess, allowance, affection, affordable, amicable, ardent,* and *afflict.*	1. Prepare a vocabulary sheet for the following words: *abrupt, advance, alter, assess, allowance, affection, affordable, amicable, ardent,* and *afflict.*	**Same.**
2. Make sure you have a piece of paper and a pencil available for each student.	2. Make sure you have a piece of paper and a pencil available for each student.	**Same.**
	3. Have the instructions for the assignment.	**Have written instructions for the assignment.**
	4. Prepare a flash card for each of the words.	**Preparing a set of flash cards.**
3. Create a worksheet.	5. Create a worksheet.	**Preparing a set of flash cards.**
Process:	**Process:**	**Process:**
Step 1: State the objective for the class.	Step 1: Assign them to come up with the pilot for a new television series.	**Don't state the objective; tell them what they have to do.**
Step 2: Pass out the vocabulary sheet.	Step 2: Form the class into small groups and pass out the word sheet.	**Both lessons pass out the worksheet, but Lesson #2 focuses on getting ready to do the assignment.**

(Continued)

(Continued)

Vocabulary Lesson #1	*Vocabulary Lesson #2*	*Difference in Lessons*
Step 3: Have the students write down a definition in their own words.	Step 3: Instruct them that their job is . . .	**Students work on the definitions in both steps, but in Lesson #2 it is not their primary business. Here, they are learning the words to be able to write the script.**
Step 4: Go to the dictionary and write down the definition.	Step 4: Monitor each group.	**Basically the same, but in Lesson #2 they are working together in groups.**
Step 5: Compare their definitions with the ones that they found in the dictionary.	Step 5: Get ready to perform.	**Basically the same, but in Lesson #2 a more active method is being used to test knowledge.**
Step 6: Have the students write a sentence for each word to show that they can use the word in its proper context.	Step 6: Tell the students one more requirement.	**Basically the same, but in Lesson #2 a more active method is being used to test knowledge.**
Step 7: Share some of their sentences and correct those examples.	Step 7: Instruct the class to check the definitions.	**Basically the same, but in Lesson #2 a more active method is being used to test knowledge.**
Step 8: Have them take a quiz.	Step 8: Share their performances.	**Basically the same, but in Lesson #2 a more active method is being used to test knowledge.**
Step 9: Go over answers as a practice for the real quiz.	Step 9: Go over answers as a practice for the real quiz.	**Basically the same, but in Lesson #2 the method is more active and participation-oriented.**

Calculating Averages

Math Lesson #1	*Math Lesson #2*	*Difference in Lessons*
Objective: Students will gain an understanding of how to calculate average numbers.	**Objective:** Students will demonstrate their ability to average numbers by correctly computing batting averages.	**Objective: The educational objective contains a skill to be demonstrated as well as a method for the students to show their increased abilities.**
Preparation Steps:	**Preparation Steps:**	**Preparation Steps:**
1. Prepare a worksheet.	1. Prepare a worksheet for batting averages.	**The worksheets are different at this step, but Lesson #2 uses Lesson #1's worksheet at the end.**
2. Make sure you have a piece of paper and a pencil available for each student.	2. Make sure you have a piece of paper and a pencil available for each student.	**Same.**
Process:	**Process:**	**Process:**
Step 1: State the objective for the class.	Step 1: Show a video clip.	**Don't state the objective; just set up what you want them to do.**
Step 2: Pass out the worksheet to each member of the class and have them work through the sample problem.	Step 2: Set up the scenario.	**Don't do the work for the students; give them a reason for wanting to know how to average numbers.**
Step 3: Review the steps of the process with the class by putting another example problem on the board.	Step 3: Pass out the worksheet to each student and instruct them that they must figure out the batting average of each player.	**Don't do all the teaching; allow the students to discover how to do it.**

(Continued)

(Continued)

Math Lesson #1	*Math Lesson #2*	*Difference in Lessons*
Step 4: Have them work on their own to complete the worksheet.	Step 4: Ask the class if anyone knows how to figure out a batting average. If a student knows how to do it, let him or her teach the rest of the class.	**Lesson #2 is a bit behind here, but the difference again is peer teaching and questioning rather than formal teaching.**
	Step 5: Have them individually, or in groups, work on the problem.	**The students can choose to work alone or in groups at this stage.**
Step 5: Go over the answers with the class making sure that they understand where they failed to arrive at the correct answer.	Step 6: Have the students share their findings. Have them explain clearly why they chose the player they did.	**One is teacher-centered, the other is student-centered.**
	Step 7: Put the following list of numbers on the board and ask the students how they would go about finding the average of the numbers on the board: 7, 23, 56, 19, 22, 6, 30, 67.	**Lesson #2 links the skills from the batting-average activity to figuring the average of a series of numbers.**
	Step 8: Have them share their findings and show the correlation between batting averages and find the average of a series of numbers.	**Lesson #2 continues to link.**

Math Lesson #1	*Math Lesson #2*	*Difference in Lessons*
Step 6: Instruct the class to turn the worksheet over and write a series of numbers of their own.	Step 9: Instruct the class to turn the worksheet over and write a series of numbers of their own.	**Same.**
Step 7: Have them find the average of their numbers. Have them compare answers with the class.	Step 10: Have them find the average of their numbers. Have them compare answers with the class.	**Same.**
Step 8: Instruct the class members to put away their worksheets. Pass out a different worksheet and have them take a quiz.	Step 11: Instruct the class members to put away their baseball worksheets. Pass out a modified worksheet from the previous lesson and have them take a quiz.	**Same.**
Step 9: Go over their answers and assign them the homework and quiz.	Step 12: Go over their answers and assign them the homework and quiz.	**Same except Lesson #2 works on the baseball worksheet to begin with.**

7

Getting Into It, HIPA Deep

The final checkpoint that units and lesson plans need to pass through to determine their fitness for dramatic learners is one that measures if they incorporate all the elements needed to internalize learning. I mention these elements separately in earlier chapters, but we need to spend some time putting them all together. They help us determine clearly if our planning efforts are aimed at increasing our ability to teach in the nexus. These elements will balance our efforts so that we include every student in our efforts to engage the dramatic learners.

Too often teachers who are determined to reach certain individuals in their class forget about meeting the learning needs of all class members. This balancing act is one of the biggest frustrations of all classroom teachers. Many are overwhelmed with the responsibility. These real feelings of angst can be reduced as we gain the skills to do our teaching in the nexus. These skills will save us running from pillar to beam in each class as we try to meet the needs of every student. If we can stand firmly in the nexus, where all learning preferences overlap, we have the best likelihood of meeting the learning needs of our students and the curricular needs established by our districts.

I was preparing to return for a follow-up visit to one of the alternative schools where I had conducted an intensive dramatic learner workshop. I called the administrator to make sure all the details of the training had been arranged, and I was greatly gratified to find that the teachers were excited and anxious for my return so they could share their successes with me.

I began my visit by observing the teachers working in the classroom. They were right. The students were responding very well to the change in approach. There was a lot of excitement and energy in the classroom. After observing all of the teachers, we gathered for the inservice portion of my visit. All the teachers and administrators were very anxious to hear what I had to say. I spent considerable time complimenting them on the modification I saw in their teaching. I told them how gratifying it was for me to see people actively applying the principles I had shared, especially when they were working so well to engage their dramatic learners.

I then asked a question that they weren't quite ready to answer. It was, "What were the students supposed to be learning?" They thought for a moment and began to respond with statements like, "to enjoy learning," "to see school as a place that is fun and engaging," "to get involved," and so on. I reaffirmed that those were all important things to be teaching, and then I rephrased my original question: "What new skills and knowledge are they gaining in this process?"

The problem these teachers were having was that they were not seeing the whole picture. They were creating a lot of excitement and fun in their classrooms by engaging the students in lots of activity. In so doing, they were completely moving away from the nexus. Their lessons lacked balance. The accompanying figure shows where their teaching was taking place.

There was no real clear curricular purpose for the activity they were generating. Their entire focus was on creating a fun and different learning environment, but they had forgotten why they were doing it. They were stuck in their attempt to get an affirmative answer to the question "Is it fun and different?"

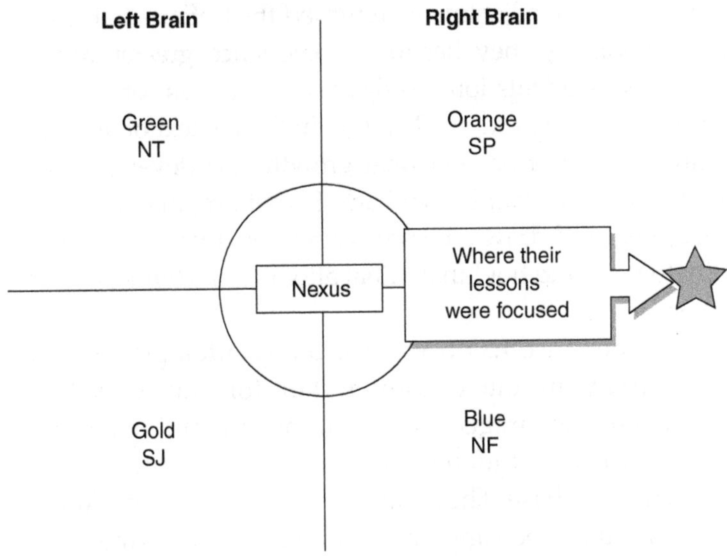

They erred when they let go of the correct definition of fun, which is "that which we enjoy, which holds our interest and causes us to search for meaning, understanding, and mastery." They were involved in fun for amusement's sake and not for the sake of increasing learning.

They had strayed from the core principles and became lost in failed practice. They had failed to consider why I asked them to make the lessons fun. This is a very common error; any time we don't understand why we are doing something, we are doing it for the wrong reason. If perpetuated, the practice will soon lose its reason altogether and turn into a dead form of what it once was. So much of our present educational practice has fallen into this abyss, and yet we hold on to it for dear life. I had to ask these teachers this question so they could make the proper adjustment: "Why are we trying to make learning *fun and different, engaging, theirs, and value based?*" They properly answered this question and immediately made the necessary adjustment to apply the foundational principles and return to sound practice.

A few simple adjustments returned their efforts to the nexus, and immediately they began to experience greater results. It doesn't take students long to figure out that fun for the sake of amusement is very empty. Real fun, in the context of any human endeavor, results from personal growth and development, not from having your hair blown back. Something may have immediate appeal and draw a person's attention, but unless it has the ability to keep and hold that initial attention, its influence doesn't last very long.

My experience has been that many attempts to increase the creativity in the classroom fail for this very reason. Teachers are encouraged to open things up and make it more engaging for the students, but in so doing, they stray from their curricular base. They start focusing on creating fun activities rather than focusing on creating more-engaging learning experiences. They move away from the nexus and become lost in an unbalanced teaching practice.

Returning to the dramatic model, we can clearly see each of the elements that are necessary to keep the lesson in the nexus. The teachers I observed were creating an exciting hook to engage their students, but that was where they stayed with their lesson. Their lessons never progressed structurally to let the students engage with the body of the lesson so students could reach the objective. When teaching isn't objective driven, it results in a series of meandering activities and efforts that lead nowhere.

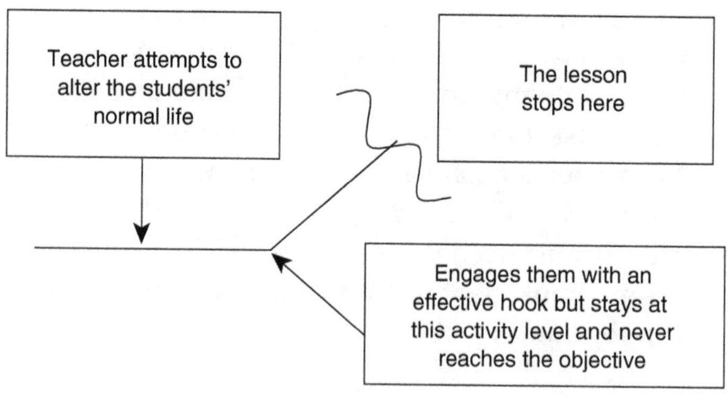

To ensure the dramatic structure is followed and the designed educational experience is complete, I look for four elements in a lesson plan. They are, hook, instruction, practice, and assessment. Of course, we must turn this into an acronym, so I refer to this as HIPA. To make sure our lesson planning efforts are sound and able to reach dramatic learners as well as the rest of our students, we must ensure that they pass the HIPA test.

Great, you're saying, a new test and another prescriptive approach to teaching. If it gains any acceptance at all, you know what will happen, right? In time it could spawn an entire army of clipboard-wielding evaluators searching every lesson for evidence of the HIPA elements. With that fear expressed, let's move forward and consider the fact that lessons that contain each of these elements are balanced in their educational approach, teach in the nexus, and reach a greater number of students. They are sound in principle, design, and practice because they allow learners to participate more fully. They are clearly objective driven and incorporate many other sound teaching practices and theories. Teachers who use each of these elements in a lesson will be able to take care of their curricular and student needs at the same time.

When we look at most traditional teaching models, we find that they are usually heavily based on only the elements of instruction and assessment. The teacher instructs while the students listen and take notes, and then at some time in the future, student knowledge is assessed by the means of a test or quiz. This model is perpetuated because most teachers feel it gives them the most control over the class and that it is the most efficient way to pass on information. If our goals were efficiency and the unloading of information, then I would have to agree. However, when individuals are concerned, efficiency is rarely the best method. I submit that more time is wasted trying to enforce a one-size-fits-all policy that doesn't attempt to accommodate the individual learning needs of all students.

If lessons that contain only the instruction and assessment elements were mapped on the following figure, we could get a

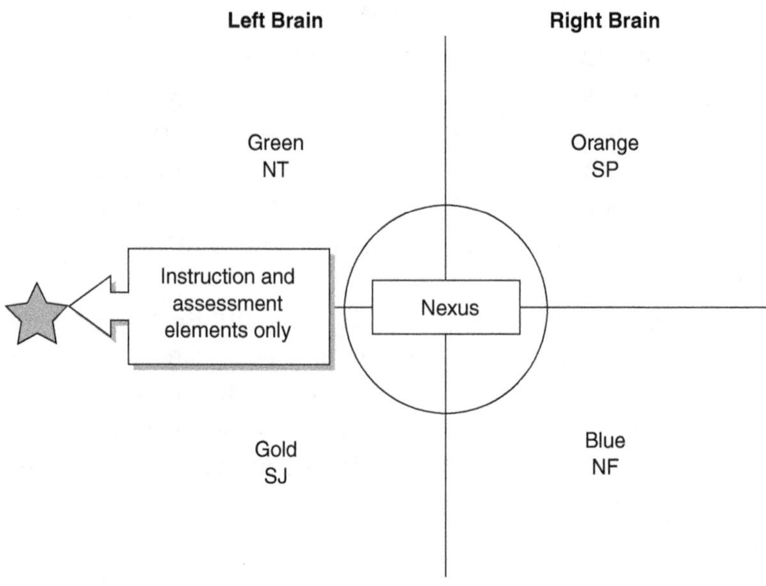

better idea why they are not able to reach every learner. The lack of balance becomes so clear that it is easy to see why we cannot hope to reach all students with one method of teaching.

In old vernacular, the instructional/assessment model is referred to as a left-brained learning approach. Its logical/sequential underpinnings often make it inaccessible to the learning preferences of the dramatic learner. This becomes even more understandable when we realize that research tells us that only 50% of our learners prefer to learn in this fashion. For this reason, the addition of the hook and practice elements to the standard lesson helps make it assessable to all learners and therefore places it in the nexus. The use of all four of the HIPA elements ensures that the lesson is instructionally sound and engaging. The presence of each of these elements gives learning a proper balance, and naturally keeps it in the nexus.

The hook and practice elements are typically seen as the more right-brain educational pieces, while the instruction and practice elements assure that the lesson is sound from the left-brain perspective. If we review for a moment the different aspects of each of these elements, we can get a better appreciation for the need of each in a sound learning experience.

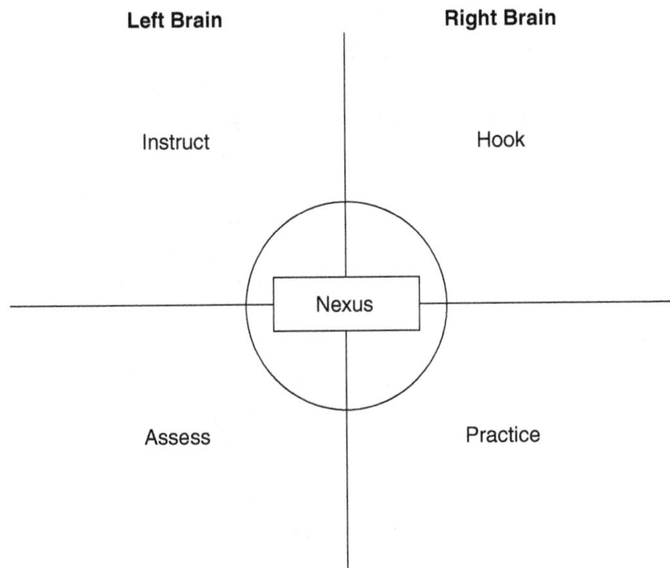

The Hook

The purpose of the hook is to initially grasp the attention of the learner. It is to channel focus and draw it to the subject at hand. It is more than an educational icebreaker; it is designed to move a student from his or her present perspective on a subject and invoke a spark of interest. When a learning experience is properly designed, it creates a kind of learning vortex that propels the learner into a field of internal learning energy that initializes a desire for understanding and intrinsic learning. The hook becomes the catalyst for the creation of this vortex.

If we turn the dramatic model upside down for a moment, as in the following figure, we can see this vortex in relation to the hook. A properly designed outcome takes the learners from their normal value of learning:

A. The hook transports learners, by way of their own interest, into the center of this learning vortex.

B. From here, the power of their own values and the desire to know something they didn't understand draws them irresistibly toward the desired outcome or objective of the lesson.

C. If the hook is designed correctly, it leads the learner automatically through the instruction and practice elements of the learning experience and brings them directly to the objective of the learning activity.

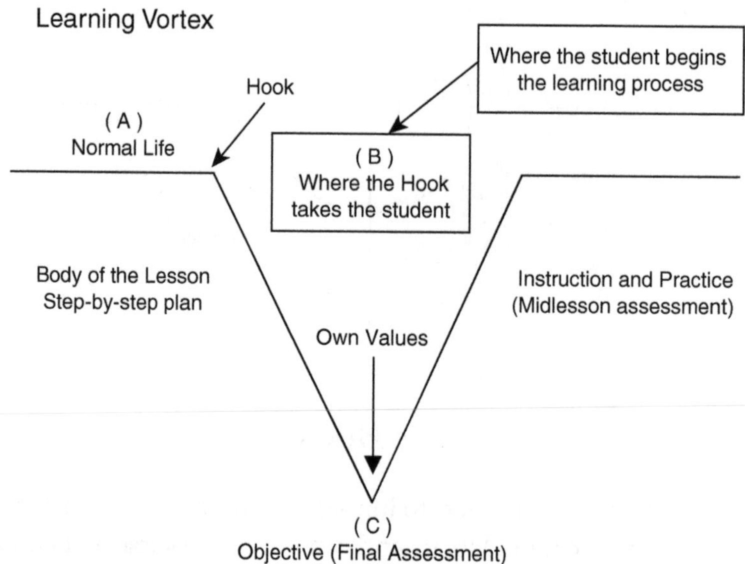

The real power of the hook phase of a learning experience is its ability to involve the indiviudal in the learning process. Many would refer to this as the self-image element of learning. We have gotten so far off base with our understanding of the effect of self-image on learning that we have factioned ourself into two camps, one that believes that self-image is the key, and another that believes that self-image has nothing to do with learning. Rather than weighing in on that subject right now, I'll simply restate that unless a learner connects personally with what he or she is learning, the process is never complete.

The hook is to draw in the learning audience (students) and get them emotionally connected with what they are about to explore. It need not be elaborate, but it has to be engaging. The hook in our man-made/natural resource lesson was the way the discovery process was structured. The fact that the class would be able to get out of their seats to explore and manipulate the items to be categorized was a large hook to draw the attention of the class members.

INSTRUCTION AND PRACTICE

The instruction and practice phases of a learning experience typically follow the hook. It is important to realize that all four of these elements need not be seen as separate. They should flow seemlessly into one; creating a totally unified lesson. It is not always necessary that you pass through one of these elements to get to the other. They are best seen as interwoven threads of the same practice.

Most educational experiences are made up of nothing but instruction. Because we are so familiar with this part of the learning process, I'll spend little time with it except to point out how it can be different. Returning to our man-made/natural resource lesson models, we can see instruction happening two different ways. In the first model, we observe a clear instructional pattern where the teacher speaks and the students listen. In the second model, we have to observe closely to identify the instructional element of the lesson. It is very much a part of the lesson, but it has become almost transparent because it is woven so carefully into the design of the lesson. In a layered fashion, the instruction is doled out to the class as necessary. The students are given their instruction on an as-needed basis so that they can master the process in a step-by-step approach. This style of instruction is a lot like the difference between the way the ancient Greek theater used exposition and how it is handled in our modern theater and films. As discussed in Chapter 5, exposition in ancient Greek plays was poured out on the audience as the first order of business. Today we are given expostion in bits and pieces to keep our interest and to keep the action moving forward. This latter style of instruction is typically more accessable to the dramatic learner.

Comparing the instruction in these two lessons also reveals a major difference in the practice element. In the first lesson, the practice phase of the lesson was almost completely separate from the instruction phase. The teacher gave her instructions first and then started the classification process. In the second lesson the instruction and practice phases were almost indistinguishable from each other and from the hook. This combining of the elements makes for a more engaging learning experience because the instruction introduces concepts that are immediately put into practice. This continuing cycle of learn, apply; learn, apply; learn, apply; more closely resembles the natural learning process that students have been involved in throughout their whole lives.

A close examination of the typical school day reveals that it is not a very natural process. The traditional instruction-assessment structure of formal education doesn't really exist in a normal life. In fact, except for PE, shop, life sciences, and fine or performing arts classes, most of the practice element of our student's education doesn't even happen in the classroom. Is it any wonder that administrators and counselors are filling these specialty classes to overflowing with dramatic learners? Teachers have turned more and more to the habit of reserving the practice element for homework assignments. Today in some school districts, almost all of the educational practice is designed to happen away from school.

This educational development has created a national trend to question the value of homework. In light of what is happening in this area, it is easy to see that this concern hasn't emerged out of thin air. It is a natural backlash from the growing numbers of teachers who send children home to practice things that have not been fully taught in school.

The educational rationale for this trend seems very sound to the teachers, administrators, and academicians that espouse and use it. Many believe that the educational system can't be everything to everybody. They note that the practice element is hard to manage in the classroom. The variables that a teacher must deal with to properly provide for this aspect of learning can turn the classroom into a very sloppy, messy, and hard-to-manage place. Practice takes time, space, and adaquate supervision. It introduces so many inconsistencies that must be managed, that it creates a logistical nightmare. Some teachers and administrators contend that, even under the best of circumstances, students never develop skills at the same rate, even if the practice component could be managed properly. Some students catch on quickly, while others languish behind and hold up the forward movement of the rest of the class.

Under the guise of this rationale, it makes sense that we send the work home so learners can spend the amount of time they need to master the subject matter on their own. Making educational practice happen away from the learning campus allows each student the freedom to practice as much or as little as he or she needs to keep up with the requirements of the system. It is neat and managable for the educator, but it works only with the smallest percentage of learners. The problem with this approach is that it isn't realistic.

It uses faulty logic that would remove the teacher almost entirely from this most important phase of learning. This argument is tantamount to deciding that because sporting events are noisy, dirty, time-consuming, and unpredictable, we should forgo the actual contest and determine a winner in some neat and orderly fashion. It removes all the drama and life from something that is supposed to be difficult in the first place. By removing the trial, however, we also remove the real reward. Learning without a little pain can produce no significant gain. By trying to reduce the pain or stress that the practice phase places on the educational system, we make learning as weak as water. We create a frustrating, unnatural enviroment that lacks completeness.

This approach to practice also fails to take into account what actually happens at home. It takes learning out of an enviroment that can be somewhat regulated and puts it at the mercy of a chaotic set of uncontrollable conditions. What happens once a student leaves the schools is no longer educationally managable. All that happens, or doesn't happen, is completely at the mercy of nonscholastic variables. What if there is no home or no place to study when the student goes home? What if no parental support or family resources are available? If there is no personal motivation to do the work, nothing will change once the individual leaves the school and enters an environment that is hostile to learning.

We must remember that it is not practice that makes perfect, it is perfect practice that makes perfect. To send a child home to do homework without first teaching him or her how it should be done is not good educational practice. What good does it do to send children home to practice something that they don't know how to do? What message is that sending to parents? What does it do to the confidence and self-image of the learner, or to the confidence others have in a system?

It seems so obvious that this practice will lead to deep frustration on the part of the learner and the parent. Why isn't it clear to those that espouse this position? It is most likely because they learn best in this style and have had the self-motivation and support to succeed in this way. The few students who are motivated and prefer to learn this way do not offset the harm that is being done to the rest of the learners. Learner frustration only leads to discouragment and disillusionment. Initial and prolonged practice belongs at school where it can be turned into personal growth and guided development. When used in this fashion, the use of the practice element at school will build the proper foundation for more and perfect practice at home.

Lest you misunderstand what I am saying, I am not against homework. In fact, I am a big supporter of it. I simply disagree with the way many fellow educators use it today. Again, I am proposing only minor adjustments to this present approach to make homework a powerful learning tool. It must become an exercise to augment what has been learned and practiced at school, rather than a time to guess and speculate what the proper practice should be. When a learning experience first hooks the interest of a learner and then provides sufficent time for engaging instruction and personal application through class-time practice, then homework becomes an important part of the learning process. It becomes a time for a student to personally assess if he or she has really mastered the skills and knowledge base that is being studied.

It is not enough to say that we need to assign homework just to teach discipline and prepare students for what is in their educational future. That argument doesn't mean anything to the dramatic learner. In fact, this faulty logic is one of the key reasons many of these individuals choose not to go on to higher education. Why should they continue to subject themselves to heavier and heavier doses of an already unbearable medicine. Homework, for them, must become something that offers an intrinsic reward in order for it to be meaningful.

One of my sons, who is a dramatic learner, came to me at the beginning of his senior year of high school and showed me the disclosure form for his English class. As we went over it together, he lamented about the number of books he would be required to read. He also pointed out that he wouldn't be able to bluff his way through the class because the teacher required in-depth reports and heavy participation in class discussions to assess student comprehension and application of the assigned literary works. As I went over the titles, I could see nothing on the list that would naturally draw the interest of my son. I knew we would be in for a long year.

As I monitored his progress, something almost magical was happening. He wasn't complaining about this class that he had dreaded. In fact, just the opposite was true. At home, on his own, he was reading. He was enjoying what he was doing. When I asked him about the class and his change of opinion, he told me that his teacher made what they read applicable to his life. Somehow she was able to help him see that *The Scarlet Letter* and other classic novels dealt with issues that he was presently grappling with.

Her ability to hook, engagingly instruct, and promote personal practice and *internalization* of themes and ideas motivated an unmotivated reader to spend hours of his time doing homework. He became engaged, and he wanted to unlock the secrets of these once worthless pages. In his reports, she allowed him to show his mastery of the concepts and themes of the works in creative and nonconvential ways. This flexibility also served to inspire his homework and personal practice time. On one such creative report alone, he spent over 50 hours when one or two hours at the computer could have produced a paper that would have covered the assignment.

The greatest part of this whole experience has been the carryover it has had on this young man as a college student. The willingness of this teacher to link learning to the values of her students was accomplished by her ability to first hook and then instruct in an engaging fashion to interest them in the concepts, and then to allow them to have class time to practice and explore the newly esteemed ideas under her watchful eye. Only when she had shepherded the discovery to the point that her students felt comfortable with practicing and exploring on their own did she send them away to expand their knowledge on their own.

This is another example of this seamless connection of elements. The whole learning process flowed together in a natural way. This teacher, and all others who have a lasting impact on the lives of their students, are willing to get knee-deep in the practice phase of learning. They do not separate practice time from the classroom experience. If a teacher leaves it out or leaves it to the mercy of the student or his or her parent(s) to figure out, they are abdicating one of the teacher's major responsibilities. This is the reason that all nexus-based lessons use the practice element as one of their most important foundations.

Assessment

The final element is assessment. This element, of course, determines the effectiveness of the learning experience. It is the element that allows the educational system, the teacher, and the student to realistically determine how things are going. When properly used, assessment is not a onetime occurrence. Rather, it is an ongoing evaluation of the progress of a learner. It, too, like the other elements, should be layered in as the learning experience takes shape, ensuring for teacher and student alike that the proper progress is taking place. It is also true that one final assessment is usually given, at the end, to determine the overall internalization of what has been taught. This is an essential part of learning. It is where the reality of an academic pursuit is determined.

There is usually no argument that assessment is an essential element in a sound educational experience. The debate typically surrounds issues such as when, how, and what kind? If we return to the examples that we have used to illustrate how to create learning experiences for dramatic learners, we will see different ways that assessment is used. In the vocabulary lesson, both examples used a quiz as the final assessment of what was learned. One of the major differences between these vocabulary lessons was how the assessment process was used at every phase of the second version of the lesson and how it was modified for dramatic learners. Built into this learning experience were evaluation points that allowed the teacher to assess without the students really knowing what was happening. Each of the multiple practice levels had its own interim assessment.

As the teacher observes the teams working together to define the words, he or she can determine if the students are obtaining the proper definitions of the words. At the writing phase, the teacher can evaluate the students' understanding of the words as they attempt to use them in the context of their story. In the rehearsal phase of the performance, a close observation can provide a second and deeper assessment of the students' abilty to contextualize the word meanings. Finally, in the performance itself, the teacher can conduct a fourth preliminary assessment in preparation for the quiz. The teacher would certainly have an accurate picture of student progress following this model. The most exciting element of this approach is that the preliminary assessments are all being conducted without the students feeling stress over their level of performance. This multilayered approach to assessment allows students to gain confidence in their internal knowledge of a subject before the final evaluation. This realistic increase in confidence reduces test anxiety, and it directly correlates positively with a student's ability to assess better on standard, logical-sequential testing instruments.

Assessment is much more accurate when it can be done in many different ways. This may fly in the face of standardized testing practices, but if students have preferences for different learning styles, it is only logical that they will have certain preferences as they relate to testing, evaluation, and assessment. If we remember that we are assessing to accurately determine how much a student has learned, it shouldn't be too difficult to modify our assessment techniques to meet the individual needs of our students.

Just this last semester, a very bright and talented student entered my office in tears. She had studied to the point of exhaustion for a midterm in another class and was panicked at the prospects of taking the standard, computer-scored test in the university's testing center. I asked her if she felt she knew the information, and she responded affirmatively. I then tested her, the best I could, from her class notes and assigned chapters. She indeed knew the material.

I suggested she go and sit down with her professor and share with him what she had shared with me. She looked at me with a terrified stare and asked if I thought that he would even listen. Her fear was that this professor would think she was stupid. I explained that if she failed the test he would know she was. She agreed to give it a try. To her surprise, he was only too happy to test her knowledge in an alternative fashion. Not only was she successful in convincing him that she had mastered the course material, she was also successful in helping him alter his assessment practices to reach the needs of other students who were having similar problems with his tests.

Educators need to remember that the best assessment doesn't necessarily take place in a formal testing setting. Assessment must be ever-present in education, but it need not be unnatural. Think of how life constantly provides its own elements of assessment. Adapting the old cliché on teachers, we could conclude with the phrase, "those who can, do; and those who can't, give a paper-and-pencil test."

In a math lesson for Title I students, I created a math assessment that consisted of students showing their mastery of basic addition and subtraction skills by participating in a relay race. Questions that were to be on an upcoming standardized test were used in the relay. The students were lined up in teams in front of three rows of 12 chairs. When an equation was given the students would race to see who could crawl under the chairs the fastest and stop at the chair that represented the correct answer. The child in a wheelchair simply rolled to the adjacent chair to indicate his answer. When the assessment first began, the teacher gave assistance so the children could correct and modify their answers. When the midlesson assessment showed that the students had a good mastery of the process, the evaluation took a new twist. The answers were no longer shared with the rest of the class, but each child's score was recorded on a test form by the teacher. This was easy to do without putting pressure on the students because their classmates remained at the end of the row of chairs. Only the teacher knew how each individual student was doing on the answers. This nonlinear assessment prepared the students remarkably well for the upcoming standardized test. Their scores had increased dramatically over those of other classes that had prepared for the test in only traditional ways.

If we examine this math lesson plan for the HIPA elements it would look like this:

Simple Addition

Educational Objective: The students will demonstrate their ability to use addition and subtraction skills to solve simple math equations by actively participating in a relay race.

Prep:

1. Create the evaluation instrument as follows and make a copy for each student. Put the name of each student

on a separate test. Divide the tests with names into three equal groups by size and math skills. Place the separated tests together on three different clipboards.

Basic Math Test		
1. 4 + 6 =	11. 8 − 5 =	21. 16 − 7 =
2. 2 + 7 =	12. 4 − 3 =	22. 3 + 8 =
3. 12 − 7 =	13. 9 + 3 =	23. 5 − 2 =
4. 8 + 4 =	14. 11 − 7 =	24. 7 − 3 =
5. 1 + 3 =	15. 3 + 5 =	25. 6 + 3 =
6. 2 + 5 =	16. 9 − 7 =	26. 4 + 8 =
7. 6 + 6 =	17. 4 + 7 =	27. 2 + 9 =
8. 7 − 5 =	18. 12 − 9 =	28. 1 + 11 =
9. 5 + 5 =	19. 6 + 6 =	29. 5 + 6 =
10. 10 − 4 =	20. 3 + 9 =	30. 12 − 4 =

Step 1: (Hook and Instruction) Tell the class you need help moving the desks back against the wall. Direct them to help you get the desks out of the way and to make three rows of 12 chairs each. (Make sure the chairs are set in a uniform fashion so that the students can crawl under them.)

Step 2: (Instruction) Break the class into the three equal teams and have each team line up in the order in which you place them in front of a row of chairs.

Step 3: (Instruction, Practice, and Informal Assessment) Once the groups are in place, tell them they are about to compete in a relay race. Have the first person in one of the lines serve as the example. Instruct this child that you are going to give her a math problem. When she has solved the problem, she is to demonstrate the correct answer by crawling under the chairs until she comes to the chair that represents the right answer. Give the equation 3 + 3 and see if the student can follow your instructions. If she crawls under the chairs and stops at the sixth chair in the row, she has correctly demonstrated that she has solved the equation. If she gets it wrong, help her correct her answer. Now make sure the rest of the class understands what they are to do. If necessary, have a few different students demonstrate what you want the class to do. (If crawling under the chairs seems too dirty or risky, set the chairs in rows and leave an aisle between each row so the students can run down the aisle and sit in the proper chair to indicate their answer.)

Step 4: (Instruction, Practice, and Midlesson Assessment) Randomly ask questions on the test, one at a time, to the rows of student in the teams. Watch how they are doing and make adjustments for those individuals or teams that need extra help. (At first you can allow the teams to work together to solve the equations. When you are sure everyone understands the process, have each child solve the problem alone.) Continue to drill the questions until each child has had several opportunities to participate. Mentally keep track of how they are doing and give appropriate time to those individuals needing a little extra practice.

Step 5: (Instruction, Practice, and Final Assessment) Go through each question (as time permits) with each member of the class using the relay format. This time use the tests (with names) on the clipboard to record their answers. (Make sure the children are seated in the order of your tests so that the process goes smoothly.)

Step 6: (Instruction, Practice, and Optional Traditional Assessment) Have the class help you reorder the desks and chairs. Once they are in order, have them sit quietly at their desks and take out a pencil. Tell them they are going to answer the same questions they just did in the relay race. Pass out a copy of the test to the students and give them adequate time to complete it.

The HIPA elements have been labeled at each step of this lesson. It should be quite apparent that the elements are not exclusive to any particular step in the lesson except for the hook. Typically, the hook is the first step of any lesson and it does not repeat during the lesson. Remember, the purpose of the hook is quite different from the other elements. Its sole purpose is to disrupt the normal life of students and draw them into a learning experience. Once this has happened, it is the job of the other elements to lead to the completion of the learning process.

The fear expressed by many teachers that keeps them from using this approach is that it takes too much time. To one such teacher, I asked, "Well, how long has your approach been taking?" She replied, "We've been at this a month and only half of the kids get it." A month is a long time. I promised her, as I do you, that if she would use this methodology she would cut this time at least in half. Dramatic learning decreases the amount of time it takes to learn anything because it draws on the natural learning skills of the students and allows for better retention.

A simple count of the elements that have been identified in this math lesson shows that the hook and instruction elements appear in Step 1. Step 2 is a brief instructional element that prepares the students to participate in the activity. Steps 3 through 6 all contain a combination of the instruction, practice, and assessment elements. These elements are a natural part of all good learning exercises. The balance they provide creates a learning atmosphere that has the ability to engage all learners, not just the dramatic learners.

Compare how these elements are used in the example lessons we have previously examined. Remember, a quick check for each of the HIPA elements gives you an immediate reading on how balanced your lesson is. It helps you to know immediately what you must do to modify your lesson so that you can move your teaching more into the nexus. It doesn't require a huge change to what you're doing already. Rather, it simply enables you to understand what you must adjust to create a learning environment that is most preferable to the dramatic learner. Please remember that a lesson that is properly balanced by HIPA elements creates the most conducive environment for *all* learners.

Natural Resources Lesson #1	*Natural Resources Lesson #2*
Process:	**Process:**
Step 1: State the objective for the class. **(Instruction)**	**Step 1:** Pass out a clipboard or other hard writing surface to each student and make sure each person has a pen or pencil. **(Instruction)**
Step 2: Ask the class if they know the difference between a natural resource and a man-made object. **(Instruction)**	**Step 2:** Take them to the space where you have laid out the items. **(Hook and Instruction)**
Step 3: Ask the class to clear off their desks. **(Instruction)**	**Step 3:** Instruct them that their job is . . . **(Instruction and Practice)**
Step 4: Show them different objects. **(Instruction and Practice)**	**Step 4:** Give them the opportunity to work. **(Practice, Instruction, and Informal Assessment)**
Step 5: Go through each item with the class to make sure that they have the right answers. **(Instruction and Assessment)**	**Step 5:** Observe the groups as they work to determine if they are applying the protocol. **(Practice, Instruction, and Informal Assessment)**
Step 6: Review for the students what they have learned by restating the definition. **(Instruction)**	**Step 6:** Assign each group or individual to be responsible for reporting their findings for certain items. **(Practice, Instruction, and Mid-lesson Assessment)**
	Step 7: Have the class restate the keys they have discovered. **(Practice, Instruction, and Mid-lesson Assessment)**

(Continued)

(Continued)

Natural Resources Lesson #1	*Natural Resources Lesson #2*
	Step 8: Spot-check for understanding. **(Practice, Instruction, and Final Assessment)** **Step 9:** (Optional) Take the class back to the classroom and give them a formal quiz. (Allow them to handle the items if they want during the quiz.) **(Practice, Instruction, and Optional Formal Assessment)**
Results	
0 Part Hook (H) 6 Parts Instruction (I) 1 Part Practice (P) 1 Part Assessment (A)	1 Part Hook (H) 9 Parts Instruction (I) 7 Parts Practice (P) 7 Parts Assessment (A)
No Lesson Balance	Complete Lesson Balance

Traditional Teaching
Outside the Nexus

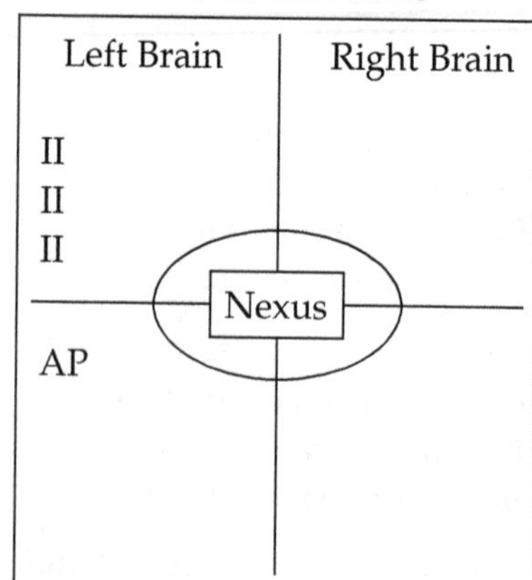

Dramatic Instruction
Within the Nexus

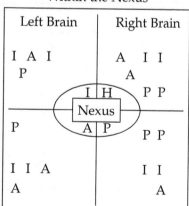

Vocabulary Lesson #1	*Vocabulary Lesson #2*
Process:	**Process:**
Step 1: State the objective for the class. **(Instruction)**	**Step 1:** Assign the class to come up with the pilot for a new television series. **(Hook and Instruction)**
Step 2: Pass out the vocabulary sheet. **(Instruction)**	**Step 2:** Form the class into small groups and pass out the word sheet. **(Instruction)**
Step 3: Have the students write a definition, in their own words. **(Instruction and Individualized Practice)**	**Step 3:** Instruct the students that their job is . . . **(Instruction)**
Step 4: Have the students go to the dictionary and write down the definitions. **(Instruction and Traditional Practice)**	**Step 4:** Monitor each group. **(Instruction, Practice, and Informal Assessment)**
Step 5: Have them compare their definitions with the ones they got from the dictionary. **(Assessment)**	**Step 5:** Get ready to perform. **(Instruction, Practice, and Informal Assessment)**
Step 6: Have the students write a sentence for each word to show that they can use the word in its proper context. **(Instruction and Traditional Practice)**	**Step 6:** Tell the students one more requirement. **(Instruction, Practice, and Informal Assessment)**
Step 7: Have them share some of their sentences and correct those examples. **(Instruction)**	**Step 7:** Instruct the class to check the definitions. **(Instruction, Practice, and Mid-lesson Assessment)**

(Continued)

(Continued)

Vocabulary Lesson #1	*Vocabulary Lesson #2*
Step 8: Have them take a quiz. **(Assessment)**	**Step 8:** Share their performances. **(Practice and Final Assessment)**
Step 9: Go over answers as a practice for the real quiz. **(Assessment)**	**Step 9:** Go over answers as a practice for the real quiz. **(Instruction, Practice, and Mid lesson Assessment)**
Results	
0 Parts Hook (H) 6 Parts Instruction (I) 3 Parts Practice (P) 2 Parts Assessment (A)	1 Part Hook (H) 8 Parts Instruction (I) 6 Parts Practice (P) 6 Parts Assessment (A)
No Lesson Balance	Complete Lesson Balance

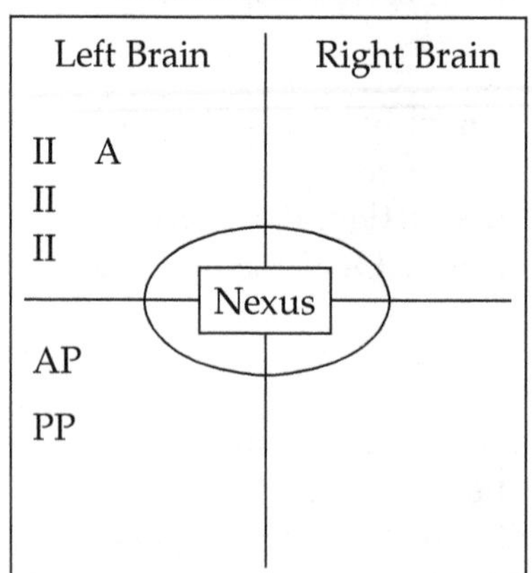

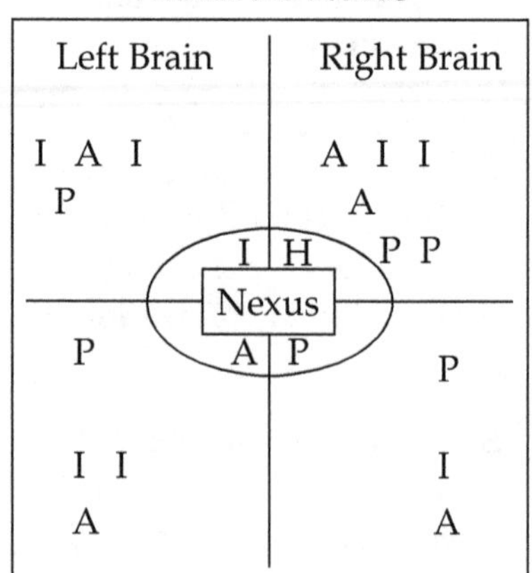

8

Learning and Self-Image

Self-image is a foundational element in the learning process. The principles of self-image must be understood to fully appreciate how important it is to enhance learning potential. Common sense should confirm the value of these principles, but it is surprising how many of us fail to use them in our daily practice. It is as if we forget that we can't positively affect learning without paying attention to the individual needs of the learner.

Principle 1: Everyone Has a Self-Image

Whether good or bad, accurate or inaccurate, self-image exists. It influences the way one interacts with everything and everybody in one's life. It usually sets the tone of a person's attitude, and in the long run, deeply affects personal behaviors and values. A person's view of himself or herself enhances or hinders access to all learning, personal growth, and development. Self-image serves as a personal bellwether for success or failure in any given situation. To ignore self-image in the educational process is tantamount to ignoring the individual learner entirely.

Principle 2: The Self-Image Can Change

Through a single major event or a series of smaller ones, individuals can change the way they feel about themselves for better or for worse. It is most common, however, for these changes to happen over time. Individuals move in and out of esteem as their actions and feelings and the actions and feelings of those around them encounter their own personal values. People who behave in accordance with their values typically have a good self-image.

Those who learn to positively navigate the shifting sands of daily life and successfully adapt to the constant flow of change and uncertainty, which is a natural part of life, develop a positive self-image. Those who become buried in these drifting sands soon lose their ability to react properly. This loss of trust in self, through the lack of ability to cope with problems, causes self-image to decrease and can result in a debilitating loss of hope. Some who lose this battle learn to cover their scars and failures with a protective layer that can pass as a good self-image. In reality, however, this layer is a false image that is bolstered by negative rather than positive actions. These individuals may appear self-assured, arrogant, or cocky. The truth, however, is that they are operating in dangerous backwaters that will never lead them into the main stream. Many dramatic learners have fallen into this trap because school is such a foreign environment for them.

Principle 3: Self-Image Development Must Be Based on the Truth

In our rush to assist students to improve their self-image, we are often tempted to tell them things that are not truthful. This is done with the best of intentions and in the hope that these individuals will believe our words and use our supportive language as a stepping-stone to personal growth and increased learning potential. Though some evidence may support the short-term value of this approach, the long-range effect is devastating to both the teacher and the student alike. The violation of this principle of truth has contributed to many of the faulty conclusions reached in this area of research.

In one such study, the researchers would take young people who were doing poorly in school and conduct what I call "the therapy of good words." In essence, the intervention on behalf of these students consisted of telling them they were good and smart kids. It smacked of a particularly humorous *Saturday Night Live* skit. Let's say that a child involved in the study had failed a particular test. The researcher would intervene on behalf of the child as follows:

Researcher: (Sitting down next to the student to offer encouragement) Well, Jada, how did you do on your test yesterday?

Student: (Looking at her desk) I don't know.

Researcher: Really? Didn't the teacher hand it back to you?

Student: Maybe, I don't remember.

Researcher: (Helping her go through her papers) Let's see if we can find it and talk about it.

Student: I don't want to.

Researcher: I know, but it's important.

Student: To you, maybe.

Researcher: That's how you feel about it now, but maybe later you'll change your mind. (Finding the test) Oh, here it is.

Student: I told you I forgot.

Researcher: That's okay, I forget things too. Let's look at this together, what do you say? It looks like you missed quite a few of them. Maybe you just didn't understand what you were supposed to do.

Student: Yeah.

Researcher: Well, let me help you out here. We'll give you a second chance on it, okay? But before we do, let's get you ready to do better this time. How do you feel about that?

Student: (Still looking at her desk) Okay.

Researcher: Great. You know what I think? I think you're a great student. You can do much better than a 20 on this test. You're much smarter than that. In fact, I think you're good enough and smart enough to be on the honor roll this semester. I'm sure that if you just tell yourself this before each test you will achieve a lot more in your life. How do you feel now?

Student: Okay.

Researcher: (Helping her clear off her desk and handing her a new test) Well, here you go. Give it another crack. I just know you'll do better this time.

I apologize for oversimplifying the process, but, essentially, this is what they were doing. Is there any doubt that the score on this new test will not be much better than the first? The most amazing thing to me is that the researchers were truly surprised when their research failed to produce better results. Is it any wonder, on the basis of these practices, that they determined that self-image development had nothing to do with improving academic skills?

This approach perfectly demonstrates the importance of this third principle. The student wasn't being fed the truth. That's not to say that this individual didn't have the potential to be a good student, but telling her she was when she wasn't demonstrating any evidence of being a good student wasn't the truth. Teachers who fall into the trap of lying to students under the guise of "building their self-image" will end up only creating larger, long-term problems for themselves and their students.

The disappointing by-product of this approach occurs every time our well-meaning untruths are confronted by reality. When this happens, the students will lose all belief in the teacher, in their own abilities, and maybe even in learning itself. Looking beyond the effect that being untruthful has on the individual, what does the rest of your class think when you openly praise work they know is substandard? What does your attempt to make someone feel good about him- or herself do to your image in the eyes of the rest of your students? What message does it send to them? Though some students may understand what you're trying to do, most of them will lose respect for you and your opinions.

Being untruthful will also adversely affect the students you have tried to support. Eventually they will have to come face-to-face with reality. When they do, your supportive but untruthful efforts will have done them no favors. In fact, one day they might even come to blame you for making them think they were better than they really are. Think of those, in your own circle of friends, whom you trust to tell you the truth, no matter what. When all is said and done, aren't they your truest friends? They are the ones you turn to in your deepest time of need because they will be honest in their assessments and stick with you through any difficulty. We can endure the truth from these individuals because they have earned our trust.

Not to avoid the almost certain misunderstanding that may follow, I must quickly emphasize that this principle is not a license to be rude or unfeeling. It is not a call to repeal diplomacy and tact. Rather, it is both a reminder that we need to be more honest in our dealings with students, and a plea that we be more truthful and yet remain supportive in our evaluation of others. This is not an oxymoron; we can be honest and supportive at the same time. For example, to students who turn in a paper that is substandard, we can focus our personal response on the positive efforts they put forth and help them feel good about what they actually accomplished. To elaborate this point, let's alter the last exchange with Jada and focus it on a written assignment rather than on a test so we can evaluate this principle in practice.

Teacher: (Returning the paper) Jada, how did it make you feel when you turned your paper in on time?

Student: (Taking the paper) I don't know.

Teacher: No, really? Stop and think about it for a minute. How did it feel to have this assignment finished?

Student: Well, I didn't dread coming to class.

Teacher: Isn't that a wonderful feeling?

Student: Kinda.

Teacher: What excited you about the topic you chose to write about?

Student: I don't know.

Teacher: You must have picked it for some reason; what was it?

Student: I don't know, I guess I've always liked horses.

Teacher: Really? I never knew that about you. You know, I can't think of an animal that has meant more to the advancement of mankind.

Student: Really?

Teacher: Sure. Did you know that there are some anthropologists who believe the horse is the one animal that kept man from becoming extinct?

Student: How's that?

Teacher: If you think about it, it makes a lot of sense. You even pointed out in your paper some of the important work horses did in the westward expansion of this country.

Student: Yeah, people used them for everything.

Teacher: You're right. I think this paper is a great start, but there is so much more you could find out and share with me and the rest of the class on this subject. We could sit down for a minute and brainstorm ways you could expand what you've done here and make it better. What do you say?

Student: I thought I was done.

Teacher: For now, if you're happy with this grade. But since you got it in on time, if you want you can look at improving this a little in these areas (go over the specific flaws in the paper) and resubmit it for a better grade. If not, you can research this topic deeper for your next paper. It's completely up to you.

Do you see the honesty in this exchange? The teacher isn't trying to build a false structure here. Instead, the approach focuses the student on how she felt when she turned her work in on time. From there, the discussion focused on the positive work that was done. There is an important distinction here between praising an individual for what she has done and helping her understand how she feels inside when she does something that is good. This does not discount the power of praise; it simply calls for it to be more focused on actual accomplishments and efforts expended. I call this *appropriate praise.* Appropriate praise is praise that is honest and accurate. It lets students know exactly what they have done right. It focuses the attention of the person being praised on how it feels to do good work and not on how it affects others. Too often individuals turn to others to make them feel good about what they have done. Looking outward for praise is not entirely a bad thing unless people get into the habit of always looking outside of themselves for validation. True self-image comes from within. It is a satisfaction with self. Helping students gain a true intrinsic appreciation of themselves should be the real goal of our attempts to increase their self-image.

Principle 4: Self-Image Development Is Understood Differently by Different People

In fact, there seem to be two very distinct camps that have formed at either end of a spectrum with only a few squatters inhabiting the lowland in between. At one end are those who hold that self-image development must be the first focus of growth and change. They could be quoted as saying, "Get people to feel good about themselves and they can do anything."

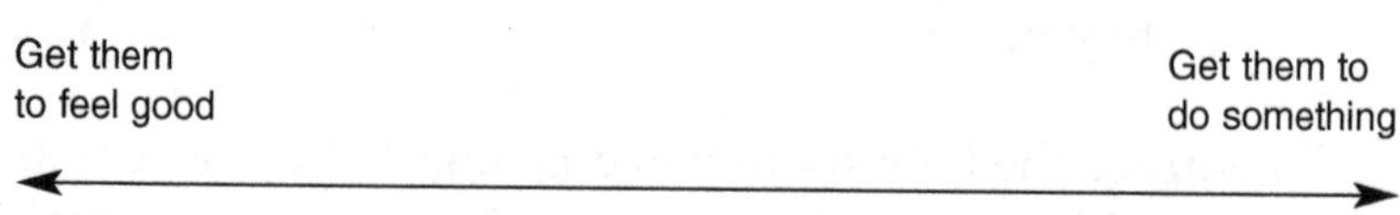

One the other end of the spectrum are those that say, "Get people to do something and then they'll feel good about themselves." These individuals often see the process of building self-image as a natural by-product of gaining a new skill or learning something new. They are just as correct in their assessment of this issue as are those in the other camp. The whole truth, however, is that the beliefs of each camp, taken alone, are just as wrong as those of the other. As with all other polarized educational beliefs, both sides of this issue have equally valid points of view, but they cannot be separated from each other. If we try to employ one approach without the other, our efforts to raise the self-image of our learners will end up incomplete and unnecessarily shallow.

The feelings-first approach fails because its single focus is only on this one aspect of raising self-image. On the other hand, efforts based solely on the work-first approach will fail as well. Any efforts to raise the self-image of our students must grow out of our ability to combine these polarized views and ideas into a unified and lasting process of growth. Its center must be focused on the student and his or her individual needs. If these principles are used to guide our practice, we will find greater success in reaching the needs of our dramatic learners as well as the rest of our students.

To better explain the need for this combined approach, let's consider the next figure. It illustrates the need for students to have a certain level of positive self-image before they can successfully participate in the learning process.

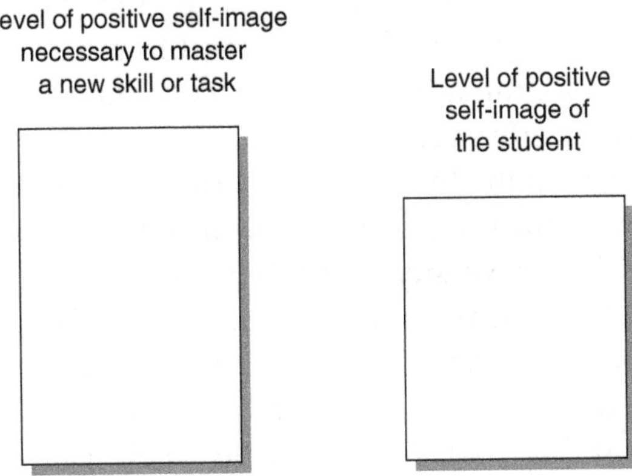

The bar on the right of this chart represents the level of positive self-image a student possesses. On the left is a representation of the level of positive self-image necessary for this same student to master a specific new skill. It is obvious that the student represented in this chart doesn't have a good enough self-image to invest in his own learning and development. In this present state, he will not be able to adapt properly to the world around him. He is frozen in place because his self-image is only good enough to maintain the present status quo in his life.

We must learn to think of self-image in our students as the capital (expendable cash) they need to invest in their future growth. Just as individuals who lack the financial capital to invest wisely in their economic future are cut off from the ability to earn dividends and interest, so students who have no educational capital are likewise cut off from a world that is open to other learners who have the wherewithal to invest. Learners in this state of educational bankruptcy cannot take advantage of any investment opportunity—even if they knew it was guaranteed to pay huge personal dividends. Their lack of faith in themselves keeps them from ever realizing their full potential.

As educators, our job must be to unify our efforts and build self-image at the same time we teach our subject matter.

As mentioned before, if we try to do one without the other, we are ignoring the first three principles mentioned in this chapter. The proper combination of all of these principles will improve self-image as it increases the learning potential of the dramatic learner. We should be careful to remember that the self-image of a dramatic learner, when it comes to school and schoolwork, is often very low.

To demonstrate this approach further, I would like to draw from a study I was involved in while still a graduate student at the University of Washington. In this small study, we worked to increase the learning potential of mentally handicapped children. These individuals had been tested, evaluated, and classified. We were told, based on their classification, that they had already reached their learning limit.

We decided to test the expectations of the staff by using an intervention that focused on building the self-image of the students as we worked to increase their skills. For lack of a better name, we called our approach "video therapy." We used a video camera to gather learning images, which we could show on TV. We were careful in our camera work and in-camera editing to paint a positive picture as our students interacted and worked with other young people who were not handicapped.

Building our model on the foundation of the first principle mentioned in this chapter, our first premise was that they already had a self-image that was based on the way they saw themselves in the world around them and the way other people treated them. We assumed that their self-image included feelings that they were not the same as other people. In keeping with the second principle, we set about to establish a protocol which we felt could assist them positively in altering their present self-image.

Our next step was to use the camera to tell the truth. The truth we wanted them to adopt was that they could increase their learning potential and skill levels with additional effort and practice. Our carefully chosen shots and angles were used to play down their differences and some of the physical problems that were obvious to the naked eye. In so doing, we carefully followed the third principle and told the truth, but we did so with diplomacy and tact. Please note that we can know something is true and build on that fact even though the learner hasn't discovered it yet. Our job is a delicate one in which we must search for and carefully expose the evidence of the truth that students have missed about themselves. Our camera became the tool for gathering such evidence.

Finally, to follow the fourth principle and combine our efforts, we harnessed our students' own natural desire to be seen by others on "TV," and in so doing, we drew their own values into the mix. We began to show these students the video we had shot. As they viewed themselves on television, something very interesting began to happen. Their whole external appearance began to change. We saw them begin to feel differently about the way they looked to others. This was accomplished because we focused on helping them appreciate the things they could already do. When this effort produced the excitement and thrill we had hoped for, we began to introduce them into different environmental situations where new tasks and situations were presented for them to master.

In this enlivened state of self-image, we never actually taught them the new tasks per se, but we placed them in a room with other youngsters who could already perform the skills we wanted our target population to master. Here, we continued to videotape their progress. As they watched and worked with a willing peer tutor, they started to do things they were unwilling to try before. The videotape recorded their progress, and we shared those carefully gathered images with them as evidence of their progress.

In the whole project, we saw our job as simply recording and sharing images of their success. We never directly taught one skill to the target population. Instead, we taught the new skill to the peer tutors who were then responsible to share what they had been taught. This process altered the expectations of our target population and created a great boost in how they felt and what they thought about themselves and their potential as learners. As we worked with these young people, we developed a chart of a methodology that became our protocol. This same protocol works well with dramatic learners.

Encouragement

This figure doesn't express anything new or exceptional, but it does demonstrate what we must do to assist others to develop a more positive self-image. The beginning point is encouragement. This is an extrinsic element, I know, but, in the initial stages, the process often must be jump-started by the teacher. This responsibility to prime the pump must fall on the teacher, who acts as the catalyst in this change process. It is okay, initially, for students to rely on our encouragement. Our job is to become effective motivators by learning to encourage different students in different ways.

What works to encourage one student will not necessarily reach another, but the more we use our understanding of learning styles, the more adept we become in this process. In the example exchange with the student (Jada) who needed to be encouraged to do more on her writing assignments, the teacher was quite adept in her ability to encourage her in this area.

Building on this first exchange, let's observe how effective encouragement could prepare Jada to expand her efforts on her next writing assignment:

Teacher: Well, are you ready for this next paper?

Student: No, I hate to write.

Teacher: Well, what did you learn from your last project?

Student: That it's hard.

Teacher: It is, you're right about that. What else did you learn?

Student: I don't know.

Teacher: Really? Nothing comes to mind?

Student: Well, I guess writing about something I like makes it a bit easier?

Teacher: Is that a question?

Student: No.

Teacher: Then you really learned that?

Student: Yes.

Teacher: It's an excellent observation. Now, how are you going to use that bit of wisdom to help you on your next paper?

Student: Can I still write about the same thing?

Teacher: Why not?

Student: Just checking.

Teacher: You just have to do five pages this time. What aspect of horses do you think you want to focus on?

Student: Actually, I was thinking about saddles . . .

Teacher: Saddles?

Student: Yeah. I read something last time about how the invention of the stirrup really changed a lot of things about riding.

Teacher: Sounds great to me. Do you know where to go to find enough information to fill five pages?

Student: Not really.

Teacher: I can point you in the right direction if you want.

Student: I do.

This simple conversation is filled with words of encouragement for the student. It is designed to lead the learner to the point where she will be willing to take the next step in the process.

Confidence

Out of our encouragement, students must gain a feeling of confidence that will motivate them to engage in activities that will move them forward personally and academically. Again, for the dramatic learner, this confidence initially needs to grow out of the efforts of the teacher. Students who already have a good self-image, as it relates to learning, are able to exercise confidence, move forward, and grow on their own. Those learners who do not, will not progress without our assistance. The confidence boost I am describing doesn't need to be extreme to be successful. It just needs to be enough to get the individuals to believe they can experience success if they put forth a little effort. Returning to the example of our writing student, her statement that she would like help in finding resources for her paper is a good indication that the encouragement offered by the teacher was successful. It appears obvious that she has gained enough confidence to attempt to put forth some of her own energy on the project.

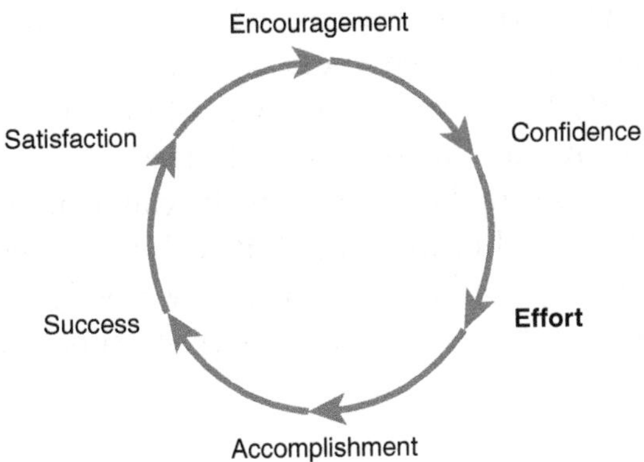

Effort

This gain in confidence is of no value unless it motivates learners to do something. Unless they become willing to invest some portion of themselves into the process, they will never grow. Here we must be doubly careful because if we encourage our students and build their confidence and they put forth some effort and fail, they will be worse off than they were when they started. We can avoid this calamity because the classroom is not the real world, and we are ultimately responsible for setting the rules and the consequences. If we do our job correctly, we can make sure their efforts are met with success.

To do this, we must remember that this is a "small to overwhelming" process. We have to acknowledge and celebrate the smallest successes. The effort phase in the accompanying figure is the buy-in point during this delicate process. Therefore, we must handle it ever so carefully or else the students will stop investing, and the cycle we wish to continue will break down.

In the example of our writing student, and in our efforts with each of our students, this self-image wheel must spin through its cycle many times in order for an entire task to be completed. It would not be unusual that at each step of the process of writing her paper, our example student would need to feel the self-image cycle completing itself before she could have the confidence to move on in completing the entire task. We see evidence that she is willing to do the initial research to get started. If her research efforts are rewarded by personal feelings of success and satisfaction, she will most likely be ready to return to her teacher to receive the proper encouragement and instruction she needs to help her be successful in drafting her outline. If she can again experience success at this level of the project, it will be the result of the cycle completing itself again. These new feelings of satisfaction will again give her the necessary personal strength to move on.

Accomplishment

To assure a sense of accomplishment, we have to design each learning event by carefully using the dramatic elements discussed in other chapters. Careful attention to the principles of sound dramatic plotting will allow a teacher to properly control the risk and the rewards of a learning experience. When the student has put forth effort and achieved an accomplishment, it should move him or her to a feeling of success, as indicated in the figure. As teachers, we must remember that the goal is not for *us* to experience these feelings of accomplishment. As rewarding as that may be for us personally, it does little to improve the self-image of our students. Our students must feel it for themselves.

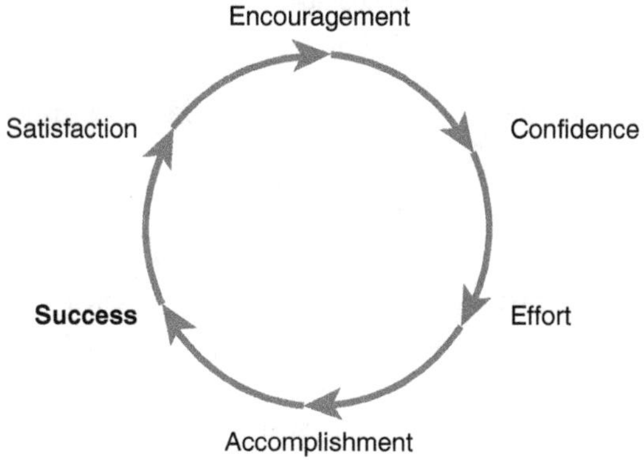

Success

In fact, if we try to measure the success our students are experiencing through the lens of our own values, we will fail in our efforts. We must learn that as we help them build their self-image, it is only their feelings of success that matter. This is one of the most frustrating aspects of this whole process. How many times have we seen the evidence of their increased success only to realize they are completely oblivious to the growth that is taking place. Our recognition of this does them no good until we can help them to see what we see. As in the research project I referenced earlier, you must find a way to capture their progress and make it apparent to them.

I have seen teachers use such tools as portfolios, videotaped performances, written evaluations, behavioral assessments, peer reviews, sample writing, and test scores as concrete evidence of growth and development. It matters not what method is used, only that it carefully charts student progress in as many ways as possible. Too often, failure in this area results from the fact that progress is charted in a way that is not meaningful to the student. This is another area where teacher creativity and alternative measuring methods can pay big dividends.

Satisfaction

Students gain a great sense of satisfaction when they can feel genuine success because of the things they have done. These feelings of satisfaction are important because they give students the personal power to move from needing extrinsic motivation to promote personal change, to beginning to rely on their own intrinsic drive as their main motivating factor. When they feel this kind of satisfaction, it becomes a reward in and of itself. It entices them to much bigger and better things. True self-satisfaction is the real high people seek in negative and destructive pursuits. Many of these counterfeit means lead to dangerous additions and other life-threatening perils. Personal satisfaction, in reality, is the illusive path to endless enlightenment and personal happiness. This is the state that Maslow refers to as self-actualization.

As teachers, we have the ability to help students move toward this utopian state of being. We can help them become more satisfied with their own evaluation of their work by learning to ask questions like, "Why do you feel this way about yourself when you do good work?" This question helps students focus on their own ability to evaluate the rewards and benefits of good work. It helps them learn to rely on their own abilities and talents. Remember, in order for feelings of improved self-image to be real and lasting, individuals must experience the satisfaction for themselves.

If our example student can succeed at the research and outline phase of the task she is attempting, the likelihood exists that she will be able to draw on her own intrinsic encouragement or initiative to tackle the rough- and final-draft stages on her own. This is our ultimate goal—to help our students build their own self-image to the point they are no longer dependent on our encouragement to move forward. When they have reached this point in their personal development, we have performed the highest duty a teacher can hope to perform.

As I interview university students who are entering our teacher-training program, I often ask them, "Tell me about your greatest teacher." Without fail, they mention an individual who did something that absolutely built their self-esteem. On the flip side of the coin, however, if I ask, "Who was the worst teacher you've ever had?" almost without exception they will say it is the one who damaged their self-image. I have conducted hundreds of these interviews, and they are for me one of the greatest evidences of the importance of self-image in the learning process.

Let me restate for emphasis: Self-esteem is tied directly to learning. If students have it, they have the wherewithal to invest in their own learning. If they don't have it, they can't invest, and the educational process has no real value even though they may be adept at going through the motions. Attending school in this frame of mind is a lot like traveling on an airplane and sitting down next to a stranger. Without interacting with this individual, there is no likelihood that you will ever have anything to do with this person once you reach your city of destination. So it is with many learners. They sit in our classrooms, day in and day out, and yet when the class is over, they go their way, and what we hoped to teach them stays behind with us. They leave us with little to show for the time they spent in our classroom. They haven't made a personal investment; therefore they have nothing to show. One of the main reasons for this disconnect is because their self-image was never enhanced enough to enable them to master the subject matter. Without this improved self image, they are never able to see themselves as individuals who can successfully tackle the subject matter or make it an important part of their own lives.

If we manage this acquisition correctly and help our students learn to invest themselves properly in the process of building self-image, as mentioned before, sooner or later our encouragement turns to their initiative. When students reach this point in their personal development, they have finally learned what they must do to increase their own self-image in positive ways. If and when this finally happens, the desire to learn and grow will become a constant part of their lives. Many individuals can look back on their lives to a particular moment in time when this kind of educational magic happened for them. Of this event or series of events, they share a common belief: "This one event—this one teacher built my self-image and changed my whole life."

One poignant example was shared in a training conference I conducted several years ago. A rather large coach shared the reason he decided to become a teacher. Holding back his emotions, he related, "I was terrible in sports. I was the last one picked. I was a big kid, so everyone thought I should be much better than I was." He continued,

> Unless you've been there yourself, you'll never know what it feels like. The teasing was devastating. Finally, one day a teacher came to my rescue. He had been out on the playground and watched me suffer as I struggled to bat and catch. He came up to me after recess and privately asked if I would like to stay after school a little bit to work with him on my skills.

His story was interrupted by his strong emotions. Almost unable to talk, he resumed his story.

> My eyes lit up, and I was filled with a strange feeling of hope. The day dragged on till school finally ended, and I ran out to the field with my glove. The teacher met me on the diamond with a bat and some balls. He first tested my skills and watched curiously as I tried in vain to catch and hit the ball. He noticed something about the way I looked at the ball and suggested that I close one of my eyes and see if it would help. When I swung the bat with my eye closed, I hit the ball! When I tried to catch with that one eye closed, I could easily see the ball! That one day changed my whole life. That one teacher changed my whole life. I became a teacher so that I could do the same thing for other children.

We all desire to be that kind of teacher. We all desire to be that kind of individual. The key lies in our ability to build self-image as we teach skills and increase understanding. It must become the major focus in what we do. As I stated before, dramatic learners often have a deluded sense of self-image, or else they have none at all. Many of these learners have come to believe that they can enhance self-image only by doing negative things. Because of this mistaken belief, they gather around negative peers, and together they walk in negative paths.

Our ability to encourage their striving for self-image in positive ways will have a long-lasting effect on more areas of their lives than just academic pursuits. It can change the entire direction of a young life. It can provide hope in a previously hopeless world. Attempts to educate that are not inherently built on the principle of building self-image are reduced to nothing more than rote exercises and meaningless drill. However, education that attempts only to make people feel good about themselves and fails to give them actual skills and new abilities is just so much smoke in the wind.

The combination of these approaches returns us to the learning nexus. It stabilizes our efforts to educate our students fully. When I seek to build the self-image of my students, I'm careful not to let them know what I am doing. It is my secret because I know it is the natural by-product of dramatic learning. I go so far as to never share the self-image-building chart with my students. I simply keep it to myself and follow its principles while working carefully to help them grow and develop in ways they have never considered.

I must reemphasize some of the pitfalls here. Remember, as we work through this process, we must control the risk. We need to get students to invest; that's our job. But we've got to make sure that when they do, they do not fail. We are in the classroom to build success. We can enhance their chances for success and accomplishment by properly controlling the risk factor. In this fashion, we can lead dramatic learners through this process without them even knowing what is happening. Some may call that manipulation, but any attempt to change the way somebody feels about something can be accurately given that negative label. To stay positive, let's remember that fostering this kind of change is the major job of education. We are not really in the business of manipulation; we are engaged in the work of enhancing personal vision and opening up a world of limitless opportunity. So rather than viewing it as manipulation, I like to refer to it as guided discovery.

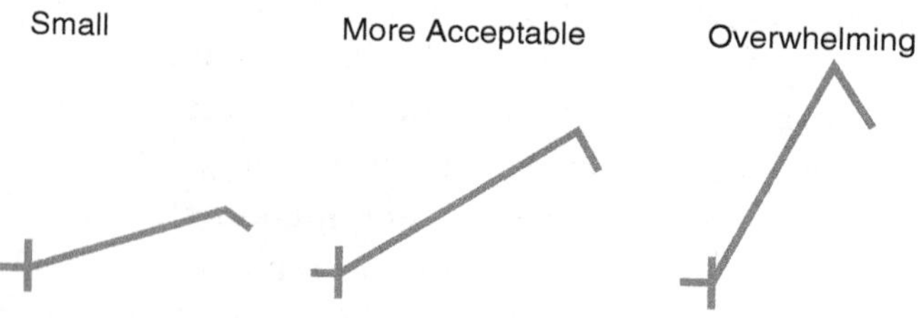

I further remind you that there really is no such thing as a self-image-building exercise, per se. In fact, when extensive efforts are exerted to overtly build self-image, the opposite effect is usually accomplished. For this reason, I want to repeat the need to teach skills and build self-image at the same time. Lesson and unit plans that rely on dramatic elements will naturally achieve this result. This is accomplished because students will gain new skills and develop an improved self-image without even being aware that changes are taking place in their lives. Learning that is fun naturally makes us feel good because it enlightens our minds as it enriches our souls. The lifting power that this gain of self-image generates can give individuals the energy to rise above their present self-imposed limitations. Positive change is the true power and reward of learning. By its very nature, real learning positively enhances the way people feel about themselves. It shakes off the shackles of self-doubt and discouragement, and it enables individuals to have complete access to these principles of personal growth and development.

9

Discipline and the Dramatic Learner

By far, the greatest number of questions I address in my university classes for beginning teachers or in seminars for seasoned veterans have to do with how to deal with undesirable student behavior. My assumption is that these behavioral concerns will only continue to grow if our educational practices maintain their present course. The seeming inability of our system to engage students fully, combined with the growing number of individuals who appear to lack the ability to exercise self-control, poses an alarming educational dilemma. This reality becomes even more frightening because it is occurring at a time of ever-increasing violence in our society and in our schools. The growing concern for discipline in the classroom is especially understandable as one studies the behavior of many dramatic learners.

It is safe to say that dramatic learners perpetrate the majority of the discipline problems that occur in school. They present a problem for a system that lacks the understanding to effectively deal with their special learning needs. For this reason it is most appropriate that we take an in-depth look at discipline and the principles and practices that are most effective in helping us reach these particular learners. Though we focus our discussion on the disciplinary needs of dramatic learners, the principles and practices covered in this chapter have application to all learners.

The concept of discipline is an interesting one. It entails much more than most people ever contemplate. Many teachers and administrators believe that discipline and punishment are synonymous terms. Though they may appear to be similar in our modern vernacular, each is a distinct and different animal. Discipline refers to discipleship, and it implies a self-imposed set of beliefs and code of conduct. The act of disciplining individuals, in the strictest sense of the word, is to actually teach them what they should do and motivate them internally to behave in a way that it is consistent with the highest ideals or values of human endeavor.

Punishment, on the other hand, has synonyms like chastisement, castigation, reprimand, retribution, or sentencing. These words connote quite a different picture from the synonyms for discipline, such as self-control, following, support, partisan, and adherence. Punishment is most often seen as a deterrent to negative behaviors. It is used to help control those who are deemed to have no self-control. It is not atypical for punishment to be viewed as nothing more than a deterrent or measure used to show somebody what not to do. It rarely contains an element that teaches what should be done in place of the unacceptable behavior. For this reason, I would like to focus clearly on this distinction as we labor to understand what we can do to help students behave in a manner that is acceptable in the classroom as well as in the rest of their lives.

To set the stage for this discussion, we must first come to an agreement on several different issues. First, the title of teacher is a huge misnomer. In reality, we have long known that nobody can teach anybody anything. Teaching is not something we can *do* to someone else without his or her willing participation. All arguments to the contrary, there is nothing we can do in the field of education without the willing cooperation of our students. I find it amazing to see how many individuals, inside and outside of the teaching profession, have no concept of this reality.

We have long accepted the cliché "You can lead a horse to water, but you can't make it drink," so why is it blasphemous to assert, "You can bus students to school, but you can't make them learn?" Students are not unlike horses. They both have minds and wills of their own. A horse knows when it's thirsty, and students know when they are curious. Anyone who has worked with either knows that there is nothing that can be done with them without first harnessing their will. Maybe the better cliché should be, "A nonthirsty horse won't drink anything," or "if you want a horse to drink, first get it good and thirsty, then lead it to water." As for students, it should read, "An incurious student won't learn anything," or "if you want students to learn, first pique their curiosity."

This reality exists because we work in one of the few fields where we cannot touch the thing we want to change. Most occupations and professions, through techniques that involve the use of specific procedures and tools, can by their own will, effort, and knowledge, change or fix the problem or challenge that exists. It is because of this common reality that education is judged so harshly by others. School board members and the public at large feel that all they have to do is provide teachers and administrators with the proper tools, and the work of learning should move forward in an uninterrupted fashion. They become easily baffled when this approach doesn't bring about immediate results. There are vast differences between educational realities and the realities of other fields of endeavor. Ignorance of these differences can easily lead outsiders to be overly critical when expenditures on facilities and technology don't immediately bring about automatic changes in learning.

In this context, imagine the mechanic with all the latest diagnostic computers and tools, standing over an engine that had a will of its own. Now I'm sure many mechanics would swear they have had this experience, but let's try and count the numbers of cars that would be placed back in service if the mechanic had to first gain the cooperation of the car before any repair work could be accomplished. If that was the reality of the automotive world, how much longer would you be stuck in the waiting room, reading six-year-old drag racing magazines, until your car was fixed?

Using another example, consider yourself the manager of a factory. You have all of the latest manufacturing and assembly tools in your assembly line. You have highly trained workers, who have received the training equivalent of a four-year college degree, operating each piece of equipment. You have the best raw materials, the best specs, and a reputation for turning out the best product. Now, with all this at your disposal, as you start up the assembly line and begin to run the raw material through, your first job is to convince the raw material to exercise its will and choose to become the product your engineers have designed.

Imagine further, how production would be affected if the parents of this raw material were hostile to the idea or if they were simply unsupportive. What if the material simply didn't get the right nutrients that day or was gathered in from a bad environment? Let's say a small amount of the material got together and began to convince the rest of the raw material that they shouldn't go along with the flow or that it wasn't such a good idea to become what everyone else was becoming. How much product would this factory produce?

This is the reality that educators face as they try to answer the discipline question. It is not offered as an excuse; it merely paints an accurate picture of the realities that are in place. Many critics of the educational process believe that schools should be run like factories, and they cannot understand why there are any real disciplinary issues. At a national educational conference, I locked horns with one such individual. As we were discussing a particularly sensitive issue about discipline, her response to the problem was, "I don't get it. Why don't you just tell them the way it is and be done with it?" This individual really believed that all that was needed was a proper procedure and instructional methodology, and then everything would begin to correct itself.

Classroom discipline problems grow out of many different sets of conditions. Some of them are within our control; others are not. Let's begin with those that are. Discipline begins with each individual teacher and his or her own preferences. What poses an extreme disciplinary threat to one teacher may not even be a concern to another. Each teacher has a different threshold for noise, talking out of turn, tardiness, back talk, joking around, foul language, late work, or any other student behavior that might be considered out of bounds. Some teachers are very tolerant of individual learning preferences and build alternative options into their assignments, while others expect students to conform to their rigid set of requirements and behavioral expectations. Some teachers find it difficult to confront negative behavior, while others can very easily face difficult disciplinary situations.

All teachers are different, so the approaches they take in dealing with disciplinary issues will naturally reflect these differences. This does not mean that districtwide policies should be set aside on a teacher-by-teacher basis, but it means that there should be flexibility in the policies to allow each teacher to meet the guidelines in their own particular way. Students can adjust easily to the different behavioral requirements of each of their teachers, just as they adjust to the differences they have encountered in their own homes or elsewhere. The real key is that each teacher develops an approach that is comfortable and still creates the proper classroom environment that is safe and secure for optimum student learning.

By stating this, I realize that I am also saying that there is not one kind of learning environment that is best. Though that is a true statement, every successful learning environment that is able to foster self-discipline and personal growth is built on the same overriding principles. These principles are mutual respect, individual integrity, security, high expectations, variety, participation, hard work, shared values, freedom to fail, and success.

It must be pointed out that these principles are not a given in most educational settings. They have to be fostered and developed through the careful investment of time and energy. Students respond quickly when they are convinced that these principles are at work in their classroom, but they will not normally respond as you might like until they have seen extensive evidence of their existence. Patience is essential for any teacher hoping to establish an environment that is highly conducive to learning at all levels. To describe this environment more fully, let's look more closely at each of these guiding principles to make sure that we are talking about the same thing.

Mutual Respect

Mutual respect refers to a willingness on the part of the teacher and the students to respect each other's needs. It requires a unique give-and-take that allows individuals to give up some of their particular needs for the good of the whole. It is a blending of minds and hearts that serves to enrich each person in return. It grows out of a dialogic teaching approach, which holds that the class as a whole, the teacher included, has all the knowledge or resources necessary to learn anything there is to learn. In this setting, teachers see themselves as facilitators of learning, rather than as bastions of accumulated knowledge.

Individual Integrity

Individual integrity means that students within the learning environment are willing to accept responsibility for learning. For this principle to exist, learners must be willing to do their fair share of the actual work of learning. They grow to accept the fact that truth and honesty are the guiding factors in all personal growth. Students who live by this principle will come to know there are no real shortcuts to learning, skill, and knowledge acquisition. This can be summed up by stating that individual integrity in learning requires students to be willing to face the truth about their own situation in life and the amount of effort they are putting into the learning process.

Security

Security is the feeling that students must have in their learning environment to allow them to try new things and venture into areas of new discovery. It is a direct result of being able to trust a teacher and other class members to allow them to try something new without the fear of ridicule if they fail. It is a feeling of peace and serenity that is experienced only when students feel a part of a team of learners who are committed to the expansion of collective and personal knowledge.

High Expectations

High expectations means that the best learning environment exists where much is required of the learner. Students who truthfully understand their potential can be more easily motivated to push themselves beyond what they previously thought was possible. These elevated expectations must be realistic and coupled with a realistic developmental plan. When these conditions exist, students stand on the verge of making incredible progress.

Variety

Variety simply refers to the need for teachers to constantly infuse change into the learning process to help keep students engaged and excited. This is not just change for the sake of change. It is the creative infusion that helps individuals gain new outlooks and perspectives. It fosters wonder, intrigue, and divergent thinking. In fact, variety does much to alleviate boredom and apathy in the classroom. The change that is fostered by variety, in and of itself, can often engender renewed energy and fire in any learning environment.

Participation

Learning without participation is a recipe for behavioral problems. It is akin to creating an atmosphere where spontaneous combustion is most likely to occur, and then acting surprised when it happens. Idle time is the most poorly spent because it has no perceived value. It can therefore be easily wasted. However, when students feel invested in their own learning as active participants, they often become too busy to cause problems. It is more rare for students to knowingly become involved in behavior that will sabotage something they really value than it is for their behavior to thwart the acquisition of something they do not see as important. Only personal participation creates personal attachment, which engages personal values into the learning process.

Hard Work

Hard work is the natural result of learning that is driven by the values of a student or a group of students. It occurs not out of teacher compulsion but as a natural extension of the students' search for understanding and subject mastery. Learning is achieved only through hard work. When students learn this principle and simultaneously discover the joy that comes from this invigorating expenditure of energy, they move to a higher level of motivation and drive. They learn the real thrill that comes from the learning process. It becomes an internal process driven by their intrinsic locus of control, and not one driven by the extrinsic demands of a teacher.

Shared Values

When a class of students begins to participate in a learning process they deem to be important, they naturally begin to gain a shared set of values. The synergism created in this environment can create the energy needed to foster learning far above what is required. Classes of students who share a deep value for the subject matter will do much in the way of self-policing to maintain the proper atmosphere that will support joint growth and development.

FREEDOM TO FAIL

Students who feel this excitement for learning need to be encouraged to step onto this unfamiliar ground. As they do, they increase their personal risk and highly accelerate their chance of failure. It is at this point of highest risk of failure that the greatest amount of real progress is achieved; therefore, as teachers we must defend this ground at all costs. Remember, the classroom is an artificial environment and we are the ones who ultimately control it. If it is designed to foster risk, it must give students the right and freedom to fail. I would even go so far as to say that it must encourage failure and view it as a positive precursor to personal growth. After all, what human endeavor worth anything has not grown out of people's willingness to repeatedly fail until they find success?

If this is not the attitude that underscores our students' efforts, their failure will be too costly, and any forward progression will cease at the slightest setback. Our students will suspend their activity and even begin to shut down their learning efforts entirely. Worse than that, in discouragement they will often revert with a vengeance to their previous behavioral patterns.

Too often, this is the condition observed in most dramatic learners. They have tried the best they can to move forward in an educational world that is foreign to them in every way. In this atmosphere, even their best efforts have been met with failure and disappointment. Is it any wonder they have become overwhelmed and discouraged in the process?

SUCCESS

The final principle is success. When learners feel the work they are doing is rewarding, the positive return far outstrips any reward they may have gotten in the past through their misbehavior. This principle directly ties discipline to the acquisition of positive self-image. When people feel good about themselves and the relationships they have with others, they will usually exhibit a high degree of positive self-discipline. Simply put, a student experiencing educational success is less apt to do negative things. In behavioral terms, we might say that everyone does what he or she does to achieve a reward. When we can make the reward for doing positive things greater than the reward for misbehavior, we have learned how to cut off negative behavior at its source.

This results from being able to work from a success base and not from a symptom base. The treatment of symptoms never leads to permanent success because a symptom rarely reveals the full nature or extent of an existing problem. When we treat only the symptom, we are engaged in a quick-fix approach that is not adequate or lasting. In the end, the deep problems are ignored and begin to fester worse under this salve of expediency. We become more successful when we deal with a problem at its source. This success will breed future successes and create an expectation of enhanced value to each individual learner. A group of students who are experiencing deep educational success rarely pose disciplinary problems. When they do, it is a result of their exuberance and anxiousness to participate. This is an enviable problem to have in a classroom.

Recently, I was observing a class in the final days of a writing unit. To the chagrin of the teacher, the class members expressed an incredible enthusiasm to have their work read. They were so excited to share their work with the rest of the class that they almost caused a riot as they clamored to go first. The teacher quickly came up with a fair method of determining a reading order, and the lesson proceeded without incident.

At the end of class time, the teacher apologized to me for the outburst of his class. He was highly embarrassed by his students' behavior, and he assured me they were normally much better behaved. In response to his concerns, I asked him to tell me what he had done to create such an overwhelming desire in his class members to read their work. I told him how commendable it was and that I had rarely seen this kind of excitement in a writing class. Relieved that I wasn't being critical of their behavior or his skill as a teacher, he explained with great personal excitement the process he had used to get his class to this point.

Interesting enough, his approach to teaching writing had encompassed each of the principles we have just discussed. He explained how he had worked hard to create a learning atmosphere that was highly respectful and safe. He explained his efforts to get them to invest and really push themselves to increase their skills as writers. He told of how he had put them in groups where students were required, through various writing activities, to push each other to excel. He articulated how they learned to deal with failure and disappointment. In the end, he talked about how rewarding the journey had been for him as a teacher and for his students.

I assured him that I preferred this outburst to the normal teeth-pulling exercise that typically precedes the sharing of student work. What he mistakenly feared I would see as a disciplinary problem, I recognized as a group of students filled with a desire to share work that they had grown to value. With this class, he had accomplished what many teachers would pay dearly to achieve. His work in this classroom is the best evidence I can offer to demonstrate what good classroom discipline is all about.

Discipline is a hard subject to broach because every situation we face is filled with so many variables. Therefore, as I have stated earlier, I prefer to approach this subject from a principle base. The principles we have just discussed are the ones I have observed in every successful classroom environment. This does not mean that each teacher who has created this kind of environment has gotten there by following the same path. It does mean that in all successful learning environments, these principles are actively at work.

In an attempt to take this discussion out of the theoretical field and move it to the practical world, I will share the thought process and practices I find useful when trying to create a healthy learning environment out of a negative one. These are suggestions that have worked for me and fit well into my teaching style. I am not suggesting they are the only way to proceed. I offer them as evidence of principle-based practice.

The first thing I do is try to be as honest with myself as possible. I have strengths and weakness when it comes to disciplinary issues. There are certain behavioral issues that are absolutely important to me as a teacher. When these conditions are not being met, I cannot function as well as I need to in my responsibility as the director of learning in my class.

Over the years, I have tried to reduce these behavioral issues to an achievable few. The more issues I create, the more time I have to spend defending them and the less time I have for the more important issues. For me, these are the important issues:

1. Everyone must treat everyone else with respect.
2. Everyone must participate.
3. One person talks at a time.
4. Knowledge acquisition may be demonstrated in many different ways.

These issues are the guiding principles behind my approach to discipline. They may not be enough for you, but that's okay. You must honestly determine what you need to be comfortable. You are, after all, ultimately responsible for setting the parameters of the learning environment inside your classroom.

Several years ago, I was asked to take over the religious instruction of a group of 11-, 12-, and 13-year-olds who had managed to run off their last four instructors. Before entering the classroom, I did a little research on their behavior and felt I understood the root of their rebellion. On my first day, I entered the class, purposefully late, and found them all sitting in a circle around the outside of the room with their chairs tipped back against the wall. Making it obvious that I noticed the way they were seated, I too took my place in the classroom by tipping my chair up against the wall. From this shared position I began to build a learning environment in which we could all be comfortable.

I had learned that the previous teachers had spent most of their instruction time trying to get the kids to sit properly in their chairs. The kids easily won the 12-to-1 battle that ensued and tied their teachers in knots by teetering back and forth on their chairs. What real difference did their sitting position make? Did the battle over chair position increase their learning potential, or did it become the issue on which the process broke down? Sometimes you have to be willing to lose a battle or two to ultimately win the war. Remember, teaching is at the core of real discipline; therefore, build your learning environment so that you are comfortable in it, but also make enough room for others to be comfortable there as well. If your world is too restrictive, it will not allow others to enter with ease and find the peace and accord they need to really belong.

My experience is that learning preferences have a great deal of bearing on a person's outlook or take on discipline. This shouldn't be too surprising when we consider the natural link between learning and discipline. As each learner has definite preferences when it comes to learning styles, the same is true when it comes to preferences in disciplinary measures. Failure to understand these preferences can be disastrous, especially when you are dealing with a dramatic learner. There are three simple overarching principles for working with these learners that should be given special consideration: Negotiate; use humor; and make them part of the solution.

NEGOTIATE

I have read many texts and articles on discipline that say never negotiate with the person who is being disciplined. Many reasons are given for this position, but most of them stem from the belief that negative actions should create their own natural or logical consequences. Our job, as disciplinarians, should be to ensure that guilty individuals face those consequences. There is sound logic in that position, but when dealing with dramatic learners in a disciplinary situation, if you do not allow them to negotiate, you move immediately out of the realm of discipline, in their minds, and into the strict world of punishment. Whoever gave this advice must never have worked with dramatic learners.

In my years of teaching and observing, there is no principle or practice of discipline that I believe in as strongly as the need to negotiate when dealing with dramatic learners. Its application almost universally produces positive results. For example, a young sixth grader once decided to rollerblade through the halls of the school. He was observed in the act and called down to the principal's office to face the music. Rather than yelling or belittling the young man for his action, the principal took him down the hall and allowed him to observe the custodian cleaning up a mess that students had caused in another area of the school.

While the young man watched the unnecessary work, the principal briefly talked about how much of the custodian's day is spent doing work that wouldn't be necessary if other people just thought about the consequences of their actions. The young man was then taken to the hallway where he had been skating. The principal asked him if he could see any evidence of his crime. There were obvious marks from the wheels and other noticeable reminders. The principal then asked a simple question: "How long do you think it will take to fix this mess?"

As they walked back to the office together, the young man was given two different consequences to face. He was then given the freedom to choose whichever one he desired. One was for him to lose recess privileges and to stay after school in detention for several days. The other was to spend time assisting the custodian in his job. The young man immediately chose to work with the custodian, even though it meant he would actually spend more time and do more work than if he had chosen the other option. The result of this wise disciplinary action reached well beyond the event itself. This young man went on to use his influence to help other kids in the school think more about their actions. His quiet but constant efforts led to the reduction of many hours of needless work by the custodial staff. His ability to negotiate, in his mind, and have some say in the process made him an ally rather than a foe. This principal had taught this young man an important lesson as he attempted to alter his behavior.

This is one simple example, but it clearly illustrates the principle of negotiation. Notice that the negotiation I am referring to is not a call to allow offending individuals to get out of anything. It is a tack that allows them to play a significant role in developing the solution. This is but one of the important principles to understand and employ when you are attempting to discipline a dramatic learner. As I list and examine other important elements, remember that I am not promising that they will all work exactly as I describe or reference. I am, however, promising that if you use these principles with dramatic learners, you will greatly increase your likelihood of success.

HUMOR

Dramatic learners respond well to humor and wit, especially when they are being disciplined. To them, humor is deeply valued. When it is used as sugar to make the medicine of discipline go down easier, they often respond more positively. This humor cannot be sarcasm, however; it must be sincere. I watched another principal catch several dramatic learners cutting class. The first words out of his mouth were, "Busted . . . busted, oh yeah." Then he started to laugh. He wasn't angry or preachy or even excited to catch them. He simply responded with humor, saying, "Walk this way to my office," in his best Groucho Marx impersonation. They all fell in line like a flock of ducklings as they headed toward his office.

They knew they were busted, and they knew they would have to face the consequences for their actions, but his response reduced the confrontation and created a common ground from which the process of discipline could begin. His use of humor didn't lessen his resolve to deal with the problem; it engaged the students. The more I watch humor used in the disciplinary process, the more I realize that it creates space and time to think and act without having to deal with a problem from a position of anger. It is like counting to 10, but it scores you points with this population. It makes you accessible and human in their eyes.

The use of humor can assist you in putting forth a front of being calm, cool, and collected during the disciplinary process. Having control of your emotions is also highly valued by these learners, even though many of them haven't learned that skill themselves. It gives you power as you work with them, rather than causing them to lose respect for you because you lose control of your emotions. They expect you to act above the fray, even though they will do everything in their power to push your buttons. The key to emotional control is doing things that buy you time to think while at the same time you draw the student into the solution. Humor is the most powerful tool I know for doing this.

Make Them Part of the Solution

The principal I have just mentioned began the disciplinary process in his office with the question, "What am I going to do with you?" He didn't start by passing out detention slips and other consequences; he sincerely asked them to help him solve the problem they had caused. At first, they thought he was kidding, but soon they learned that they were going to have to become part of the solution. Some tried to see if this approach was a sign of weakness, but they soon learned they were mistaken. In a logical and respectful way, this administrator listened to and recognized their perspectives as he kept the focus of their discussion on their specific behavioral problem. He did not stray from the discipline policies of the school, and still he found the latitude to provide them with alternative consequences that were meaningful and appropriate.

Each young man left his office on a positive note. They knew exactly what had happened, but it was done in a way that gained their respect and cooperation. They knew they had broken the rules—that wasn't even the question. Dramatic learners usually know exactly what they are doing. They are willing to gamble with rules because they know they will get away with things more often than they'll get caught. When caught, they are willing to face the consequences if they are dealt with in an acceptable fashion. They take risks for the reward they'll get if they aren't caught. Sometimes they risk just for the thrill of breaking a stupid rule. They are driven by these kinds of rewards. This kind of behavioral motivation is foreign to many teachers and administrators. More often than not, these students' behavior can be altered if they are offered an alternative reward they value more than the reward for breaking the rules. Remember, if it is more rewarding for them to do what you want them to do than it is for them to do what they want to do, you will be successful in altering their behavior.

I may be letting the cat out of the bag here, but this is why coaches, shop teachers, drama teachers, art teachers, music teachers, and any other gatekeepers of exciting extracurricular programs seem to have magical control over these "problem kids." The real secret is that these teachers control the activities that these kids really value. This is what really gives these teachers the control that others envy. They can and do use the students' natural value to participate in these activities as a tool to help control their unwanted behavior. This is the same idea that has spawned the no-pass, no-play rules that govern most extracurricular activity participation. The only downside of this motivation is that it is extrinsic. If the students only conform for the sake of the activity, once the threat of not being able to participate in the activity is taken away, they will usually revert to their normal behavioral or educational patterns.

Discipline Don'ts

There are several very important discipline don'ts that I need to mention when working with dramatic learners. These don'ts may work for other learners, but they are guaranteed to fail with this population. I will not list them in any particular order as far as importance is concerned, but I highly advise you to spend some time evaluating these items in light of your present disciplinary practices. You might find you will gain better results from refraining from doing these don't s than you will by adopting the do's that have already been discussed.

Don't escalate the tension level. If you try to increase the emotional pressure or intensity of the situation on dramatic learners to get them to change their behavior, you will usually end up creating an ever-increasing struggle that they will become more and more determined to win.

Don't try to compete with them. This is closely related to the previous item because the result of this competition will resemble what happens if you try to increase the tension. They will aptly accept the challenge and continually escalate the situation until you give up. Their natural competitive nature will take over, and you will often find out the hard way that they have the endurance to outlast your best efforts to beat them at their own game.

Don't get on their bad side. They can become a very formidable enemy, and we have enough of those without purposefully creating new ones. (This is one of the problems that the use of humor helps to avoid.)

Don't try to solve their problems. If you try, they may seem grateful, but actually, they will ultimately claim no ownership or responsibility for your solution. If it is not their solution, they will not follow through with it, and you will become increasingly frustrated trying to get them to follow your plan rather than helping them actually change their behavior.

Don't criticize them for being dramatic learners. If you do, they will turn it back on you and explain all their shortcomings as inherited traits they cannot overcome. They will learn quickly to play any game that you introduce better than you can play it. They also seem to find a way to turn your own words and rules against you.

Don't use physical force. It will only build resentment and create a potentially explosive situation. For some dramatic learners, physical force is seen as a personal affront. To others, it is a quick and easy price to pay for their "crime." It is often the consequence of choice because of the fact that it is over quickly and allows them to get back sooner to what they really want to be doing. Remember, they possess great physical endurance, and it might be true that it hurts you more than it hurts them.

Don't be afraid to do something unusual. The unexpected approach will often work best with this population because it catches them off guard.

Don't expect blind obedience. They will not do something simply because it's the way that it has always been and is supposed to be done. Remember, they often believe that rules are something meant for other people to follow, and respect is something they only have to give to those who have earned it. It is not something given out of deference to age or position.

Don't be vague. If you beat around the bush and don't get to the point, you will lose respect in their eyes. Meet them straight up, tell it like it is, and avoid long protracted lectures.

Don't use guilt. Guilt doesn't motivate dramatic learners. They usually view guilt trips as a weak and emotional attempt to manipulate them into doing what you want. They are present-oriented individuals, and guilt trips attempt to take people back in time. If you haven't noticed this already, the use of guilt with this population usually causes them to shrug their shoulders and give you a look that says, "So what?"

For the sake of comparison, I list the discipline do's and don'ts for those learners who are more comfortable with mainstream educational practices. In most cases, it will be easy to note that the principles which work for this group are completely opposite to those that work with dramatic learners.

As you compare these lists, see how many of these do's and don'ts you are using in your failed attempts to discipline dramatic learners.

DISCIPLINE DO'S FOR MORE TRADITIONAL LEARNERS

- Make sure you clearly state the problem so that they fully understand what they did wrong.
- Ask them to tell you what behavior would have been more appropriate in the given situation.
- Formulate a plan for them to follow that allows them to make restitution for what they did wrong.
- Ask them to commit to follow the plan.
- Allow them to do makeup work to compensate for what they lost by their misbehavior. (This will sometimes be an effective approach to take with dramatic learners.)
- Continually reinforce their strengths to make sure they don't believe that their mistakes make them bad students.
- Be professional in showing respect for them and the situation.
- Show concern for them personally and for their feelings.
- Listen compassionately to their side of the issue, and be careful not to make them think you have cut short their attempt to explain themselves.
- Continue to appreciate their positive qualities.
- Focus your disciplinary efforts only on the behavior at hand.
- Show empathy and understanding for their situation.
- Make sure they clearly understand the impact their negative behavior has had on other people.
- Use their natural feelings of guilt at doing something wrong to motivate them to change their behavior.

Discipline Don'ts for More Traditional Learners

- Don't discipline in anger where you appear to be mean or vindictive.
- Don't be so businesslike that you are short with them.
- Don't use derogatory words.
- Don't raise your voice or yell.
- Don't appear cold or impersonal.
- Don't make it a personal issue.
- Don't get carried away emotionally.
- Don't bring up their past behaviors.
- Don't be unfair or extreme in the consequences you prescribe.
- Don't ignore their normally good behavior.
- Don't be inconsistent with them. Make everything you do seem fair.

One final note before I leave this topic. I have found that it is best for all learners, regardless of their style, to be disciplined in private. Reexamining the first example I gave of the young rollerblader and the principal, you see that he took the time to deal with this child alone and away from others. There was no grandstanding or posturing. Everything said and done was for the benefit of the student alone. In the privacy of that action, there is an unspoken message of personal interest that is powerfully sent.

Having said that, much of what we have to deal with in the classroom requires immediate attention and cannot be done in private. Those public moments handled in anger or haste will create new problems that typically outweigh any present concerns. It is therefore necessary to follow up any public discipline with private time, clarification, and reinforcement. Private time can also be created within the typical classroom setting by assigning individual or group projects. When you are not lecturing and the class members are engaged in their project work, it is very easy to privately approach a student and quietly address a behavioral problem. Private discipline is more respectful, and it keeps the student from having to continue to escalate the misbehavior to save face in front of his or her peers.

To conclude this discussion on discipline, I will cover a few private principles that work for me when I need to help students learn to alter their behavior. They are so basic that I hesitate to mention them, but I am always surprised how well they work when I suggest them to others. I apologize ahead of time for their pedestrian nature. I find, however, that when it comes to behavioral issues, the simpler approach is usually more effective.

George's Axioms on Discipline

Fun Trumps the Need to Discipline

(This is a restatement for emphasis.) When students have fun and are engaged in the learning process, they are involved in positive educational behavior. They are on task and doing the work of learning. In this mind-set, students will do almost anything to sustain the thrill of learning. When they are not having fun, they will do almost anything to get out of it.

Say What You Mean

Never say something you are not willing to do. For example, if you say, "I'm not going to talk until you're quiet," make sure you don't. When you say, "The next person to get out of their seat will have to stay after class," make sure they do. If you say you will and then you don't, you are only undermining the power of your word. In time, you will lose all credibility. Having said that, there will always be times when you can't follow through with what you say. In those rare cases, make sure you let the class know you realize that you are backing down, and explain to them candidly why you've decided to change your mind.

Keep Them off Guard

Constantly do things students don't expect in your discipline practices. For example, if you use an assertive-discipline model, instead of writing the names of the students on the board who are misbehaving, change things around. Without saying anything, start putting up the names of students who are doing good things. When they complain that they haven't done anything wrong and that their name is on the board unjustly, tell them that you placed their name on the board because of something good they did. Ask the members of the class if they are able to identify the behavior that warranted the special recognition. Every time anything else happens that's good, write that person's name on the board and see if the class members can identify the reason. You'll be surprised how big a difference this simple reversal of the normal practice will make in your classroom.

Another example of a simple variation is to notice a student's particularly exceptional behavior and then ask him to stay after class. This will make the student wonder throughout the rest of the class period what it was that he did wrong. When he meets with you, tell him what you observed and thank him for his willingness to participate and add so much to the class. In the same light, start calling home and talking to the parent(s) or guardian(s) of students who are really working hard or behaving well. You can also try a real zinger that works wonders. Give a note to a student who has done something really well in your class and tell her to take it home and give it to her parents. Don't tell her what it is or why you're giving it to her. It will have a remarkable impact.

In each of these examples, we are just taking a normally negative practice and turning it around so we begin to reward positive behavior rather than negative behavior. Again, the difference between discipline and punishment is that punishment tells someone what not to do, while discipline teaches someone how to behave properly. How many other common discipline techniques can you alter with similar results? Remember, the goal is to keep them off guard.

Discipline by Proximity

The more physically removed students are from a teacher, the more likely they are to misbehave. For this reason, dramatic learners often like to sit in the rear of the room. To circumvent this practice, I like to treat my classroom as my own territory. In it, there is no place that I cannot be, and there is no classroom arrangement that cannot be used. In the same regard, I work hard to establish that there is no place the students can identify as my dominant teaching area. In one lesson, I may stand at the front, sit in the back, walk up and down the aisles, ask someone to trade seats with me while he or she take notes at the board, look out the window, or stand on my head. I do this so the students will see that it is a normal part of my teaching practice to be anywhere and everywhere in the classroom at the same time.

This is not because I'm nervous, but so I can put myself wherever I need to be the classroom without the students trying to interpret, "why is he there?" This practice gives me the latitude to move over and stand by a couple of talkative students without them feeling I am only there because they are talking. Rarely when I position myself between talkers do they continue on with their conversation. My sleepy students find it very hard to drop off when I am constantly brushing by them or giving instructions while standing next to their desks.

If I give myself permission to be anywhere in the room at any time, I also give myself permission to change the physical structure of the classroom to suit the needs of any given lesson. When this happens, students get used to sitting in different places and working with different students in nontraditional classroom setups. I find that a very simple and effective hook for any lesson is accomplished by just changing the arrangement of the desks and chairs in the room. By controlling the distance between the students and myself, I can constantly alter the classroom environment in a way that gives me ultimate freedom and access to the students as I deem necessary to properly deal with their behavior.

Because I establish a precedent that it's okay for me to be anywhere in the room, I can move close to a student and help her work quietly on an individual assignment, I can get in the middle of a group project and ask questions to help them move forward, I can sit back and observe, or do anything else I need to do to ensure the success of an activity.

Proximity allows me to add or subtract pressure on the learners. It gives me power to eavesdrop and peek over shoulders so I can make accurate assessments of the understanding and grasp a student has on the present project or assignment. It gives me complete freedom to mentor and coach, rather than to just lecture. Even simpler than any of the reasons I've previously given, it's just different enough to keep the students off guard and create a sense of variety in the classroom.

Proximity also increases teacher access. It makes me more available to my students. Often the student who is afraid to ask a question in front of the whole class will be willing to stop me when I am standing near him and ask for assistance. It gives me a great opportunity to make one-on-one contact with each student, in each class, each day. I also use proximity as a means to put myself at eye level with each student and to strike the posture of a coach and mentor rather than that of a lecturer. In this more respectful posture, some students will willingly open up when otherwise they might remain aloof. I find that it sends a message of personal care and concern for each learner. It gives me the space and time to draw as near to them emotionally as I do physically.

As in anything, propriety is important when it comes to proximity. You don't want to get so close that you make yourself or your students uncomfortable. You don't want to move around the room at a rate that makes your students dizzy or that keeps you from having to participate in other forms of exercise. When used correctly, proximity is an excellent nonconfrontational way to alter behavior.

Make Your Discipline Transparent

Transparent discipline is discipline that can be identified only by the one doing the discipline. It takes many forms in the way of practice, but its guiding principle is to alter behavior without being intrusive. Discipline by proximity is one of its simplest forms. If I can change students' behavior by just moving to another place in the room, I have accomplished my objective without them even becoming overtly aware of what I have done. This is what makes it transparent. Some other examples are ignoring a negative behavior, praising a positive one, changing the stimulus when students are acting out by focusing their attention on something interesting, or using humor to deal with an activity that is not acceptable. The goal again is to alter behavior without bringing attention to the fact that that is what you are doing. It is the art of being subtle when dealing with unwanted behavior.

A kindergarten teacher I'm familiar with uses the best example of this practice that I have ever seen. Whenever there is an altercation between two students, it is arbitrated by a small sock puppet. The children have learned to bring their grievances before a small school mouse worn on the hand of the teacher. Sometimes when she sees a problem brewing, she puts on the puppet and comes and sits next to the children who are having the problem. She begins the whole process by asking a simple question in the squeaky voice of her puppet: "What seems to be the trouble here?" The students often request that the mouse mediate their problems. However the mediation is initiated, it is very interesting to watch the children plead their cases before this mouse, as if it were a real person. They even forget that the teacher is the one actually operating the puppet and helping settle the disagreement. Though she is ultimately controlling the outcome of the situation and providing discipline for her students, her efforts are transparent to them.

In a high school setting, one teacher has established a model where all disciplinary issues are handled through a peer-review group. This approach is almost the same as the mouse tribunal, but it is more age-appropriate. The students are given the responsibility to manage their own behavior, and they are often much more strict with each other than the teacher would ever be. Because of the structure she has established, this teacher's effort to establish acceptable classroom and interpersonal behavior is completely transparent to the students. They truly believe they are the ones in charge, and they act more responsibly because of it.

These two examples demonstrate complete disciplinary structures that have been developed by teachers to help make their discipline transparent. Other teachers use transparent discipline simply by trying as often as possible to correct behavior without directly confronting it. Some of these more subtle efforts are used every day in the classroom. They include squelching a quarrel without a reprimand by finding another red crayon, stopping a side conversation by asking one of the offending parties to answer a question or work at the board, stopping a pending confrontation by apologizing for a lack of understanding, or easing students' fear of failure by accepting the offer of another student to come to their assistance. These cases may not seem to be disciplinary situations, but they are or could easily become so if not handled properly. A teacher who uses transparent discipline has learned to use a soft and gentle hand to carefully direct students back where they belong. It takes patience and a willingness to reach out to the offending parties in a way that helps them save face and gives them an easy way back.

Transparent discipline also means recognizing a problem before it escalates. Teachers who have the ability to survey the whole classroom while dealing with the needs of individuals have mastered an important aspect of transparent discipline. The respect that a student gains for a teacher who "has eyes in the back of her head" stops a lot of negative behavior before it even begins. This quality can be easily enhanced in teachers who simply learn to position themselves in the classroom where they can see everyone at the same time. This ability grows out of constant efforts to monitor the behavior of each student while effectively using proximity to reduce problems that might be brewing.

Use the Least Restrictive Alternatives

My last axiom cautions that teachers should use the least amount of intervention possible to effectively solve a problem.

This does not mean you allow undesirable behavior to take over your classroom, but it means that you use a series of progressively increasing alternatives until you find the one that alters the behavior. There is no need to use a sledgehammer to drive home a point if it can be done with a glance or a stare. I have observed many teachers who have resorted to yelling and name-calling as their first tactic for trying to alter an undesirable behavior. It was effective in changing the behavior in the short term, but the long-range effect on the culprit and the rest of the class was devastating.

I am not advocating that teachers should go through a litany of prescribed intervention before they actually get down to business. Instead, I find if I use a few transparent discipline techniques before I get more overt, I can often change the behavior before I have to confront it directly. In one class I was teaching, a student kept talking to his neighbor and I wanted it to stop. My first intervention was to use proximity and stand close to him. It worked, and I didn't have to do anything else. In another class, I attempted to deal with a similar situation in the same way. The first tactic didn't work; so I had to take my efforts to a different level because the student didn't get the hint when I tried to use proximity to stop the talking. I therefore put myself in a position where I could make direct eye contact with the individual. This didn't work either; so I had to use a more restrictive alternative. My third attempt was to sit down next to the student when the rest of the class was working on an individual assignment and ask her politely to refrain from talking during class. This third intervention proved successful. Certainly, I've had occasions when students have had to be asked to leave class, but they are very rare. In those cases, I felt confident that I had done all I could do before resorting to the most restrictive alternative.

As I mentioned at the beginning of this chapter, there is no magic formula for success in this difficult process. There is no quick-fix method. If, however, we approach discipline with the thought in mind that we are there to teach something, and if we demonstrate respect for the individual as we do, our efforts will become more successful and personally satisfying.

I believe this reality is the best we can hope for because we can only gain positive ground in this area by the willing participation of the misbehaving student. It is a journey of trial and error and of great frustration. It is one that can get easier as we become more proficient. We can never forget that each individual student has different needs and may respond to our best efforts in a way we never dreamed possible. For some students, our best efforts may simply not be good enough. The best we can realistically hope for is that we have given it our best shot. For this reason, principles rather than practice must drive our actions, and patience must be our watchword.

Conclusion

We must conclude this journey where we began. It is our shared dreams and aspirations to make a difference in the lives of our students that must drive us on. Ideally, you have been able to find a few morsels of my experience that will help you on your way. My message is very simple. We just need to be wiser than we have been in the past. If we can see our way to reduce the complexity of all learning theories and practices down to a few simple guiding principles, our noble dreams can gain wings. If we can band together as pilgrims headed to the same destination and truly recognize that our real strength is in our difference of opinion, then we will finally stand on the common ground from which we all can progress.

For many of us to come to this place, we must finally be willing to admit that the best and right way to educate all students varies depending on the individual needs of the learner. The acceptance of this fact is not an admission of weakness or shortcoming; it is the actual bonding agent that will hold us all together and propel our profession ahead into great new worlds of success. It will allow us to rediscover the true joy of learning and enable us to pass it on with more regularity to rising generations.

If we can find a common belief, our anatomy of learning, we can build on the past and move our whole field forward. The simple principles we must cling to are the same ones that have given the real fire to our dream. They are simultaneously tangible and elusive, but so are all things that edify the human soul. If we can remember that the awe of learning grows out of our natural desire for personal discovery, we will never lose our way.

The principles I have proposed are very simple. I repeat them here for the sake of clarity and summary.

1. Learning in the natural world, away from man-made structures, requires the active involvement of the learner. Therefore, nothing can be learned without the willing participation and effort of the learner.
2. Life without drama is meaningless and uninspiring. Therefore, learning that is not built on dramatic elements is also meaningless and uninspiring.
3. Learning must be value based. Therefore, when teaching takes into account the values and preferences of a learner, he or she will be motivated to participate.
4. Learning must be fun. Therefore, when the first three conditions exist, learning becomes the most rewarding, engaging, and fun activity in life.

Everything else I have written to this point means nothing without the context of these four simple principles. They are the North Star of my teaching practice. In the roughest of seas and on the blackest of nights, I know I can return to these principles to regain my bearings. I also know that when I stray from them I end up in uncharted and dangerous waters. I apologize if they seem too simple, but I am firm in my commitment to them.

In over 20 years of training teachers, I have seen the validity of these principles played out over and over again in the lives of learners of all ages. I find that they have universal application in all educational environments. It doesn't matter, therefore, if the learning is happening on the bedroom floor of a three-year-old child, beside a stream, in a formal classroom, behind prison walls, in a university lab, or in a corporate boardroom. Learning is learning.

I challenge you to examine these principles and ideas and see if they can bring greater success to your teaching efforts. I repeat my simple promise that you will be more successful if you learn to apply them than you have been without them. This has been my motivation for putting these things in writing. I wish you the best of luck in your efforts to reach the learning needs of all your students, but most especially your dramatic learners. I invite you to respond to me so we can continue down this road together.

Appendix

The following information has been compiled to assist readers who are not fully conversant with the ideas and methodologies that have been used over the years to understand human behavior in terms of personality or learning styles. From the earliest recorded history, theories have been postulated about why people behave and learn the way they do. The ancient Egyptians believed there were four different and distinct personality types, as did the ancient Greeks.

Hippocrates, the father of medicine, believed these four different temperaments or personalities were a result of an imbalance in the body's major organs. He believed that good emotional and physical health was achieved through a proper balance in the respective abilities of the heart, lungs, liver, and kidneys to produce bodily fluids or humors. He called his four different personality types after these humors: namely melancholic, choleric, phlegmatic, and sanguine. Several other ancient Greek physicians built on and expanded his original observations.

It is interesting to note that in modern times, a significant amount of the major work that has come forward on personality and learning styles is generally in harmony with the work of these ancient observers and physicians. The founding father of this modern research is Swiss psychologist Carl Jung. His foundational work in the area of psychological types and preferences has spawned the development of many different instruments and approaches designed to accurately measure the personality attributes that he identified. It is important to note that much of Jung's work was overshadowed by that of his contemporary, Sigmund Freud. Since the rush to adopt Freudian psychological positions has finally passed, many individuals, who once overlooked Jung's work, now find it remarkably sound. Jung's research provides strong evidence to support his main observation: that human behavior was not random. He identified opposite preferences within people, which helped to determine how they generally approach life and their daily decisions.

These opposite preferences are extroversion/introversion, sensing/intuition, and thinking/feeling. To Jung, each individual was born with a specific predisposition to these preferences. He observed the habitual exercise of individual choice consistent with these preferences, and he noted that these patterns of decisions could be used to help understand the fundamental differences in people better.

In the early 1940s, a mother-and-daughter team, Isabel Myers and Katharine Briggs, combined the recently translated works of Jung with their own findings and created an instrument called the Myers-Briggs Type Indicator (MBTI). Today it is one of the most widely used personality surveys. Their instrument expanded on the work of Jung and identified four opposite scales, rather than the three that he had identified.

These scales are extroversion and introversion, thinking and feeling, judging and perceiving, and sensing and intuition. Their original self-assessment survey contained 160 questions and was used to identify 16 different and distinct personality types. These personality types are designated by a four-letter code that corresponds with individuals' preferences as they relate to the four opposite scales mentioned above. The first letter of each of the scales is used to identify the strongest preference between the opposite elements: (E) for extroversion, (I) for introversion, (T) for thinking, (F) for feeling, (J) for judging, (P) for perceiving, (S) for sensing, and (N) for intuition (because the letter "I" was already used as the designator for introversion). A detailed discussion of what each of these designators means can be found in Chapter 3. The 16 different MBTI personality styles are identified as follows:

Myers-Briggs Type Indicators	
1. ISTJ	Meaning that the individual typically prefers introversion over extroversion, sensing over intuition, thinking over feeling, and judging over perceiving.
2. ISTP	Meaning that the individual typically prefers introversion over extroversion, sensing over intuition, thinking over feeling, and perceiving over judging.
3. ESTP	Meaning that the individual typically prefers extroversion over introversion, sensing over intuition, thinking over feeling, and perceiving over judging.
4. ESTJ	Meaning that the individual typically prefers extroversion over introversion, sensing over intuition, thinking over feeling, and judging over perceiving.
5. ISFJ	Meaning that the individual typically prefers introversion over extroversion, sensing over intuition, feeling over thinking, and judging over perceiving.
6. ISFP	Meaning that the individual typically prefers introversion over extroversion, sensing over intuition, feeling over thinking, and perceiving over judging.
7. ESFP	Meaning that the individual typically prefers extroversion over introversion, sensing over intuition, feeling over thinking, and perceiving over judging.
8. ESFJ	Meaning that the individual typically prefers extroversion over introversion, sensing over intuition, feeling over thinking, and judging over perceiving.
9. INFJ	Meaning that the individual typically prefers introversion over extroversion, intuition over sensing, feeling over thinking, and judging over perceiving.
10. INFP	Meaning that the individual typically prefers introversion over extroversion, intuition over sensing, feeling over thinking, and perceiving over judging.
11. ENFP	Meaning that the individual typically prefers extroversion over introversion, intuition over sensing, feeling over thinking, and perceiving over judging.

(Continued)

(Continued)

Myers-Briggs Type Indicators	
12. ENFJ	Meaning that the individual typically prefers extroversion over introversion, intuition over sensing, feeling over thinking, and judging over perceiving.
13. INTJ	Meaning that the individual typically prefers introversion over extroversion, intuition over sensing, thinking over feeling, and judging over perceiving.
14. INTP	Meaning that the individual typically prefers introversion over extroversion, intuition over sensing, thinking over feeling, and perceiving over judging.
15. ENTP	Meaning that the individual typically prefers extroversion over introversion, intuition over sensing, thinking over feeling, and perceiving over judging.
16. ENTJ	Meaning that the individual typically prefers extroversion over introversion, intuition over sensing, thinking over feeling, and judging over perceiving.

These designations for the different styles are very cumbersome and more clinical than user-friendly. In most cases, individuals who have taken the MBTI cannot remember how they scored. Even if they do, they have little collateral understanding of what the four letters represent. Typically, they do not have the ability to use the information in a way that enhances how they deal with their own life situations or their interactions with others. For this reason, several individuals have attempted to create instruments that followed the same principles in a way that is easier to use and which is more accessible to the general population. David Keirsey was one such individual. A behavioral psychologist, Keirsey simplified the MBTI process and developed the concept of personality temperaments. Each of his temperaments was originally identified by letters corresponding to the MBTI designations. It is interesting to note that in his research, Keirsey returned to four major temperaments that align rather well with those of the ancient Greeks. Keirsey's four temperaments are shown here:

Keirsey's Temperaments	
1. NF	Meaning that the individual typically uses intuition as his or her main information- or stimuli-gathering preference and uses feeling as the preferred method for processing information or other stimuli.
2. NT	Meaning that the individual typically uses intuition as his or her main information- or stimuli-gathering preference and uses thinking as the preferred method for processing information or other stimuli.
3. SJ	Meaning that the individual typically uses sensing as his or her main information- or stimuli-gathering preference and uses judging as the preferred method for processing information or other stimuli.
4. SP	Meaning that the individual typically uses sensing as his or her main information- or stimuli-gathering preference and uses perceiving as the preferred method for processing information or other stimuli.

From Keirsey's research, several instruments have been developed which use colors as the designators for the different temperaments. Clime International uses the colors Blue, Green, Gold, and Orange. Several other instruments use the same or different colors to identify the different styles. In the case of the Clime instrument, colors were chosen to delineate the preferences because (1) the color vernacular had already been established as common terminology in many educational circles, (2) colors have fewer negative connotations, as far as labels go, and (3) colors are more memorable than the four-letter MBTI codes.

The MBTI, the Keirsey Temperament Sorter, colors instruments, and other such instruments that are based on the Jungian foundation are all attempting to measure the same elements that relate to individual preference. The Clime International instrument is designed to go beyond personality preferences of the other instruments and use these same principles to measure individual preferences as they relate to learning.

Learning styles related to personality preferences have a deeper affinity to the values of individual learners, and therefore appear to be a more accurate measure. The next figure illustrates how these three approaches overlap with many of the most widely used Jungian-based instruments. This figure combines several of the identifiers used in the different instruments and approaches so that similarities are readily apparent.

Clime International	Blue	Gold	Green	Orange
Ancient Egyptians	Nun (Water)	Geb (Earth)	Shu (air)	Ra (Sun/ Fire)
Greeks Hippocrates	Melancholic	Choleric	Phlegmatic	Sanguine
Greeks Paracelsus	Nymph	Gnome	Sylph	Salamander
Jung	Feeler	Sensor	Thinker	Intuitor
Kretschmer	Hyperesthetic	Depressive	Anesthetic	Hypomanic
Fromm	Receptive	Hoarding	Marketing	Exploiting
Adickes	Dogmatic	Traditional	Agnostic	Innovative
Spranger	Religious	Economic	Theoretic	Artistic
MBTI	ENFJ, ENFP, INFJ, INFP	ESTJ, ESFJ, ISTJ, ISFJ	ENTJ, ENTP, INTJ, INTP	ESTP, ESFP, ISTP, ISFP
Merrill	Amiable	Driver	Analytical	Expressive
Keirsey	NF	SJ	NT	SP

Another added benefit of the colors approach used by Clime International is that it allows for more flexibility in the scoring of preferences. As with most human endeavors, it is highly unlikely that the majority of individuals will have preferences that are on the outer limits of available choices. It is more typical for individuals to have preferences that fall into a normal bell curve, rather than ones at the extreme ends of the spectrum.

As shown in the following figure, a young woman, for example, who prefers extroversion over introversion as her method of interaction is not likely to be so high in her preference that it precludes her from having the ability to function as an introvert:

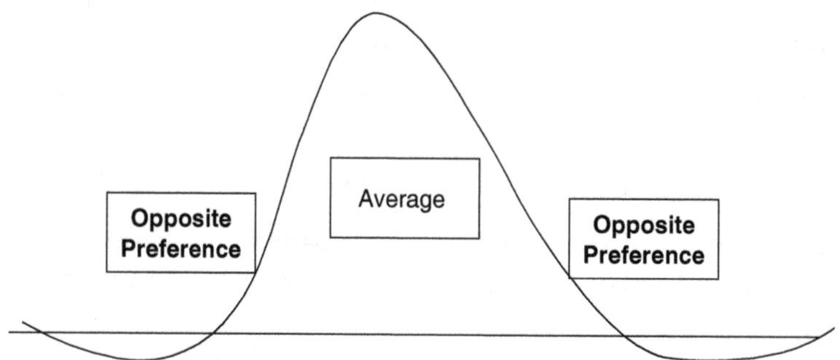

The same is true for all of the MBTI scales. In the Clime International instrument, there is room for individuals to have blended preferences. The following figure provides a more in-depth look at the color designators and how they relate directly with the 16 MBTI designators:

Traditional Left-Brain Learners		*Nontraditional Right-Brain Learners*	
GOLD (SJ)	GREEN (NT)	ORANGE (SP)	BLUE (NF)
ESTJ	ENTJ	ESTP	ENFJ
Extroverted Gold With Green	Extroverted Green With Gold	Extroverted Orange With Green	Extroverted Blue With Gold
"Supervisor"	"Field Marshal"	"Promoter"	"Teacher"

(Continued)

(Continued)

Traditional Left-Brain Learners		*Nontraditional Right-Brain Learners*	
ISTJ	INTJ	ISTP	INFJ
Introverted Gold With Green	Introverted Green With Gold	Introverted Orange With Green	Introverted Blue With Gold
"Inspector"	"Planner"	"Crafter"	"Prophet"
ESFJ	ENTP	ESFP	ENFP
Extroverted Gold With Blue	Extroverted Green With Orange	Extroverted Orange With Blue	Extroverted Blue With Orange
"Provider"	"Inventor"	"Performer"	"Revealer"
ISFJ	INTP	ISFP	INFP
Introverted Gold With Blue	Introverted Green With Orange	Introverted Orange With Blue	Introverted Blue With Orange
"Protector"	"Designer"	"Composer"	"Healer"

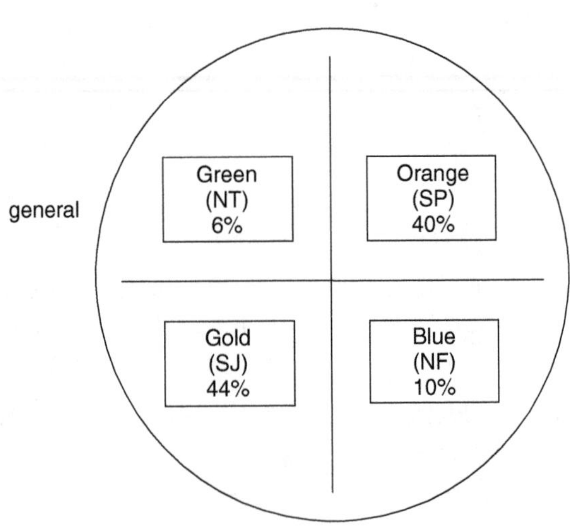

According to David Keirsey, as he describes in his book *Please Understand Me II*, the general population breaks down as follows:

These general population figures become very interesting when we compare them to the percentages of teachers in each preference. David Keirsey's numbers reveal that 52% of all teachers and administrators are Gold or SJ, 36% are Blue or NF, 4% are Orange or SP, and 8% are Green or NT. The numbers put out by the Center for Applications of Psychological Type (CAPT) in the *CAPT Atlas of Type Tables* are a little more conservative, but still reveal why dramatic learners (mostly Oranges and Greens) have such a hard time in school.

Percentages of Teachers by Color

Level	*Gold SJ*	*Blue NF*	*Green NT*	*Orange SP*
Preschool	41.0	35.0	12.0	12.0
Elementary	49.4	27.1	10.3	13.2
Middle/Jr. HS	44.7	28.9	15.2	11.2
High School	42.3	34.2	16.1	7.4
Adult	40.2	30.1	12.2	17.5
Jr. College	35.3	34.4	23.2	7.1
University	29.8	32.7	31.2	6.3
Average	40.4	31.8	17.2	10.7

When we further consider that younger students are often in a more Orange developmental phase, we can see how few teachers have the same learning style as dramatic learners. It should be obvious from these numbers that the Blue and Gold students are well represented by teachers, as far as the sharing of learning style is concerned. School is a good fit for these students because it is compatible with their social, structural, and personal values. The following figure illustrates how underrepresented dramatic learners are in the K–12 world of public education:

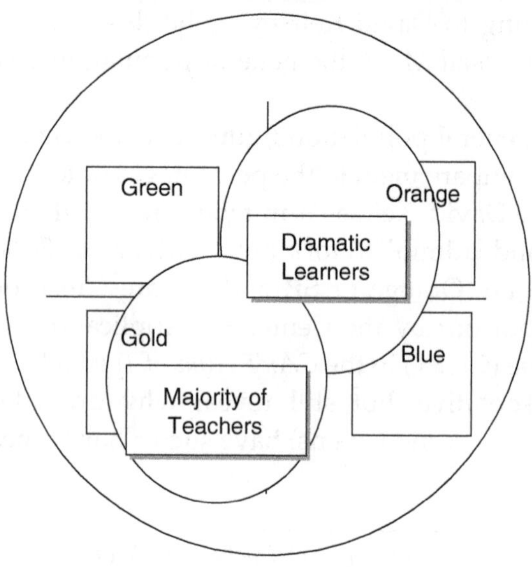

To bring all this information together so the learning needs of each individual can be better understood, I will outline the learning preferences of each style by color. For the sake of the proper context, it is important to remember that the majority of dramatic learners are Orange and Green or they have Orange or Green as a strong secondary preference. I will include a narrative description and an outline of the learning and the teaching preferences by color. As you read these, it will be helpful to compare and contrast the different styles. It is also very revealing to look at your own teaching preference and compare it with the learning preferences of the other styles. Gold and Orange are opposite styles, as are Blue and Green. Typically, teachers have the hardest time reaching students who have the opposite style as their first or second preference.

Blue Learning Styles

Feelings are at the core of Blue learning. If these students feel individual support from their teacher and their fellow students, there is no limit to what they can accomplish. Person-to-person interaction is an essential part of their style; without it, learning is not something they typically value. When they can learn new things while working, interacting, and communicating with others students, they will fully engage.

The best educational environment for Blue learners is one without conflict or an intense feeling of competition. Activities or assignments that allow them to collaborate and use their creative energy are highly favored. Blues typically like to please others, and they will go out of their way to help everyone fit in; therefore, harmony and peace in a classroom is very important to them. Often they will give up what they really want just to maintain a sense of harmony.

Blues need to be made to feel part of the educational process. It is essential that their feelings are validated as they learn. They respond well to a more democratic classroom approach. When they are made part of the team, they will expend considerable personal energy to help keep things running smoothly. They need to receive a lot of emotional support and feedback. Personal, one-on-one interaction with the teacher is repaid many times over. Writing complementary comments on their papers or using other personal touches that connect you to them are highly appreciated and noticed by Blue learners. Compliments are much better tools for correcting behavior than criticism. In fact a good ratio to use with a Blue student would be about five compliments to one criticism. That's five compliments to cushion the blow before and/or after the constructive criticism. They must believe that your criticism is given out of a genuine concern for their well-being.

Blues will usually do their schoolwork, if for no other reason than they don't want to disappoint their teacher. If, however, they are forced to choose between doing schoolwork and caring for the needs of a friend, the friend will usually come first. A good rule of thumb for understanding a Blue learner is that people and feelings come before any other considerations.

Blues are usually very well behaved students. They can often get off base if they are sitting near their friends in class.

This is because it is often more important for them to communicate with their peers than it is to listen to a lecture. If their feelings get hurt, however (and this can happen very easily), they can pull inside and shut themselves off from the very support they thrive on to feel good about themselves. They can usually be put back on track by having someone privately remind them that their behavior is hurting other people. Remember, their feelings and the feelings of others are their first consideration.

They typically enjoy subjects that are people-oriented, such as English, history, humanities, psychology, creative writing, languages, drama, art, dance, music, and other social sciences. Sadly, they tend to shy away from the solitary and analytical subjects like math or science. When they are able to see the value that these subject areas could have in helping them assist others, they can quickly make a connection to a subject area which otherwise would have little or no interest to them.

The opposite learning and teaching style of the Blue is the Green.

Keys for Teaching Blue Students

- Make sure they know you care about them personally.
- Focus on feeling, not just on facts.
- Create a pleasant and inviting learning environment.
- Create assignments that require students to use their creative abilities to complete.
- Reward them with small personal interactions such as notes, smiles, approving looks, and so forth.
- Teach principles, not facts.
- Create learning teams.
- Allow them to do open-book work.
- Assess their knowledge in creative ways.
- Be enthusiastic about the students and the subject matter.
- Be happy and upbeat.
- Smile and laugh a lot.

- Don't give "assignments," get them involved in "projects."
- Use their own values and interests to motivate their learning.
- Be whimsical and allow them to do the same.
- Show care for the individual learner.
- Create a harmonious classroom environment.
- Focus rules on helping each other excel.
- Focus class discussions on subjects at the feeling level as well as the intellectual level.
- Use multisensory and imaginative lessons.
- Use open discussions.
- Use cooperative learning techniques that avoid the creation of winners and losers.
- Make sure people come before any other consideration.

Gold Learning Styles

Structure and order are at the core of Gold learning. These learners need to have the confidence that they are learning in an environment that is well organized and planned out. Confusion, chaos, and disorder are very unsettling and frustrating to a Gold learner. The person-to-person interaction they need to have with their teacher is one that is professional and traditional. Normal teacher/student roles are expected and preferred in the classroom.

They are normally very obedient and respectful of teachers and administrators. Gold learners are traditionally hardworking and dedicated students who receive great personal satisfaction from doing their work well and on time. They fully appreciate detailed course outlines and syllabi and need firm direction and clearly defined details to feel completely comfortable with their coursework and assignments. Once they know precisely what is expected in an assignment, they will usually be diligent in getting their work done without a lot of outside coaxing or reminding. Often they will take detailed notes during class and remind the teacher of details or class requirements that might be skipped. In many ways, they are ideal students.

The learning process for a Gold learner needs to be straightforward and systematic. Because they are sensory in the way they gather information, they can become overly concerned with achieving perfection. This drive to excel scholastically will internally motivate them to work hard to get A's in their coursework, but sometimes, in the process, they miss the real purpose of learning along the way. Gold students are pleasers, especially when it comes to people in authority. They will do the right thing because they know it's the way things are supposed to be done. Their strong sense of loyalty and duty often earns them the negative label of teacher's pet. They love to take positions of leadership or service, and they strive to help the teacher maintain the proper order and structure they believe should exist in a classroom.

Gold learners are better assessed in more traditional paper-and-pencil tests. They prefer activities that are more fact and knowledge based, rather than ones that are more speculative or open to personal interpretation. They respond well to a more traditional teacher-centered classroom approach.

They need things to be fair and believe that students should pull their own weight. However, they appreciate opportunities for extra credit to help make up for any oversights which might occur. They are motivated by tangible educational rewards such as certificates, medals, trophies, good grades, honor rolls, and so on. They respond well to verbal praise and acknowledgment of their good efforts. The more tangible the feedback, the more clear it is for them. Their desire for these kinds of rewards can be used to keep them on task and help them put forth the effort necessary to grow and develop through most of their personal challenges and difficulties.

Gold learners will usually do their schoolwork because it is the right thing to do. Often they will be self-motivated to do their homework before they will do anything else. They are naturally motivated by duty and responsibility, and believe that work must come before play. A good rule of thumb for understanding a Gold learner is that real happiness is achieved by having everything in life in its proper order.

Gold learners typically enjoy traditional subjects, but they will work to succeed in classes they don't naturally enjoy, simply because it is required. There is no particular subject that they shy away from except those that are highly theoretical, subjectively assessed, and/or lack hard black-and-white answers. Courses that are touchy-feely and have no clear criterion for assessment tend to make them uncomfortable.

The opposite learning and teaching style of the Gold is the Orange.

Keys for Teaching Gold Students

- Make sure you treat them professionally and with respect.
- Focus on traditional approaches.
- Make sure all learning expectations are clearly explained and outlined.
- Reward them in tangible ways.
- Teach in a step-by-step fashion.
- Be highly organized and establish a predictable routine.
- Follow your own rules and make sure the class does as well.
- Be fair and just.
- Clearly explain what behavior is acceptable and expect them to do the right thing.
- Teachers must be professional.
- The classroom must be orderly and traditional.
- Class discussion must be kept on subject and not allowed to wander off in unrelated areas.
- Lessons and assignments need to be clearly focused, direct, and organized with specific goals, objectives, and modes of assessment.
- When assigning group projects, create clearly identifiable tasks and responsibilities.

- Help them see there is more than one right answer to many questions.
- Provide opportunities for makeup work.
- Be prompt in grading and provide specific feedback on their tests and assignments.
- Give them opportunities to take notes.
- Give them enough time to do an assignment well.
- Let them work in leadership or service positions.

Green Learning Styles

Green learners make up a large percentage of dramatic learners. The reason is that they have a natural desire to learn, but a nontraditional preference for how and what they want to learn. Thinking and analyzing are at the core of Green learning. If this style of learner believes his or her teacher is competent, then, and only then, can learning happen in the classroom. Green learners develop deep contempt for teachers they believe do not know more about a subject than do they.

They love to learn in impersonal and theoretical ways. Group projects are not highly motivating unless they are able to work with a group of like-minded individuals. They often like to learn in solitude, and they prefer to use the teacher as a resource. When motivated, they are the most independent and dedicated of all students in the acquisition of knowledge. When they are not, they can be the most challenging to deal with. They will engage in learning only when they are personally interested in it.

The best interactions with Green learners are often those that allow them to share something they have learned or that has increased their understanding in a particular area of interest. These learners are filled with endless why questions. Teachers who learn to channel and satisfy their real need to know why will gain the unique ability to reach them where it counts. This does not mean that teachers need to know all the answers; they just need to recognize that these learners are generally more inquisitive, and therefore need teachers who are competent in helping them find the answers they need.

Green learners, like their Gold counterparts, need sufficient time to complete tasks. Often, if they feel they are not given enough time to complete an assignment to their personal satisfaction, they will not do it at all. Activities or assignments need to be meaningful. Assignments need to help these individuals actually increase their knowledge in a subject area or help them demonstrate, in a meaningful way, what they already know. Anything that is perceived as busywork will be devalued by these learners.

Greens are more interested in pleasing themselves and expanding their own areas of knowledge and interest than they are in pleasing others. It is usually not important for them to feel like they fit in with the rest of the class. In fact, many relish the fact that they are different and do not follow the herd mentality of their conforming classmates. Often they will maintain a course of dialogue or action they believe to be the moral or intellectual high ground, even if it causes disharmony and disrupts the normal flow of the traditional learning process. They are usually not afraid of conflict or heated debates, as long as the discussion focuses on ideas and concepts and not feelings or emotions.

Greens feel a need to challenge established procedures and methodologies. This is not out of any dark desire to establish a state of anarchy in the classroom; they just believe there is always a better way to do something. You could say their motto is, "If it isn't broken, it still has room for improvement." They respond well to a more democratic classroom approach. Like their Blue and Orange peers, they like to take some ownership in the establishment of their learning environment. They have strong preferences when it comes to these issues. They do not need to receive a lot of personal emotional support, but they need real support for their ideas and their thinking skills. Teacher compliments must be truthful, sincere, and accurate or else these learners quickly lose respect for their teacher. Green learners are their own worst critics. They shine best when given creative opportunities to share with an appreciative audience the things they have learned.

Greens will usually do their schoolwork if they can see it will get them where they want to go, or if they are personally interested in doing it. They will not do it simply to please others or to keep harmony. Often, if they think a job is too simple for them, they will not do it at all. A good rule of thumb for understanding a Green learner is that learning is a joy in and of itself. They don't need the motivation of a grade to spur them. In fact, many turn their backs on grades as arbitrary indicators of gained knowledge. For this reason, it is useful to help them learn how to play the educational game for their own benefit and not for the benefit of others.

Introverted Greens are usually very well behaved students. Their quiet nature concerns their teachers and parents who don't understand introversion. Extroverted Greens can appear to be Orange unless you really know the difference. Their outward nature is what makes them look and act Orange, but inwardly they are motivated by the Green preferences that have been previously listed. Both the extrovert and the introvert can often get off base when they begin to go down a channel of personal interest. They are typically very good at beginning projects and research, but they are not as good at completing them. It is so easy for their vast natural interests to lead them from one topic of interest to another. Therefore, it is essential to help them learn to focus their energies and complete their tasks and assignments. Remember, their thinking and analytical skills are most important to them. When you respect them in those areas, you are opening the door to their souls.

Greens can enjoy and excel in any subject. Many are drawn to the science and math fields because these subjects readily reward their thought-based learning preferences and analytical nature. They often tend to gravitate to fields that allow for the exploration of new ideas and concepts and ones that they believe will not relegate them to the task of memorizing things that are only seen as black-and-white. When educationally motivated, they can be found in any field of pursuit or subject area that challenges their minds and expands their understanding.

The opposite learning and teaching style of the Green is the Blue.

Keys for Teaching Green Students

- Be competent as a teacher.
- Avoid approaches that are black-and-white or that seem to rely on feelings or baseless conjecture.
- Make learning as individual as possible.
- Create a stimulating and research-oriented classroom environment.
- Create assignments that are thought provoking, meaningful, and require students to use their analytical and creative abilities.
- Recognize them for their ability to think and work with new ideas.
- Teach theories, not just facts.
- Create meaningful, compatible research teams.
- Allow them to focus their learning in a field related to their own interest.
- Assess their knowledge in as many alternative ways as possible.
- Provide multiple and continuous access to learning resources.
- Serve as a learning resource to your students.
- Be willing to use quiz-type formats for teaching.
- Help them to understand the real-life whys of an assignment.
- Provide opportunities for them to assist others in learning what they know.
- Provide opportunities for them to develop alternative approaches and assessments.
- Put them in the role of a researcher or scientist.
- Be personally inquisitive, and reward their inquisitive nature.
- Let them experiment.
- Rules must be flexible and reasonable.

- Class discussion must focus on facts, theories, and proper analysis of data, information, and knowledge.
- Lessons need to engage the mind of the learner.
- Students need to be free to follow their own educational agenda, as far as academically possible.
- Cooperative learning is best when like-minded people are allowed to work together.
- Individual knowledge acquisition needs to come before any other consideration.
- Assignments need to be thought provoking and meaningful.

ORANGE LEARNING STYLES

Orange learners make up the largest percentage of dramatic learners. This is because fun and excitement are at the core of Orange learning, and these elements are usually seen as the antithesis of most traditional educational approaches. These learners need to gain an understanding that learning can be the greatest rush of all. When they do, they can gain a voracious appetite for learning and knowledge acquisition. Traditional lessons, lectures, worksheets, structure, and repetition are very unsettling and frustrating to Orange learners.

They need teachers who are willing to laugh and learn with them. They often see normal teacher/student roles as stifling to the learning process. Teachers of Orange students would do well to see themselves more in terms of coaches than traditional classroom teachers.

Orange learners are often seen as the troublemakers and jokers in class. They do not naturally show respect for teachers and administrators. In their eyes, people in positions of authority deserve no special honor or treatment for the sake of their age or position alone. Respect is something that has to be earned. Often, to the chagrin of parents, teachers, administrators, and others in authority these learners will treat adults as equals.

They are not traditionally hardworking or dedicated students. This does not mean that they aren't hardworking by nature. On the contrary, they have tireless ability and stamina that can boggle the mind when they are involved in pursuits that are valuable to them. Many Oranges have come to believe that school is their last choice when it comes to the spending of their time. They often attend school only because they are forced to, and, therefore, they seek every opportunity to be somewhere else. Many will stay in school for the social or extracurricular activities, but those who are not drawn by either of these factors often drop out if they do not have the proper parental or peer support.

They are typically unorganized and unprepared for class. They are not usually impressed by a detailed course outline or syllabus; rather, they see it as evidence of the traditional classroom structure they dislike. They do, however, need clear direction to be successful. Once they know what is expected and what it means to them personally, they will usually do their work. It isn't always on time or up to the standards of the teacher, but it is often done. They typically do not take class notes, learn, or memorize in traditional ways.

The learning process for Orange learners, as with the Gold learners, needs to be straightforward and systematic. Because Oranges are sensory in the way they gather information, they need to be able to deal with things in a very practical way. If they can't see the immediate reason for learning something, they will often dismiss it as stupid or boring. Orange students are more interested in how they feel about things than how others feel. They often let their gut response to an issue or a situation determine what they will do, and they often act without thought of the consequences to themselves or others. For this reason, they often get in trouble even before they know what they did wrong. Teachers who can learn to ignore these outbursts can often gain the respect of these learners very easily. That isn't to say that the students should be allowed to get away with bad behavior. It is to say that the teacher who learns to ignore some of the first impulses of these students will often avoid many unnecessary confrontations.

Oranges love to perform in front of the class and take positions of leadership. This kind of attention is a great reward for them. Though they may not deserve these kinds of privileges, they will grab the spotlight one way or another. It is best, then, when this attention seeking happens with the teacher's blessing. This show of support, from a teacher, can often win much-needed buy-in by the student and his or her peers. Oranges' natural physical propensity usually means that they are better assessed when a variety of methods are employed. The more ways that can be used to test what they have learned, the more accurately they can demonstrate their knowledge and skill acquisition. Traditional paper-and-pencil tests are often the least accurate way to assess what they know. For this reason, they often do not see themselves as being good test takers.

Because they do not pay close attention to deadlines, extra-credit work offers them a much-needed second chance to make up for their oversights and procrastination. They thrive in learning environments that give them several options rather than environments that are totally rigid and spelled out. They are not always motivated by good grades or other tangible academic rewards; therefore, teachers often need to find alternative methods for rewarding their work and behavior. Providing immediate tangible rewards that are deemed important seems to work really well. Free time or extra privileges for completed assignments are examples of these kinds of tangible rewards. They respond well to verbal praise, but something they can see, feel, and use is more valuable.

Homework is not the strength of an Orange learner. Play will typically have a higher priority than will work. Therefore, if homework or other assignments are seen as something that is fun to do, those assignments will move up quickly on their priority list. Because these learners are not usually self-motivated when it comes to schoolwork, it is good for a teacher to provide constant reminders of upcoming due dates and tests. A good rule of thumb for understanding Orange learners is, when they think learning is fun, they will go to great lengths to participate.

The opposite learning and teaching style of the Orange is the Gold.

Keys for Teaching Orange Students

- Teachers must be engaging and fun.
- The classroom must be stimulating and active.
- Focus on nontraditional approaches.
- Make sure all learning expectations are clearly explained and presented in a step-by-step process.
- Create a learning environment that is engaging and full of variety.
- Create assignments that have specific goals, objectives, and modes of assessment, but don't share these with the students.
- Teach them to enjoy doing Gold things.
- Be flexible.
- Allow them to be involved in the discipline and rule-making process.
- Be willing to negotiate.
- Be willing to overlook certain behaviors.
- Make sure to remind them continually concerning due dates and assignments.
- Use humor.
- Establish an unobtrusive routine.
- Class discussion must be lively and entertaining.
- Lessons need to be fun, flexible, and hands-on.
- When working together in a group, each person needs to have a clearly delineated responsibility.
- Help them learn to keep on task.
- Provide opportunities for makeup work.
- Provide opportunities for alternative assignments.
- Use learning games and activities.
- Let them work in leadership or service positions.
- Lessons need to be high energy, multisensory, and physical.
- People need to learn by doing.

- Cooperative learning must create a sense of healthy competition.
- The reward for learning needs to be as immediate and tangible as possible.
- Assignments need to be creative and fulfilling.

As you consider the way each learner prefers to be taught, it may be interesting to compare these learning styles with the teaching styles listed below. It should become immediately apparent why you are able to easily reach those learners whose style matches the way you teach. It should also help to see why you may have problems meeting the learning needs of those with opposite educational preferences. How much power would you gain as a teacher if you could learn to enhance your teaching abilities by using the teaching preferences of other educators?

Blue Teaching Preferences

- Seek to nurture students.
- Focus on feelings and educating the whole student.
- Provide positive feedback for students.
- Seek to build the student first.
- Foster one-on-one interaction.
- Create multisensory learning activities.
- Create a safe, peaceful, and harmonious learning environment.
- Seek to create a democratic learning environment and disciplinary structure.
- Want to be well-liked by the students.
- Encourage cooperative learning situations.
- Often create their own lesson handouts and other educational material.
- Use creative and unconventional instructional approaches.
- Find ways to grade effort as well as achievement.
- Avoid confrontation and do not enjoy dealing with disciplinary issues.

Green Teaching Preferences

- Seek to create an analytical learning environment.
- Expect students to be naturally interested in learning.
- Create logical and theoretical approaches to subject matter.
- Seek to inspire the intellect of their students.
- Rely on lecture/Socratic method for presenting information.
- Are flexible in their approach to lesson planning.
- Create research-based learning projects.
- Seek to create an independent learning environment.
- Strive to maintain a high level of content knowledge and/or subject competency.
- Encourage divergent thinking.
- Expect students to be self-disciplined.
- Use creative and unconventional instructional approaches.
- Use scientific exploration as a means to foster greater learning.
- Focus more on the intellectual needs of the students, not on their emotional needs.

Gold Teaching Preferences

- Create highly structured learning environments.
- Focus on the standards and assigned curricular issues as the basis for their work in the classroom.
- Follow very traditional teaching practices.
- Create and follow detailed lesson plans.
- Use concrete and no-nonsense learning activities.
- Establish firm disciplinary guidelines.
- Create and maintain a neat and orderly classroom.
- Rely highly on lecture as their main instructional tool.
- Want to be seen as a professional in the eyes of their students and other educators.
- Encourage school-based learning projects and activities.
- Rely on the educational material that is made available through the district.

- Expect students to be responsible.
- Rely on standard and traditional grading approaches.
- Assess through standard pencil-and-paper testing.

ORANGE TEACHING PREFERENCES

- Create highly interactive and engaging learning environments.
- Seek to bring fun and humor to the classroom.
- Use very spontaneous teaching practices.
- Loosely follow open-ended and unstructured lesson plans.
- Use hands-on, kinesthetic learning activities.
- Use unstructured and varying disciplinary approaches.
- Enjoy an active, busy, and even noisy classroom.
- Rely on entertaining presentations and learning activities as their main instructional tools.
- Want to be seen as an entertaining teacher in the eyes of their students.
- Encourage hands-on learning projects and activities.
- Create their own approach to required course content.
- Expect students to engage in the learning process.
- Rely on creative grading approaches.
- Assess student knowledge in as many ways as possible.

References

Aristotle. (1987). *The poetics of Aristotle* (S. Halliwell, Trans.). Chapel Hill: University of North Carolina Press.

Ball, W. (1984). *A sense of direction.* New York: Drama.

Darling-Hammond, L. (1997). Education, equity, and the right to learn. In J. I. Goodlad & T. J. McMannon (Eds.), *The public purpose of education and schooling* (pp. 41–54). San Francisco: Jossey-Bass.

Gardiner, H. (1991). *The unschooled mind: How children think and how schools should teach.* New York: Basic Books.

Gilkey, L. (1966). *Shantung compound.* San Francisco: Harper Press.

Keirsey, D. (1998). *Please understand me II.* Del Mar, CA: Prometheus Nemesis.

Keirsey, D., & Bates, M. (1978). *Please understand me.* Del Mar, CA: Prometheus Nemesis.

Macdaid, G., McCaulley, M., & Kainz, R. (1991). *CAPT atlas of type tables.* Gainesville, FL: CAPT.

Index

CORWIN
PRESS

CPSIA information can be obtained
at www.ICGtesting.com
Printed in the USA
FFHW011632190719
53713255-59424FF

9 781412 914857